By the same author:

Scattered Under The Rising Sun: The Gordon Highlanders in the Far East 1941–1945 (Pen & Sword Military, Barnsley, 2012)

St Valéry And Its Aftermath

The Gordon Highlanders Captured in France in 1940

Stewart Mitchell

Pen & Sword
MILITARY

First published in Great Britain in 2017 by
Pen & Sword Military
an imprint of
Pen & Sword Books Ltd
47 Church Street
Barnsley
South Yorkshire
S70 2AS

ISBN 978 1 47388 658 2

A CIP catalogue record for this book is available from the British Library

Typeset in Ehrhardt by
Mac Style Ltd, Bridlington, East Yorkshire
Printed and bound in the UK by CPI Group (UK) Ltd,
Croydon, CR0 4YY

Pen & Sword Books Ltd incorporates the imprints of Pen & Sword
Archaeology, Atlas, Aviation, Battleground, Discovery, Family History,
History, Maritime, Military, Naval, Politics, Railways, Select, Transport,
True Crime, Fiction, Frontline Books, Leo Cooper, Praetorian Press,
Seaforth Publishing and Wharncliffe.

For a complete list of Pen & Sword titles please contact
PEN & SWORD BOOKS LIMITED
47 Church Street, Barnsley, South Yorkshire, S70 2AS, England
E-mail: enquiries@pen-and-sword.co.uk
Website: www.pen-and-sword.co.uk

Contents

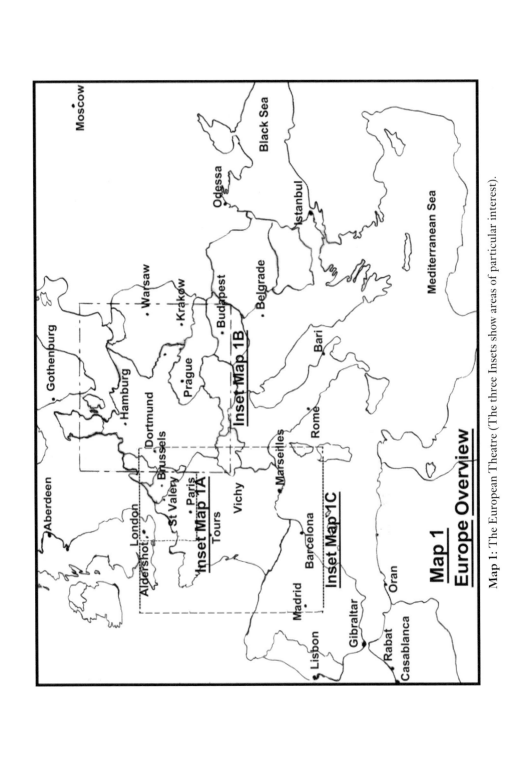

Map 1: The European Theatre (The three Insets show areas of particular interest).

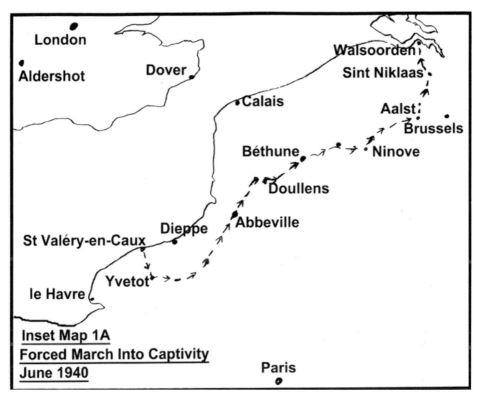

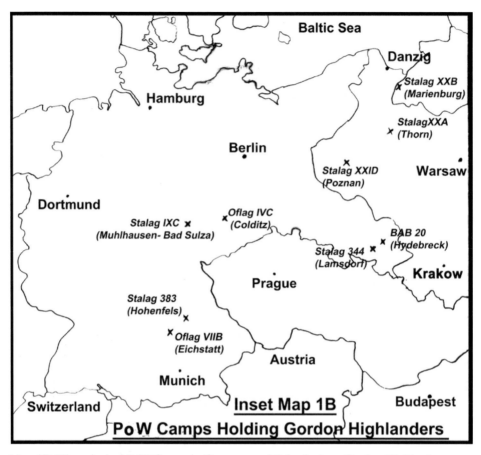

Map 1B: The principal PoW Camps in Germany and Poland where Gordon Highlanders were imprisoned.

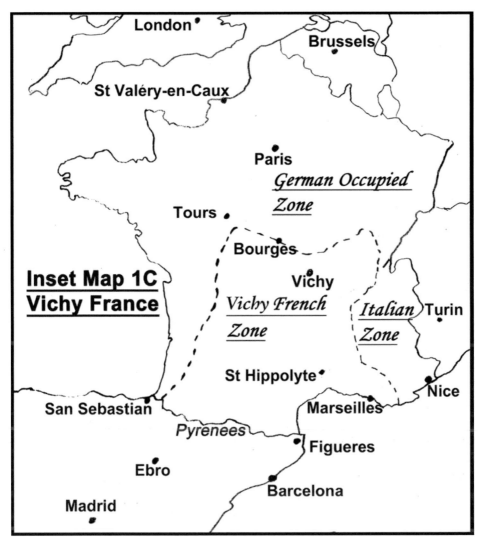

Map 1C: Vichy France. The Division of France after the Armistice with Germany and Italy. (Escaping and evading PoWs ranged over this whole area, including Belgium and Northern Spain)

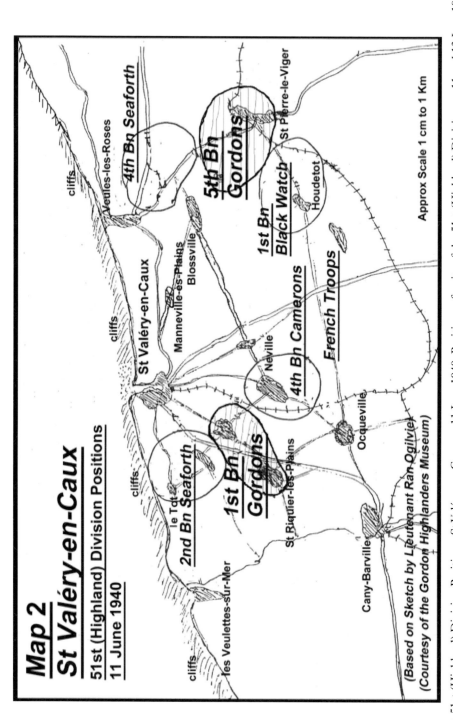

Map 2: 51st (Highland) Division Positions, St Valéry-en-Caux on 11 June 1940. Positions of units of the 51st (Highland) Division on 11 and 12 June 1940. (Based on a sketch drawn by Lieutenant Ran Ogilvie – Courtesy of the Gordon Highlanders Museum)

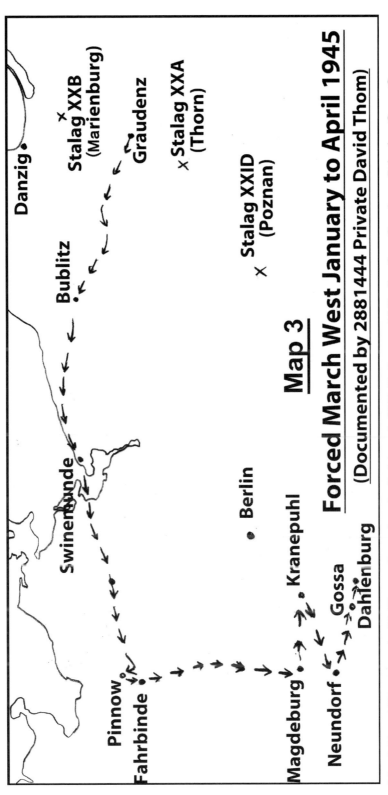

Map 3: Forced Winter march of PoWs away from advancing Red Army in 1945. (A distance of 640 miles, from Graudence, Poland, to Gossa, Germany, over the period from 20 January to 24 April 1945 – Courtesy of Sandy Thom)

Acknowledgements

This book could not have been written without the support and assistance of many people. Firstly, I would like to thank the Chairman, Lieutenant Colonel Charlie Sloan, and the Trustees of the Gordon Highlanders Regimental Trust and the Gordon Highlanders' Museum for their support and permission to reproduce material from the Museum's collection. Special thanks are also due to the Museum's Executive Director (Bryan Snelling), the Curators (Jesper Ericsson and Ruth Duncan), the Museum's Administration Officer (Morag Mitchell), the members of the Museum Research Team (Major Malcolm Ross, Charles Reid, Bert Innes, Gordon Third, Anne Clark and David Rennie) and the Regimental Secretary (Major Grenville Irvine-Fortescue) for their invaluable assistance. I would also like to thank Lieutenant General Sir Peter Graham for writing the Foreword and for his valued support and encouragement.

During the period I carried out the research for this book it was a sad fact that few of the men who served with the Regiment in 1940 were still alive to tell their story in person. I am particularly grateful, therefore, to Mr James Nicol who was the first to tell me about his story and set me on the journey which has resulted in the completion of this book. His account was complemented by William Maitland and William Harper (the latter a Seaforth Highlander, also captured at St Valéry-en-Caux) both of whom have now sadly passed away. I wish also to thank family members of many of the other Gordon Highlanders who had served with the Regiment and contacted me with information about their loved ones. These included Cecil Hutcheon, Roy King, Stanley Robertson, Moira Mapely, Henry Tobin, Gordon Steel, Isobel McRae, Francis Knowles, Arthur Durward, Flo Walterson, Margaret Cormack, Lewis Gibbon, John Inglis, George Reid, Gordon Reid, Hellen Mutch, Bruce Milton, Rob Wilson, Caroline Hastie, Johnny Jarvis, Peter Rennie, Kath Hope, Marina Alexander, Jane and Alan Harper and many others. Their assistance was invaluable in expanding my knowledge and gave me access to family photographs and documents never published before. These depicted events and personal details of the individuals' and the Battalion's experiences during the period which is described and illustrated in this book.

Prior to this project being undertaken, a number of Gordon Highlanders who had been prisoners of war had produced their own unpublished accounts which were extremely helpful to me. Through his daughters, June and Alison, I was fortunate to receive the detailed diary written by Alex Watt and similarly invaluable assistance was received from Sandy Thom with a memoir written by his father, David Thom, and from Hamish McLennan providing the memoir written by his father, George McLennan, about himself and his brother Johnny McLennan. A number of Gordon Highlanders kept diaries which still survive in the family archives. Among these were Albert King, Albert Robertson and Gordon Reid, whose sons Roy King, Ron Robertson and Gordon Reid, generously allowed me to use these for my research. In addition, the unpublished memoirs of Maurice R. Maclean (*A Prisoner of the Reich*) and Bill Reaper (*The 'Orra' Loon Goes To France*), William Anderson and Ran Ogilvie are included in the archives of the Gordon Highlanders' Museum. These and other significant documents and photographs from many families have proved invaluable in piecing together the collective story of the men of the Regiment caught up in the momentous events in France in 1940.

I would also like to acknowledge my use of information contained in the rich source of material at the National Archives, Kew, London (Files WO344, WO373 & WO392); Aberdeen City Library's newspaper archives and the Commonwealth War Graves Commission. In addition, John Clinch was extremely helpful in providing information on escaping PoWs down the Comète Line. Last, but by no means least, I would also like to thank my wife, Hilda, and my daughters Hilary, Nicola and Judith, for their support and encouragement over the years it has taken to research and write this book. There are many other people who have assisted and it would take too long to name them all, but all of their assistance is gratefully acknowledged.

Every effort has been made to ensure that facts presented in this book are wholly accurate and faithfully reproduce information passed to me. However, if any discrepancy or inaccuracy has occurred I apologise in advance.

Foreword

By Lieutenant General Sir Peter Graham KCB CBE
Last Colonel of The Gordon Highlanders

Having completed *Scattered Under The Rising Sun*, his successful and moving book about the 2nd Battalion The Gordon Highlanders as prisoners of the Japanese, Stewart Mitchell has turned his attention and research to the Gordon Highlanders who had been prisoners of war of the Germans. They had a different experience. In some peoples' minds their time as prisoners had not been as hard as those who had been captured at Singapore and who had to work on the Thai-Burma Railway.

I remember well once having a discussion about this with Lieutenant Colonel Reggie Lees MBE, one of the most inspirational officers of the 2nd Battalion, who had kept morale high in the camps he was in by refusing to be dominated by the Japanese and absolutely certain the war would be won by the Allies. He was a remarkable and wonderful man. 'Peter,' he said, 'we had a much easier time than the people like your father in law, David Morren. We all had to work on the railway. So we fought on in the sense that we upset the building of the railway by altering angles of supports for bridges, putting white ants on the vines holding the supports in order to destroy them, undermining the railway sleepers so they would weaken more quickly and working as slowly as possible to delay the project. We could continue to fight. In Europe, officers captured by the Nazis were not allowed to work, could only plan and try and effect escapes, lecture each other on educational subjects which might be useful to them after the war but there was little they could do to do real damage to the German war effort. They had a dreadful time – a stupefying time.' I could understand Reggie's thoughts but I am not sure I could agree with him.

This carefully and sensitively researched book shows how inventive, determined and ingenious so many Gordon German prisoners of war were. It is a story about people who did not know how long they would be imprisoned. These people found themselves incarcerated by a ruthless enemy and fought back by planning escapes, some of which were successful, many were not, but of course all of them added to the workload and concerns of the German Army and Government. It is a story which demonstrates the great guts and ingenuity of the Gordon prisoners of war; the way they looked after each other and the extraordinary lengths they went to try and reach home. Indeed some of the journeys they made in Europe are quite amazing, long, hazardous and with huge risk. Many of them suffered from their experiences but most of them said nothing about their experiences on return to their families. Indeed at one point Stewart Mitchell though of calling this book, *He never spoke about it.*

Stewart Mitchell has written a moving, unusual and very interesting book. There are not many books about prisoners of war and their life in the camps and on the run. He has brought to life so many stories that would have been lost forever. The Gordon Highlanders and their families are extremely grateful to him for this second book completing a pair. Like the first book it is a testament to the determined courage, ingenuity, luck and spirit of the Gordon Highlanders under duress. What a fantastic group of men they were, supported by their distant families. We owe Stewart a great debt for his interest, hard work and commitment and I thank him sincerely for what he has done for the old Regiment.

Peter Graham
2016

Introduction

In the annals of the Second World War it is natural that there is a great deal written and spoken about world leaders such as Winston Churchill, Franklin D. Roosevelt, Joseph Stalin and Adolf Hitler. Similarly we would expect there to be recognition of the role of prominent soldiers such as Field Marshal Bernard Montgomery, General Dwight D. Eisenhower and Erwin Rommel. In contrast, popular culture often concentrates on momentous battles, Special Forces, American GIs and Dad's Army. Unfortunately, rarely do we hear the story of the ordinary British soldier and among this circle there is an even more invisible band; they are the prisoners of war (PoWs).

There was, for some, a stigma attached to prisoners of war, a feeling the general population had that somehow they had given in too easily or had an easy time in a PoW camp, playing football and generally loafing around while others were continuing to fight and die for their country. The truth was, however, very different to the general belief. Thousands of men had no choice but to surrender as ordered. This was the case at St Valéry-en-Caux in June 1940, where a whole division was ordered to lay down its arms. Singapore, in February 1942, where some 60,000 British and Australian soldiers were ordered to surrender, was a very similar situation. These orders came from the top of the chain of command, i.e. the generals in charge, although there were other situations, such as the men left behind at Dunkirk, unselfishly holding the perimeter to let others escape, condemned by their orders to death or captivity. This public misconception was not helped by the PoWs themselves. They were generally reluctant to talk about their experiences and the most common comment families say about the men involved is 'he never spoke about it'. It is hoped that this book will shine a light into the world of the men of the Gordon Highlanders captured in France in 1940. Most, although not all, were captured at St Valéry-en-Caux with the 51st (Highland) Division, an event which had a disproportionate impact on the North and North-East areas of Scotland and has been etched deep into the local psyche.

Their experiences of brutal treatment and general hardship endured with cheerfulness and humour are told here through the words of the men themselves, mostly for the first time. From this group of men, almost all from ordinary humble backgrounds, springs a story of incredible courage and resourcefulness. They applied themselves to dangerous and novel situations, worked in sub-zero temperatures on farms in Eastern Europe, down salt or coal mines and in various factories. They encountered many nationalities, including French, Germans, Arabs, Poles, Czechs, Russians, learning local languages to engage with the local populace, often receiving their assistance and sometimes forming lasting friendships. Many made daring escape attempts and were forced to live off the land, offering to work or begging or stealing food and clothes, anything to avoid recapture. Their numerous escapes often meant travelling alone, or with one or two comrades, through countries they could not have dreamt of visiting before the war. This was in a time before television and globalization made every country and its cuisine appear commonplace. It was also at a time where foreign travel for the ordinary man was inconceivable, so the situation these men found themselves was utterly novel. Despite all this, their spirit remained defiant.

At St Valéry many other units were forced to surrender alongside the Gordon Highlanders. These included other Highland infantry regiments and their supporting corps. Their story is equally valid but this book attempts only to tell the story of the Gordon Highlanders.

Chapter 1

Hoping for the Best – Planning for the Worst

The Gordon Highlanders, like most infantry regiments of the British Army, operated an integrated three part organizational arrangement. These comprised a Regimental HQ or 'Depot' (Aberdeen, in the case of the Gordon Highlanders) and two Regular battalions (staffed by full-time, career, soldiers), each of a nominal strength of thirty officers and 930 other ranks, together with some twenty attached specialist trades from other Corps, e.g. the Royal Army Medical Corps (RAMC) and the Royal Army Ordnance Corps (RAOC). In addition there were the Territorial Army battalions (TA) for part-time soldiers and the Gordon Highlanders had the 4th (Aberdeen City) Battalion, the 5th/7th (5th Buchan & Formartine merged with the 7th Deeside) Battalion, the 6th (Banff & Donside) Battalion. At any particular time, only one Regular Battalion (1st or 2nd) would serve at 'home' (i.e. somewhere in the UK) while the other was overseas (i.e. somewhere in the British Empire). However, at the end of 1934 neither of these battalions was actually in the UK. The 2nd Battalion had been posted to Gibraltar in October 1934. The 1st were in the throes of returning home, bound for Redford Barracks, Edinburgh, returning from fifteen years' continuous overseas service, in Turkey (March 1920); Malta (November 1921); India (1925) and Palestine (1934).

However, an extraordinary opportunity was afforded by the positions of the 1st and 2nd Battalions at the beginning of 1935. As the 1st Battalion sailed home from Palestine they were allowed to make a special call at Gibraltar to meet up with their 'brethren' of the 2nd Battalion, commanded by Lieutenant Colonel George Burney. The previous meeting of the two battalions in peacetime took place in 1898 in India. General Sir Ian Hamilton, the Colonel of the Regiment, travelled out especially to take part in this event. (The Colonel of the Regiment is an honorary ceremonial position and not to be confused with the military rank of colonel. This title is generally conferred on retired senior officers who have a close link to the regiment. In both these respects Sir Ian was undoubtedly qualified.) The two battalions paraded together, creating a magnificent spectacle enjoyed by dignitaries, the soldiers and the public. An inspection was carried out by the Governor, General Sir Charles Harrington GCB GBE DSO.

In September 1935 the long-awaited move of the 'home of the Regiment', the Regimental Training Depot and HQ, at Castlehill Barracks, took place with the opening of the new barracks at the Bridge of Don. The ceremony was presided over by the 11th Marquis of Huntly (The Duke of Gordon) whose ancestor, the 5th Duke, had raised the Gordon Highlanders in 1794 and whose tartan was adopted by the Regiment. There were many other dignitaries present, including the Marquis of Aberdeen and the Colonel of the Regiment, eighty-two-year-old General Sir Ian Hamilton. Sir Ian had led the parade, which marched from Castlehill to the new Gordon Barracks, cheered all the way by crowds lining the streets. These new barracks were spacious and modern and situated at the northern edge of the city.

As the bells rang in the New Year of 1938 they were also signalling the ringing of changes for the 1st Battalion Gordon Highlanders. The year started routinely enough but no one could predict this was in reality the year that began the countdown towards another war in Europe. The Battalion's activities in Edinburgh included many ceremonial duties, such as the changing of the Castle Guard on Edinburgh Castle's Esplanade, while the band had played at the Scotland versus Wales rugby international at Murrayfield. Ceremonial duties apart, much of their time had also been taken up with the move to modernize and mechanize the British Army, which involved a great deal of training with the new Bren guns and anti-tank rifles.

The TA also moved into the mechanized era. In June 1938 the 5th/7th Battalion decided their annual camp and route march through Aberdeenshire should be mechanized. Their first leg was from Ellon to Haddo, the seat of the Marquis of Aberdeen, which involved an eight-mile march, with the trucks being loaded as if for active service. Along the way their progress was interrupted by the RAF dropping flour bombs to simulate an air attack, with several direct hits being scored. From Haddo the Battalion was fully mechanized with over fifty vehicles involved, including thirty trucks, twelve buses and ten cars. Over the next three days they covered sixty miles to Ballater, during which crowds cheered their progress as the men debussed to march through the various towns and larger villages en route. This increased the morale of the soldiers, appealed to the patriotic sprit of the public and possibly encouraged other young men in that community to enlist. As a further feather in their caps, the Battalion was awarded the Freedom of the Burgh of Banchory. A ceremony to mark this was held on 25 June 1938, when the whole Battalion formed up in the town square. The honour was conferred on the Battalion by the Provost, James M. Burnett, presenting a scroll in a silver cylinder, engraved with the Banchory coat of arms and the Regimental crest, to the Commanding Officer, Lieutenant Colonel Alick Buchanan-Smith OBE TD. In exercising their new right, the Battalion marched through the town with bayonets fixed.

The weather was particularly inclement for June, with torrential rain making life uncomfortable for the men spending so much time marching or under canvas. The whole camp and manoeuvres lasted for a fortnight and a BBC Outside Broadcast Unit followed their progress. This was originally planned as a trial, not for transmission, but the producer considered the results were so good that the material was broadcast to the nation. Among their adventures was a night exercise which involved the erection of a bridge over the River Dee, with the assistance of the Royal Engineers of 51st (Highland) Division. The rain had swollen the river so that the strong current proved a challenge and threatened the success of the operation. After an arduous forty-eight hours without sleep, they were successfully across the river but still had some way to march, in the torrential rain, to reach their camp. Meanwhile, the drummers and pipers were more fortunate and had gone directly to the encampment and pitched their own tents. The Quartermaster, Bill Craig, was the hero of the hour when, considering the weather conditions, he ordered that tents be pitched for the whole Battalion. On their arrival the remainder of the Battalion were relieved and delighted at the sight that greeted them as they had not looked forward to the prospect of pitching their own tents in sodden ground before they could rest. Once a meal had been served and a tot of rum issued most were asleep instantly.

Refreshed, the plan for the next day was for a march over the Cairn o' Mount to Laurencekirk. (The Cairn o' Mount is a 454-metre-high mountain pass through the Grampian Mountains which has served as a military route since Roman times.) The Commanding Officer (CO) considered that the continuing foul weather made this exercise inadvisable but, at the suggestion of some of his officers, the men were given the option to volunteer for this or travel by mechanized transport. To the CO's pleasant surprise, all but fifteen men volunteered. Overall the annual camp and route march was considered an achievement of logistics and endurance which was accomplished successfully in extremely difficult conditions. The CO was justifiably proud of his men's achievements, whilst they knew it was an experience they were glad to have done but that none would easily forget.

For the 1st Battalion, the news was of their new posting to Talavera Barracks, Aldershot, Hampshire. This was greeted with mixed feelings. Some referred to Aldershot as the 'sunny south' whereas others were sorry to leave Auld Reekie, as Edinburgh is known. The 1st Battalion's correspondent to the Regimental magazine, *The Tiger & Sphinx*, wrote of sorrow at leaving the many good friends made in Scotland's capital and now having to turn their attention to 'the grim reality of Aldershot'. This posting was for four years and at this time there was no suggestion that this would not be the case. January 1938 not only brought news of their posting south but also that of a new Commanding Officer. Lieutenant Colonel J.M. Hamilton DSO had completed his tenure of the post and was succeeded by Lieutenant Colonel C.M. Usher OBE. Usher was an eminent sportsman in his own right, having played rugby at international level sixteen times, captaining Scotland in 1920 and 1921 while serving as a young lieutenant of the Gordons.

Another character of the 1st Battalion came to the public's attention in the United States of America when, in January 1938, the *Washington Post* printed a front-page article featuring 'Champ' the 1st Battalion's mascot. The men blushed to hear their dog, which they all held in great affection, described as 'the mascot of one of the world's most famous outfits of fighting men'. Champ adopted the Regiment, rather than the usual alternative arrangement, when the 1st Battalion's Military and Pipe bands were on a tour of South Africa as part of the 1936 Empire Exhibition. Champ, a handsome brown dog, attached himself to the pipe band at Braamfontein Barracks, Johannesburg, in the first week of their tour and just refused to go away. He was a quick learner and knew the roll of the drums preceded the playing of the National Anthem. On hearing the drums roll he would march on to the bandstand and stand at attention on his haunches. On parades, Champ led the pipers and barked at people who got in the way. According to the Bandmaster, William Norris Campbell LARM ARCM,

Champ had an ear for music, liked the sound of the bagpipes and was the only South African in the Gordon Highlanders. At the end of the four-month tour, Lieutenant Stuart cabled the British Board of Agriculture and Fisheries for permission to take Champ back to Scotland and this was approved, subject to the usual quarantine arrangements. At their final concert in Johannesburg, the city's Caledonian Society presented Champ with a collar and a first-class ticket to Edinburgh. After his quarantine in Southampton, he re-joined the Regiment in Edinburgh and settled down quickly, appearing not to miss the sunshine of his former homeland. He was a particular favourite with the boy soldiers and they were pictured with him and his handler, Private Arthur Smith, in the *Tiger & Sphinx* in 1938.

When the 1st Battalion arrived in Aldershot on 16 March 1938 they immediately made an impression. They paraded through the town, en route to their barracks, led by the Pipes and Drums of the 1st Battalion Argyll and Sutherland Highlanders. They didn't have very long to settle in when they were involved with the visit of King George VI and Queen Elizabeth to Aldershot on 12 April, which included the Gordons demonstrating an infantry and tank attack. In June they took part in the tremendous spectacle of the world famous Aldershot Searchlight Tattoo which included two more royal visitors in the shape of the young Princesses Elizabeth and Margaret, who came to the children's daytime rehearsal. Towards the end of the year they were also involved in a review of mechanized troops by King Carol of Rumania and the Gordons were able to show off an entire company of mechanized infantry accompanied by a Bren-gun carrier platoon drawn up in battle order.

Undoubtedly, the most disturbing aspect of 1938 was the Czechoslovakian Crisis. The Sudetenland, areas of Czechoslovakia where the inhabitants were mostly German speaking, became a focus for Hitler's expansionist ambitions in February 1938. This prompted a crisis in Britain and France as the formation of Czechoslovakia had been part of the settlement after the Great War and for a time tensions were running high. Reinforcements, in the form of a draft of newly-trained men, were sent to Aldershot from the Depot in Aberdeen. They were given a great send off from friends and families. A photograph of this event featured in the local newspaper showing them waving their Glengarry bonnets from the train with the caption 'A Cheery farewell from Depot Gordon Highlanders who left from Aberdeen Station for Aldershot where they will join the 1st Battalion which is going to Czechoslovakia'. On the outside of the carriages the men had written in chalk various satirical and patriotic slogans such as 'To heil with Hitler'. Among this group was George Clyne who, like many others, had only recently completed his basic training.

The 1930s was a tumultuous decade for Europe and there was some disquiet about what the next turn of events would mean for the country. The 1st Battalion Gordon Highlanders were at one point on six hours' notice of mobilization to be sent to central Europe, with one draft already embarked at Southampton, only to be recalled the next day. This immediate crisis was avoided following the 'Munich Agreement' between the German Chancellor, Adolf Hitler, and the British Prime Minister, Neville Chamberlain. Despite the latter's claims of the agreement bringing 'peace for our time' this has since been widely regarded as an act of appeasement but Britain was not ready for another war.

The Czechoslovakian crisis did, however, serve as a wake-up call to the government. As a consequence it was recognized that the British Army was too small to counter the rising military strength of Hitler's Germany and a serious effort was undertaken to expand the Army, including doubling the size of the Territorial Army. Britain was in a state of economic depression in the 1930s and in the rural area of the North-East of Scotland a large proportion of the population were working in agriculture, where traditionally incomes were very low. The Territorial Army was a popular pastime in these austere times, where men would meet and socialize in the local drill hall. They were also enticed by the small bounty payable and the attraction of the two-week annual camp, which was not only as good as a holiday they could not otherwise afford, but they also received the same pay as a Regular soldier for the duration of the camp. Harry Tobin enlisted into the 5th/7th Battalion (TA) Gordon Highlanders in 1937, shortly after his 17th birthday. He was persuaded to join up by Captain Bill Lawrie, whose civilian occupation was as the physical education teacher at Bucksburn Intermediate School. Bucksburn, situated on the western outskirts of Aberdeen, was home to the Battalion's Headquarters. HQ Company included many local men who were workers at the nearby Stoneywood and Mugiemoss paper mills. In 1938 their summer camp was near Drumlithie, south of Stonehaven in the Howe o' the Mearns. While in the TA Harry learned to drive in an army truck, helped on by his cousin, also Harry

Tobin, who was the Battalion Transport Sergeant. Harry found his new skill very useful as he found a civilian job as a driver.

For the Gordon Highlanders the Army expansion resulted in a large number of recruits into all their TA Battalions. For example the 4th Battalion reported they were at full establishment while the 5th/7th had a surplus. Historically the 7th Battalion had drawn recruits from the Shetland Islands, but no effort had been made to include the islands since the end of the Great War. When the assistant adjutant visited Shetland in the spring of 1939 he recruited over 100 men in a very short time. The expansion meant the formation of new units, for example the 5th/7th Battalion Gordon Highlanders was, on the eve of the Second World War, split and its two First World War components restored. The 5th Battalion's area was Buchan and Formartine, while the 7th Battalion covered Kincardine, Deeside and the Shetland Isles. Lieutenant Colonel Alick Buchanan-Smith, who had commanded the 5th/7th Battalion, commanded the 5th while Lieutenant Colonel J.N. Reid took over temporary command of the 7th.

In view of the deteriorating international situation and the rise of Nazi Germany, with the increasingly belligerent approach of Adolf Hitler, Leslie Hore-Belisha, Secretary of State for War, persuaded the cabinet of Neville Chamberlain's government to introduce a limited form of conscription. As a result, Parliament passed the Military Training Act on 26 May 1939. This Act applied to males aged 20 and 21 years old who were to be called up for six months' full-time military training and then to be transferred to the Reserves. This was the UK's first act of peacetime conscription and was intended to be temporary in nature. Men called up were to be known as 'militiamen' to distinguish them from the Regular army. To emphasize this distinction, each man was issued with a suit in addition to a uniform. There was one registration date under the Act, on Saturday, 3 June 1939. Understandably, but significantly, registration under this Act was not required for men who had already enlisted into the Territorial Army, which in some minds was an incentive to join the part-time TA rather than spend a compulsory six months in the army fulltime. Charles Morrison, from Aberlour on Speyside, turned 20 years old in April 1939 but was unaware of the requirement of this legislation and the implications for him. However, by chance, at seven o'clock one evening, he heard a radio announcement about the imminent implementation of the new legislation. The BBC accent on the crackling radio also went on to inform him that those who had enlisted into any Territorial Volunteer unit by midnight that same evening, only five hours later, were exempt from the conscription. Charles, a shoe salesman, had no military ambitions and did not relish the prospect of a full-time posting into the army when the less onerous, in his opinion, requirements of the TA were the alternative. Unfortunately for Charles, normal business hours were over for the day but he was determined to try and sign up before the midnight deadline. There was one small glimmer of hope as he sought the help of the local recruiting officer, Sergeant Geddes. He told Charles there was a TA dance taking place that night in Dufftown, Banffshire, and that the duty officer would have the authority to sign his enlistment form. With Sergeant Geddes in tow he made the seven-mile dash to Dufftown, like Cinderella, with a midnight deadline but hurrying to arrive rather than depart by the witching hour.

On arrival at the dance venue he was introduced to Captain Spence, the duty officer. To Charles's surprise Captain Spence mentioned they had met before but Charles couldn't recall what this occasion had been. Then it dawned. The previous year he had played against this officer in a competition at Dufftown Golf Course, a match which Charles had narrowly won. Anxiously, he wondered if his journey had been in vain. Would Captain Spence secure his revenge by not co-operating in his scheme? However, there was only one hiccup in the process. A list of questions on the enlistment form was read out for Charles to answer. His embarrassment came when Captain Spence passed the form to a young lady present to ask one final question. This was 'are you in the habit of wetting the bed?', whereupon the assembled company collapsed in laughter, drowning out his reply. Captain Spence, having exacted his revenge, duly signed the form. Charles was relieved as he had narrowly avoided conscription, becoming 2881803 Private Morrison, C., and the newest recruit into the Territorial Army, 6th Battalion Gordon Highlanders.

In the spring and summer of 1939 everyone was still hoping and convincing themselves there would be no war. This was not the case however, at the Royal Military College, Sandhurst. Raonuill (Gaelic for Ranald, but he was affectionately known as Ran) Ogilvie was undergoing his officer training where he and his fellow cadets all believed there was little question that there would be a war and were pretty sure they would be involved in fighting pretty soon.

This was reinforced by the work going on in the grounds building air raid shelters against possible bombing.

The first contingent of 150 militiamen, drawn from the traditional recruiting area of the Gordon Highlanders (Aberdeen, Aberdeenshire, Banffshire & Kincardine), reported to Gordon Barracks, Aberdeen, on Saturday 15 July 1939. To accommodate this large influx of men a number of corrugated iron Nissen huts had been erected. Among the recruits who arrived on this first day were Harry Milne, Albert King, Robert Hastie, Gordon Reid and Bill Reaper, their small suitcases containing only a few treasured personal possessions as the War Office provided everything else, down to toothbrushes and shaving kits. On presentation of their call-up papers at the guardroom, the conscripts, unsure of how they should behave, were met by a sergeant and led across the parade square for their induction into army life. This was a dramatic change for most, involving strict discipline and communal living. The conscripts were from a wide variety of civilian backgrounds; for example, Harry Milne was a milkman, Albert King a plasterer, Robert Hastie had part trained as an accountant and worked in his family's business of ships' chandlers and trawler owners, Gordon Reid was a solicitor's clerk and Bill Reaper a farm servant. They were all welcomed and addressed in the dining hall by Major Norman, the officer commanding the Gordon Barracks Infantry Training Centre, who explained to them that, although they could not leave the barracks without permission, there was a room available every day where they could receive their family or friends and have tea with them.

Their first day consisted of enrolment, a medical examination and the issue of clothing and kit, then generally getting to know their surroundings. In this process they were allocated their army numbers with Harry being allocated 2882814; Gordon's number was just three digits higher (2882817) while Albert was allocated the consecutive number (2882818). There was no time wasted in getting them into the army's ways and they paraded in uniform for the first time on the day after their arrival. The plan was for them to spend two months doing preliminary training at Gordon Barracks after which they were to be sent to Aldershot to spend a further four months with the 1st Battalion for additional training and to a man they expected to return to their civilian occupation after six months. Bill Reaper described this new experience as being so different from his civilian life it was 'like a trip to Mars'. His pay was one shilling and sixpence per day (7.5p), much less than he earned on the farm but he considered the food as 'out of this world'. His daily diet on the farm had been very plain, comprising of porridge or brose (simply oatmeal mixed with boiling water and salt) for breakfast, with other meals being mainly soup, or potatoes, with only the occasional piece of meat. For example, he confessed he had never even seen a tomato, let alone tasted one. At the Bridge of Don Barracks Reveille was at 5.00 a.m., which was not a problem for him, and then two hours were spent cleaning and polishing his kit, which was then laid out on his bed in a regulation manner for inspection. Thereafter there was time for personal hygiene matters before being marched off for breakfast. There was the familiar porridge for breakfast but the difference was it was followed by bacon, liver and onion.

Whilst this novel body of men were undergoing their basic training they attracted quite a bit of media attention as well as visits from several VIPs to see how they were progressing. The first of these, on 23 July 1939, was Major General Sir James Burnett of Leys DSO, who was Colonel of the Gordon Highlanders, closely followed, on 8 August 1939 by Major General Victor M. Fortune CB DSO, General Officer Commanding (GOC) of 51st (Highland) Division. General Fortune had a previous association with the Gordon Highlanders when he was commander of 5 Infantry Brigade, which included the 2nd Battalion Gordon Highlanders while they were stationed in Aldershot; however, his part in their fortunes was a matter for the future. Brigadier Milorad Radovitch, the Military Attaché to the Yugoslavian Legation in London, also visited Gordon Barracks on Monday 21 August 1939 to see the training of the militiamen and see them parade. His visit also made possible a family reunion between Mrs Radovitch and her mother. The General's wife was an Aberdonian by birth who went to Serbia to serve as a nurse during the Great War where she met and fell in love with Radovitch, at that time a young junior officer. They had married in Aberdeen in 1919 and their two daughters were travelling with them. A dress rehearsal for this important inspection by the general had taken place a few days earlier with the militiamen's first public parade down Union Street, Aberdeen's main thoroughfare, on the occasion of the commemoration of the Aberdeen Branch of the Old Contemptibles. (These were men who had gone over to France in 1914 to face the first onslaught of the German advance whom the Kaiser reputedly described as a 'contemptible little army', a phrase which resonated with the men themselves and gave rise to the name of the first wave of the British Army to serve in that war.)

In addition to these high profile visits, the militiamen did not lack a social life. During August 1939 they put on a concert in the barracks to a large audience of their fellow militiamen and families from the married quarters. The men themselves provided most of the entertainment, including a hill-billy band, and several individuals playing the accordion, the piano, the cornet and singing cornkisters, traditional Scots ballads which generally have a humorous or satirical theme sung in the Doric – a strong distinctive dialect of Scots spoken widely, but almost exclusively, in the North-East of Scotland.

After the initial six weeks' basic training the first batch of militiamen were transferred to the Beach Ballroom to undergo training in more technical aspects of their duties, such as how to use, clean and re-assemble a machine gun. Conditions in these venues were far from satisfactory. For example, there was an inadequate number of wash basins for the number of men so long troughs, supplied only with cold water, were set up outside to allow men to wash and shave, although a limited number of showers were available at a school nearby. This transfer did, however, make way for the second batch of 150 militiamen, who were ordered to report on 15 September 1939 with a third batch commencing training on 15 October 1939. However, events overtook the original plan with Germany's invasion of Poland on 1 September and Britain's declaration of war two days later. By this date not even the first cohort of militiamen had completed their training, so all were immediately catapulted into the army for the duration of the war, rather than any possible transfer to the reserves and the early return to civilian life they had expected.

As part of the Munich agreement, signed on 30 September 1938, when Adolf Hitler and Neville Chamberlain settled the Sudetenland question, there was an understanding that this was an end to all of Germany's territorial claims. However, Hitler did not keep his word on this. Only six months later Germany seized the whole of Czechoslovakia and was pressing for the inclusion of the city of Danzig, modern day Gdansk, into the Third Reich. There was some history to this latter issue which had been a source of conflict between Germany and the Polish state for many years. After the end of the Great War the borders of Poland were the subject of intense discussion as part of the

Versailles Treaty. It was agreed that access to the sea was an imperative for the viability of the Polish state. To facilitate this, the Polish Corridor was created, along with making Danzig a 'free city' administered by the League of Nations. In the post-war period this corridor, which separated East Prussia from the rest of Germany, created a source of tension between Germany and Poland. The Polish government were extremely concerned by the increasingly belligerent tone coming from Berlin but were reassured to a degree when Britain and France guaranteed the integrity of the Polish borders.

On the morning of Friday 1 September 1939 there was a meeting of the Cabinet in 10 Downing Street, chaired by Neville Chamberlain. The unfolding and confused reports that Germany had invaded Poland were discussed and agreement reached on the wording of an ultimatum to be delivered to the German government. The wording was unambiguous. This required that the German government give a satisfactory assurance that all aggressive action against Poland would cease and German forces would be withdrawn promptly from Polish territory, otherwise the United Kingdom would, without hesitation, fulfil their obligations to Poland. This, in effect, warned Germany that, unless their actions in Poland ceased, Britain and France would declare war, although the government desperately hoped this could still be avoided. The Cabinet also agreed that the British Army, including the Territorial Army, should be mobilized immediately, together with a general call up of reservists.

In common with regimental and battalion headquarters all over the country, at around seven o'clock that evening, a telegram, with the word 'Priority' emblazoned in large letters across the bright red envelope, was delivered to the headquarters of the 5th Battalion Gordon Highlanders at Bucksburn. The duty officer opened this to find it was short and to the point. The short message was entirely uncompromising. It read. 'Priority. 5th Gordons Mobilize. Acknowledge'. This was followed two days later by another telegram which was equally brief, stating 'War has broken out with Germany. Acknowledge'.

Naturally, other battalions of the Gordon Highlanders received similar orders but there was a contrast in the logistics required to fulfil the requirement to mobilize between Territorial Army battalions, such as the 5th, compared with the 1st which was comprised entirely of Regulars. When news reached the 1st Battalion they were under canvas at the annual brigade camp. They paraded immediately and, after leaving a rear party to strike camp, marched, led by the Drums and Pipes, the twelve miles back to Talavera Barracks, Aldershot. (It should be noted here that the term 'Drums and Pipes' is historically more accurate than the more usual Pipes and Drums. The reason for this is that when the Highland regiments were being raised in the eighteenth century, the British Army had no such rank as Piper, only Drummer. Officers would, however, try to get their pipers listed as drummers so that they could earn the higher rate of pay. It is interesting to note, therefore, that only one Scottish regiment commemorates this historical point correctly. It is never the 'Pipes and Drums' but always the 'Drums and Pipes' of the Gordon Highlanders.)

The 5th Battalion drew its men from north-east Aberdeenshire, so the mobilization brought men from Fraserburgh and Peterhead area, some forty miles distant, by train. The junction of the branch lines from these towns joined in the village of Maud for the onward journey to Bucksburn. Situated in the heart of the rolling Buchan countryside, where world-renowned Aberdeen Angus cattle grazed on the rich grasslands, the centre of the small village of Maud was dominated by a livestock auction mart. The arrival in the village that Saturday of a large body of soldiers was something novel. For eight-year-old Jack Webster, the son of a local farmer and livestock auctioneer, there was an air of excitement. His attention was immediately drawn to the officer giving orders, who ably accomplished the transfer of men, with all their associated equipment, to the Aberdeen-bound train. This was Captain Nelson Keith, who in civilian life was a maths teacher at Fraserburgh Academy. At 39-years-old, he was an experienced Territorial Army soldier, but quite old to be on active service and soon to serve with the British Expeditionary Force (BEF) in France. (By a strange quirk of fate, many years later Jack, who became a well-known journalist and author, married Captain Keith's daughter, Eden.) The announcement of the general mobilization meant that families now had to come to terms with the stark reality that the men of their family were going away to fight another war. This was especially true for Mrs Bella Steel from Dyce, Aberdeenshire, who had four sons called up. Francis, William and Alan were all with the 5th Battalion Gordon Highlanders while Harry was with the Queen's Own Cameron Highlanders, all serving with 51st (Highland) Division, a seemingly immaterial detail which would come to have an immense significance on their futures.

That weekend the organizational activity, all of which required detailed planning, was hectic. On arrival at Bucksburn the officers stayed at the Strathcona Club, a house within the Rowett Institute, while the other ranks were in billets locally, having their meals provided in the works canteen of nearby Stoneywood paper mill. The first issue to be resolved was that the separation of the 5th/7th Battalion, which had been planned for the beginning of October, had not occurred, so this was a priority. The 5th were bound for the south and the 7th were to stay in Aberdeenshire. Those men of the 5th Battalion who were too young to serve overseas or had bad eyesight, varicose veins or flat feet, were weeded out. These men, provided that they were not completely unfit, were transferred to the 7th Battalion. Then war duty roles had to be assigned to the non-combatant men such as the pipe band. George McLennan, a piper, recalled the men of HQ Company were detailed to various platoons and duties. Pipers and drummers were to be stretcher bearers and he was detailed to be medical orderly of the Battalion, although, at this time he was ignorant of first aid, except for the little knowledge gained in the Boy Scouts.

By comparison, the 1st Battalion were fighting fit, already stationed in Aldershot, and their level of preparedness was high, although their numbers were not yet at full war establishment. This was partly addressed on 4 September when 199 reservists arrived at Aldershot and a second party, including some officers, arrived the next day. Lieutenant Ran Ogilvie had been sent up to the Depot in Aberdeen to escort the reservists to Aldershot and found the Bridge of Don Barracks a hive of activity as the reservists mustered and were issued with their kit. These included Alex Hardie, Jim Moir, Bill Lawrie and Tommy Bass. They marched to the railway station behind the Depot pipers and the pavements were crowded with people who cheered the column to the echo, an experience that Ran never forgot. Their journey by train down to Aldershot was somewhat tedious as the mobilization of the army, over the entire country, brought chaos to the railways as extra troop trains were laid on. Once back in Aldershot, the Battalion's readiness was utilized almost immediately and, as part of the British Expeditionary Force (BEF), they began to depart for Southampton on 20 September, the main body arriving at Cherbourg, France, on the morning of the 23rd to form part of 1st Infantry Division.

Company Quartermaster Sergeant Joe Skinner hardly had time to get his breath as these events unfolded. He had enlisted into the Gordon Highlanders in 1919 and risen steadily through the ranks. He had served with the 2nd Battalion in Northern Ireland, Aldershot, Gibraltar and Singapore. As a senior NCO he was allowed to have his family with him on foreign postings and they enjoyed life in the sun and he and his family were well known within the Battalion. He was promoted to colour sergeant (CQMS) in October 1938 and anticipated finishing his service there in a few short years but fate had a different direction in mind. When the 1st Battalion in Aldershot required an experienced quartermaster sergeant he was posted back to the UK at the beginning of August 1939. When he and his wife, Mary, and five children embarked at Singapore the possibility of war seemed a very long way off. Their ship arrived at Southampton the day war was declared and they made their way to Aldershot to find the Battalion already mobilizing. The married quarters were being closed and the families had to return to their relatives, making space to accommodate additional troops in the barracks. Their daughter, Margaret, was impressed by the large bonfire made with the furniture from the married quarters. The family travelled north to stay with Mary's family in Peterhead while Joe remained with the Battalion, trading tropical sun for a cool soggy northern France. He soon saw a further promotion to acting sergeant major but subsequent events meant this was never officially confirmed.

The Territorial Army units were generally not quite ready for overseas service immediately. Not only were they not fully trained, their numbers were also well below their war establishment. The 4th Battalion, which had been converted into a machine-gun battalion, spent their first month in the Aberdeen area and a further month at Aldershot, receiving specialized machine-gun training and being strengthened by the addition of reservists with machine-gun experience. They then embarked for France, arriving at Cherbourg on the morning of 4 November, claiming the distinction of being the first Territorial Army unit to join the BEF in France, with Regimental Sergeant Major Irwin Webster being the first TA soldier down the gangplank and setting foot in France. The 5th and 6th Battalions, both elements of 51st (Highland) Division were later in joining their regimental comrades in France. Before leaving for the south, the 5th Battalion paraded their colours at Stoneywood before laying them up for safe keeping. They were inspected by the Colonel of the Regiment, Major

General Sir James Burnett of Leys Bt CB CMG DSO, who had commanded a brigade during the First World War. He was a distinguished soldier who was Mentioned in Despatches eleven times and awarded the Distinguished Service Order twice. On 6 October 1939 the Battalion marched from Bucksburn to Aberdeen Railway station departing to Cove, Hampshire, where they took up residence in Morval Barracks. The 6th Battalion left from their headquarters at Keith around the same time, also heading for Hampshire and were stationed at Delville. The strength of the battalions was increased by the posting of men from the 7th Battalion, which remained in Banchory, and further drafts of militiamen.

The next ten weeks were spent in training to bring the units up to scratch, including lectures on various topics, such as their duty to escape if captured. Mechanized movement exercises were also being undertaken. During one of these intensive training exercises, on 6 October 1939, the 5th Battalion had its first casualty. During the night, while on manoeuvres on Salisbury Plain, one of the Bren-gun carriers went into a shallow ditch where some of the signallers were sleeping and Private Cyril Dunn was caught under the vehicle. His arm was dragged over the track and George McLennan had his first real test as a medic, having to crawl under the carrier to support Cyril's body so that his arm would not suffer more damage. The track had to be carefully unfastened to release him. On arrival at the military hospital both of them were soaked in his blood. His arm was practically torn out, but he recovered, although his right arm became withered and useless, so he was declared unfit for further military service.

Both the 5th and 6th Battalions moved to Aldershot at the beginning of December 1939. In the intervening period the War Office had decided that the kilt was no longer suitable dress for modern warfare and that only battle-dress would be worn on active service, although the kilt was permitted for ceremonial duties and while men were on leave. This was not welcome news to the Highland regiments who took the wearing of the kilt as an inalienable right. The place of highland dress as an integral part of the regiment's character is underlined by the apparent need by the Commanding Officer of the 1st Battalion (Lieutenant Colonel Dougie Usher OBE) to decree in Battalion Orders, issued on 29 March 1939:

The practice of wearing pants when dressed in the kilt is contrary to the traditions of Highland Regiments. This practice will cease forthwith. Pants may only be worn under the kilt when attending dances and when taking part in Highland Dancing. Disciplinary action will be taken against any soldier contravening this order.

The 5th Battalion decided to make the passing of the kilt into a solemn affair and appropriately Bonfire (Guy Fawkes) Night was set as the date for their protest. On 5 November 1939 a woodpile was erected on the barrack square. Playing a *piobaireachd* (pibroch), the Battalion pipers then led a party of officers who carried an effigy wearing a kilt and glengarry to the pile, with the men of the Battalion following at a slow march. The effigy bore a strong resemblance to Adolf Hitler and its right arm was held raised in the Nazi salute. It was then soaked in petrol and a torch applied with the result that the effigy was consumed and collapsed in the blaze, which resulted in a rousing cheer from the assembled company. One officer rushed forward and snatched a small remnant of the kilt from the flames and placed it in a barrow. This was ceremonially marched to a 'grave' nearby where it was solemnly buried to the strains of a lament. The ceremony drew to a close with drinks all round while the pipers played the stirring march 'The Back o' Benachie'. A grey granite pillar, inscribed with details of the event on each of its four faces, was commissioned from an Aberdeen granite merchant to mark the occasion and designate the spot where this ceremony had taken place. Unfortunately, by the time the pillar was delivered to Aldershot the Battalion had moved to France so it was not erected there. After the war it was returned to Aberdeen and now has pride of place near the entrance of the Gordon Highlanders' Museum, Aberdeen. One face reads:

When you burn our kilt you roast our pride. You can take away the tartan but you cannot quench the spirit of The Gordons.

In December the 5th Battalion moved from Morval Barracks to Badajos Barracks, Aldershot. They were sad to leave their temporary home but the morale of the men was high and the mood jovial. Drum Major A. Wilson composed a song, entitled *The 5th Gordons Farewell To Morval* to mark the occasion which gently poked fun at some of the characters of the Battalion, such as Platoon Sergeant Major (PSM) Bert Mackie, the Pioneer Sergeant, Pipe Major (Sergeant) George Cruickshank and Captain (later Major) Bill Craig, the Quartermaster who had been the hero of the hour, at Banchory in 1938.

The 5th Gordons Farewell to Morval

It was on a cold December Morning
And the order, battle dress for all
The gay Gordons started packing
As 2 o'clock they left Morval.

PSM Mackie did his bit
His Pioneers did rally
They had the Gordons' standard down
As the noise ceased from Reveille.

Pipe Major Cruickshank on his toes
To get the wardrobe empty
As he carried out (dead men)
I lost count at twenty.

Militia, Guardsmen and Reserves
Whom the gallant 5th signed on
Stood back and talked of old Shin Ack
While Bucksburn carried on.

The Quarties started grousing
The RQMS was there
And sorted out their troubles
As he scratched, where there once grew hair.

Now Morval Camp had many a fault
Captain Craig's work, sure was no dud
And although the complaints were not of the huts
We could hardly just blame him for the (mud).

And then the boys did gather
Just to glance at their old home
And they'll say, after seeing Badajos
Morval is a HOME SWEET HOME.

As the RSM shouted 'Battalion'
The 5th all braced up as one
The band who were now at the ready
To play Morval's lament to the gone.

The command to advance had been given
As each man by the guardroom did pass
Might have ever so sweet many memories
But Morval stands out to the last'.

(Reproduced by Courtesy of Gordon Steel)

It was clear that deployment to France was near and men were given embarkation leave. Brothers Archie, Jack and Billy Hutcheon, who lived at School Croft, Belhelvie, Aberdeenshire, had all enlisted into the 5th Battalion Gordon Highlanders. Jack (aged 34) and Billy (aged 23) enlisted together in April 1939, receiving consecutive Army service numbers. Their brother, Archie (aged 24), had enlisted twelve months earlier. Their youngest brother, Jimmy, did not want to be left out so had also tried to enlist but was rejected as too young. He was keen to be doing his bit, so he joined the Home Guard until his call-up papers came through. They were a close-knit family with Jack, Bill and Jimmy all working at Balmedie Quarry, while Archie worked on a local farm. The three older brothers all served in the same company of the Battalion and were among those to get a few days leave just before embarkation to France. They came back to School Croft for Christmas. Their mother, Christina, and Jack's wife Mary were delighted to see them while Jack's two sons, Jackie & Cecil, were thrilled to have their dad home to play with them again. Christina Hutcheon was pleased to have the whole family sit down to their Christmas meal together. Like many others, the Neilson family arranged a visit to the local photographer's studio for a family photograph before William (Bill) left home in 1939. This was duly taken with Bill, in uniform, standing proudly behind his wife, their baby daughter Florence on her knee, while he rested his hand lovingly on the shoulder of their 4–year-old son James, standing by her side. The future was uncertain and these families knew this could be the last occasion they would all be together. This also played a part in the decisions of Robert Little and William Wilson (2880032) to marry. David Spink spent Christmas Eve with David Thom's family in Peterhead and they hung up their stockings and Santa left them both a wallet.

The declaration of war had a profound effect on many men who were already in a romantic relationship. In the first few days after war was declared (from 4 to 14 September 1939) there was, in the experience of Aberdeen District Registrars, 'a situation, without parallel'. There was a threefold increase in the number of marriages registered in Aberdeen, rising from a pre-war average of thirty-five per week to 110. One feature told it all: most of the men who brought their brides before a minister or sheriff were in uniform. One man who was unable to marry his sweetheart before his posting south was Charlie Irvine. Charlie and his brother Eddie joined the Bucksburn Company of the 5th Battalion Gordon Highlanders in 1938. Charlie joined up in order to learn how to drive; his test was to drive from the Drill Hall in Bucksburn for about four miles, mainly on the main road to Inverness, so this was not too difficult. Both brothers were also among those given a few days home leave before embarking for France and Charlie married his sweetheart, Peg, on 29 December 1939. There was no time for any honeymoon as he had to rejoin his unit the following day but little did he know that any plans for his next leave would be on hold as he would not see Peg again for five and a half years. Robert Little was married that Christmas but not so fortunate were Alex Watt (2875918) and his fiancée, Alice. They were all set to wed with the guest list made but it was agreed the nuptials would wait until Alex's next leave but as Alex wryly put it, 'Adolf Hitler intervened'.

There were a few ceremonial duties to perform before embarkation to join the BEF in France. King George VI and Queen Elizabeth visited 51st (Highland) Division on 18 January 1940. The 5th and 6th Battalions, together with other units of the Division, lined Wellington Avenue, Aldershot, which Their Majesties walked and reportedly remarked how well the men were turned out, particularly bearing in mind the short service of many of them. The following day both battalions paraded together again, under command of

Brigadier George Burney, who had relinquished command of the 2nd Battalion Gordon Highlanders in Singapore in January 1938. On this occasion they were joined by 1st Canadian Division, which included the 48th Highlanders of Canada, allied to the Gordons, and the 75th Toronto Scottish whose affiliation to the London Scottish (a Territorial unit of the Gordon Highlanders) also made them a part of the Gordons' family. They were inspected by the Colonel of The Regiment Sir James L.G. Burnett of Leys Bt CB CMG DSO who took the salute as they marched past to the massed Pipes and Drums of 153 Brigade, of which 5th and 6th Gordons were units. This was an occasion with both a first and a last. It was the first time that an allied Regiment had paraded with the Gordon Highlanders but it was the last time these units would officially be seen wearing the kilt.

The Highland Division was now ready for action and the Gordons embarked for France. They began leaving Aldershot for Southampton on 29 January and were ferried across the Channel on the HMTs *Lady of Mann* and *Ben-my-Chree*, both owned by the Isle of Man Steam Packet Company but repainted grey and pressed into naval service as personnel carriers (both vessels later saw service at Dunkirk and on D Day). The daylight crossing of the convoy had an escort of two destroyers but there was no threat. The 5th Battalion disembarked at le Havre on 30 January with the 6th Battalion arriving the next day. Douglas Davidson, one of the fresh militiamen with the 5th Battalion, wrote home just a few days later to reassure his family he was safe. He was not allowed to say where he was but did mention he had spent about two days at sea. He described his experience crossing the English Channel by writing, 'It was a fairly good crossing but I was forced to feed the fishes on the way over.' Although now in France the units were still not at full strength, for example the 5th had a complement of only 607 men (23 Officers, 10 Warrant Officers, 19 Sergeants, 44 Corporals and 511 other ranks) but this was increased by further drafts, mainly of militiamen bringing the numbers up to 784 by the end of March but still almost 25 per cent under full war establishment. This was symptomatic of the problem faced by the entire British Army which had been starved of resources for many years while Germany had re-armed with modern weaponry and built up its armed forces by a considerable degree. One man who had expected to be among those arriving in France, with the 5th Battalion Gordon Highlanders, was Francis Steel. He watched his three brothers, William, Alan and Harry, leave with a very heavy heart. He was a despatch rider and, one very dark night while making a delivery with the blackout slit limiting the brightness of his headlight, he collided with a cow which had wandered onto the road. The inevitable consequence was that he crashed and broke his wrist and was declared unfit to travel to France. Francis was shortly afterwards transferred to the Royal Engineers and carried out highly sensitive work for the duration of the war but his brothers all had very different experiences.

The weather in France proved to be a problem. The winter of 1939-40 was the coldest for half a century with even the English Channel freezing at Boulogne. The cold weather made the men feel miserable. Douglas Davidson, in his first letter to his parents from France, at the beginning of February 1940, wrote:

> we are billeted in a barn up to our eyes in mud. We had a very hard frost at the beginning of the week and the telephone poles and the trees snapped like matchsticks. There was about two inches of ice on the telephone wires.

There was also difficulty in starting the trucks with the fuel or sump oil freezing. A roster was organized to start up the vehicles every hour and sometimes, if there was a heavy frost, the engines were left to run all night to prevent them from freezing as there was no anti-freeze available. The two battalions were stationed in the Lilliers–Béthune area just south-east of Lille. Many of the men were billeted in the area and made friends with the local townsfolk in this fine old city who, in the words of Walter Young, 'were kind and interested in them'. So the Gordons settled in to their new surroundings. There was no shortage of novelty items in the shops and those men who had young children or sweethearts at home were keen to keep in touch. Corporal David Greig, a veteran of the Great War, sent letters and novelty postcards home to his young daughter Isobel while Piper Gordon Reid (2880758) sent 'all his love' with a coloured picture postcard, embroidered with the words, 'From Your Soldier Boy', to his sweetheart, Lila Duthie, whom he married after the war.

The 1st Battalion's Commanding officer Lieutenant Colonel C. (Dougie) Usher OBE left the Battalion on 22 February to take up the appointment of Area Commandant at Saint-Malo, for which he was promoted to full colonel. He was given a tremendous send off by all the ranks of the Battalion, who lined the streets whilst the sergeants pulled his car along with eleven pipers playing in front. Only three days later the 5th Battalion received an honoured guest at Béthune, in the person of French Général Fagalle. Escorted by the Adjutant, Major Rupert Christie, he inspected the Guard of Honour provided, while the local population enjoyed the spectacle of the Battalion's Drums and Pipes parade and play in the main square of the town. This all contributed to the friendly relationship between the French people and the Gordon Highlanders, much of which had been fostered in the previous war and continues to the present. The occasion was a success and the following day Major Christie received a short personal handwritten note from the divisional commander, Major General Fortune. The note read:

> Dear Christie, just a line to congratulate you on your Guard for General Fagalle. The men were well turned out and smart. A credit to you and your Batt'n. Yours, Victor Fortune.

The High Command had been considering the standard of training of the Territorial divisions in France and decided it would be beneficial if each brigade exchanged one Territorial battalion for a battalion of Regulars. In 153 Brigade this was accomplished by exchanging the 6th Battalion for the 1st Battalion who were expected to bring some additional experience and professionalism. (The other partner in 153 Brigade was 4th Battalion Black Watch (Royal Highland Regiment).) The substitution of the 1st Battalion for the 6th Battalion Gordon Highlanders from 1st Infantry Division to 51st (Highland) Division and vice-versa took place at the beginning of March 1940. This event was not allowed to pass without some ceremony. The 1st Battalion paraded at Cysoing on 6 March 1940. General Sir Harold Alexander, the divisional commander, came and said his farewell while Brigadier Charles Hudson VC intimated how sorry he was to lose them from 2 Infantry Brigade. The next day they departed, marching off to strains of the band of the 2nd Battalion Staffordshire Regiment.

As they prepared to leave the 51st (Highland) Division fold, the men of the 6th Battalion had no real idea where they were bound and after six months of the phoney war many individuals believed they were headed back home. Corporal Jimmy Nicol was in the 5th Battalion but had originally enlisted into the 6th, in which his father also served. He grew up in Insch, Aberdeenshire, and when he left school became an apprentice blacksmith there. Following in his father's footsteps he enlisted into the local 6th Battalion Gordon Highlanders but when he was offered a new position working in Hatton of Cruden, near Peterhead, he transferred to the 5th Battalion, which was based locally. His previous service meant he knew a lot of the 6th Battalion men well, so when they heard of their move, with the rumour being this was back to the UK, his old friends started to pull his leg, saying he was in the wrong battalion now! As events eventually unfolded, this friendly taunt was, ironically, an ominous prophecy.

After a march of three miles the 1st and 6th Battalions met at Seclin, where old friends had a chance to exchange news. In this all-Gordons' affair, Brigadier George Burney, a Gordon Highlander himself, welcomed the 1st Battalion as part of 153 Brigade and bade farewell to the 6th. (George Burney was a Gordon through and through, a son of the Regiment, his father being Brigadier General Herbert Henry Burney.) As the 1st Battalion neared their final destination their hearts were gladdened by the sound of the pipes. They were met by the 5th Battalion's Pipe Band who played them the final four miles to their destination at Allennes-les-Marais, marching past General Fortune on the way. There was still work to be done, however, and next day a detachment of two companies was sent to Arras to dig a twenty-five mile trench for a telephone cable. In addition, much work was done in improving the defences in this locality.

The 4th and 6th Battalions settled in the west, part of the force which, in the event of enemy invasion, would move forward into Belgium and take up positions along the Dyle Canal. The role of 51st (Highland) Division changed. They were placed under French command and ordered to move over 200 miles south-west to the Saar region. In preparation for this move Second Lieutenant Ran Ogilvie was astonished to discover the commander of the troop of Royal Engineers who arrived to take over his platoon's billets was none other than Second Lieutenant Iain Ogilvie, his brother, who had been in the TA but had just been released from his reserved occupation as a civil engineer and so was immediately commissioned into the Royal Engineers, all unknown to Ran.

There was now a sense that the 'phoney war' was at an end. German forces had attacked Denmark and Norway and were concentrated on the borders of Holland and Belgium. The Gordons braced themselves for what the future might hold.

Chapter 2

The Battle for France

At first things were relatively quiet and the normal routines of army life in the field continued, equipment still had to be maintained and serviced and supplies had to be procured and purchased locally. Charles Morrison (2881803) who had a role in this was despatched on a regular basis to Metz to pick up the beer ration for Headquarters Company from a local brewery. The brewer's daughter was very pretty and he was delighted his regular collection gave him ample opportunities to pay her a visit. One day she proved useful when he had an unusual problem. The tap on the mess beer barrel became faulty and so would not pour. This was seen as nothing short of a calamity requiring immediate action. Charles's schoolboy French did not extend to the word for the tap so he consulted his would be sweetheart who was able to inform him this was 'robinet' so off he went into an ironmonger in Metz to ask for a replacement tap for the barrel. In his best schoolboy French he enquired 'Bonjour monsieur, je veux un robinet?' He was flabbergasted when the elderly shopkeeper replied in a broad Scottish accent, 'Aye it will be a tap yer needin' is it laddie?!' Apparently this man was a Great War veteran who had returned to Metz after the war and married a pretty French girl. They both had a good laugh about the incident.

Shortly after arrival in the Saar area the 5th Battalion had its first death while on active service, although this was not from enemy action. George Sutherland, one of the Shetland men who had enlisted in the spring of 1939, died as a result of a drowning accident in the River Moselle. At the beginning of May 1940, the 51st (Highland) Division took up positions in the Maginot Line, relieving some French units. Both the 1st and 5th Battalions Gordon Highlanders were stationed in close proximity to each other, near Budling, some twenty miles north of the strategic town of Metz and just south of the German frontier. It was not long before 1st Gordon's C Company encountered enemy activity, with their positions in the front line (*Ligne de Contact*) being raided on the night of 3 May. This was successfully beaten off, as was a repeated action the following night.

Early in the morning of 10 May 1940, when they were in the *Ligne de Receul*, a position a few miles behind the most forward posts, the start of the German offensive was signalled by the message to 'Man battle stations at once. This is not a practice'. However, there was little activity in their sector, although they could hear the battle raging not far away and there were reports that the town of Metz was being bombed. They did not have to wait long for the battle to reach their positions and they came increasingly under shellfire. Private James Campbell became their first casualty. He received a shrapnel wound to his arm, which was treated by George McLennan, and was sent down the line for further treatment but died two days later. This day, 10 May 1940, did not just mark the start of the German offensive on the Western Front but coincidentally was also the day that Winston Churchill took office as British Prime Minister, following the resignation of Neville Chamberlain. Prior to this he had been the First Lord of The Admiralty, an office of state which he had held in two world wars.

The Gordons suffered many casualties in an operation to relieve the 4th Battalion Black Watch, in the forward positions of the *Ligne de Contact*. Harry Tobin (2878125) had a lucky escape when a bullet stuck his rifle butt. This was not his only close shave. About a week later he had another near miss when a bullet passed through a fold in his trousers without him receiving a scratch. One of the serious problems for the British forces at this time was communication with the forward positions. Radios were still not in universal service and, in any event, were not wholly reliable and so fixed telephone lines were employed. The problem with these was that they were frequently being cut by enemy bombardment and messages could only be transmitted by runners and despatch riders.

On 12 May 1940 an advance party of 5th Gordons went forward to start the relief and gain intelligence. At this time, the enemy, who probably noticed their movement, began a strong action to take the forward position at Betting which was held but this forward position was isolated. The next morning, after an artillery barrage on 51st (Highland) Division's front, there was a determined enemy infantry advance. Again the forward positions were vulnerable and, in the ensuing battle, Second Lieutenant Douglas Innes was wounded and their position, at Petit Wölscher, seized. He and seven other Gordon Highlanders were captured. In addition two other Gordons were killed and Second Lieutenant Innes's wounds also proved fatal. He died in captivity six days later. This was a baptism of fire for the Gordons. In these desperate circumstances there were valiant attempts to reach and relieve the forward positions, being manned by a mixture of Gordons and Black Watch. A combined fighting patrol was mounted and under the leadership of Lieutenant Johnny Rhodes, supported by Second Lieutenant Ran Ogilvie, fought their way through to the isolated post at Betting and evacuated the men back to their own lines, capturing a German officer in the process. Lieutenant Rhodes was awarded the Military Cross for his actions. Johnny Rhodes was not the only one to gain distinction during this time for demonstrating courage under fire. On 15 May Private James Brown showed a total disregard of the danger in conveying orders and messages to forward posts after the telephone lines had been cut by shellfire. His citation read: 'He repeatedly displayed great initiative and courage under heavy machine gun fire in maintaining contact with the forward posts when communication with them was of vital importance'. His bravery was recognized at the highest level with the recommendation for his Military Medal being made by Major General Victor Fortune CB DSO.

This battle was the first serious action by the 5th Gordons but their Commanding Officer, Lieutenant Colonel Alick Buchanan-Smith, was not present to witness how well they had weathered the challenge. He was a sick man and returned to the UK with a serious case of shingles, which had been dogging him for some time. He saw his Battalion move forward before his departure, having relinquished his command. Initially Major Rupert Christie, who had deputized for him in the past, acted as a caretaker CO until Major J. Clark, of the 1st Battalion, could take over.

The next few days saw some intense action, with the focus for the Gordons being the front held by the 5th Battalion. Again a forward post was in trouble, this time at Heydwald, just half a mile from Petit Wölscher, where the danger had been earlier. Captain Lawrie, D Company Commander, was unable to make contact with his men at Heydwald and with a depleted force himself he was desperately trying to hold on to his own position. PSM Charlie Fullerton's platoon was on the forward edge of Heydwald wood and had suffered from the heavy shelling which was followed up by an infantry attack, which they repelled. Unable to make contact with the Company HQ, Charlie set off alone and got through and then led a fighting patrol, with stretcher bearers, back to his platoon and evacuated the wounded. This done, he led a successful attack on Bois Cawe, captured ten prisoners and killed around twenty others. Lieutenant H. 'Ginger' Gall was ordered to mount a fighting patrol to rescue the men in the vulnerable forward posts but was met by fierce resistance from the enemy, who were now holding the positions at Heydwald. With this situation now hopeless the patrol covered the withdrawal of the remnants of D Company, an action for which Gall was also awarded the Military Cross. Despite these brave endeavours, seventy-five men of D Company remained cut off and so became prisoners in this action, among them Private Harold Doyle. Harry and the others were taken away from the front to Comlere, where he, and two other Gordons, were selected for interrogation by a senior German officer, before being taken to a transit camp at Linberg with the others. So began their five long years of imprisonment.

The 51st (Highland) Division, including the Gordons, then moved into reserve but the increasingly desperate situation meant this was short lived. At about this time Jack Caldwell received some bad news. He was called to the company command post where a sergeant from the RAMC was waiting to speak to him and told him that his brother, George, who was serving with 154th Field Ambulance, part of 51st (Highland) Division, had been killed. There was also some devastating news for Donald Peglar whose twin brother George was killed on 16 May. The twins had enlisted as boy soldiers, being given consecutive Army service numbers and were both posted to India in 1931; they had performed all their service with the Regiment together. In the midst of this sadness Lieutenant James Sinclair received the joyful news that his wife had given birth to a baby daughter (Hellen) on 8 May, the first child to be born to any soldier of the re-formed 5th Battalion. To mark the occasion, Lieutenant Colonel Alick Buchanan-Smith sent, on behalf of the officers of the Battalion, an engraved silver christening cup to Sinclair's family in Fraserburgh with the handwritten message: 'With every good wish and prayers for the safe return of her Father.' None of them imagined that it would be another five years before he was able to return home.

The Division was now cut off from the rest of the BEF by the unexpected German panzer thrust through the densely-wooded Ardennes, so they remained under French command. The French Second Army was trying to hold back a strong German offensive on the Somme and the French high command ordered the transfer of the 51st (Highland) Division to this front. This was, on the face of it, a chaotic manoeuvre which saw parties of the Gordons split between rail and road transport to travel to their destination by completely different routes. Since transport was limited the 5th Battalion decided to store their drums at Metz before going south. Those making this decision were either unaware or dismissive that a fate similar to that which had befallen the 2nd Battalion's drums at Ostend in 1914 could recur. In October 1914 Willie Graham, who would go on to command the 2nd Battalion in Singapore, was only a young second lieutenant who, finding the transport wagons grossly overloaded, decided to leave the seven drums in the save keeping of the local gendarmerie at Ostend, not expecting the city to be overrun by the German army within a few weeks. The drums were not recovered until 1934 when the Colonel of the Regiment (General Sir Ian Hamilton) made a personal approach to President Hindenburg of Germany, then Head of State in name only as Adolf Hitler had come to power, and requested the return of the drums. This was agreed and Sir Ian and other representatives of the Regiment travelled to Germany where the drums were returned to the Gordons with a great deal of ceremony.

On 22 May 1940 the 51st (Highland) Division set off for the Somme, their mechanized transport taking the more or less direct route through Varennes, Vitry-le-François Sézanne, Gisors to a position south-west of Bresle, covering a distance of over 300 miles in convoy. The men on the rail parties travelled by a more circuitous route, heading around the south of Paris, via Vitry-le-François, Troyes and Amboise then looping back north-east through le Mans to Rouen before being bussed to the rendezvous area, covering a distance of over 400 miles. This was all completed by 30 May and the next day the Division moved forward, across the River Bresle, to take up positions in the front line to block the advancing Germans.

The objective for the 1st and 5th Gordons was to be in position for the major offensive planned by the French on 4 June and they took over their positions in the preceding days. Being in such close proximity with the enemy was not without risk and casualties were sustained from shellfire over these two days, with twelve men killed. These included Captain Bill Diack, commanding C Company of the 5th Gordons, and his batman, Andrew McIntosh, who, in the afternoon of 2 June, were reconnoitring the position they were to take over that night. While driving to the company command post the pair were killed by shellfire. Shelling was intense at the village of Behen, where the Gordons were at this time. George McLennan, a stretcher bearer and first aider was hunting for the Regimental Aid Post (RAP). In the confusion stretcher bearers with casualties were having difficulty in finding it. George noticed there were shrapnel fragments glowing white all over the road and when he entered the RAP he found the Medical Officer examining Joe Johnston, the orderly room driver. Joe had been hit in the back by a piece of shrapnel which had passed straight through, from back to front, but his wound was so serious there was nothing they could do for him and he died within twenty minutes. By a strange coincidence two of the 1st Battalion's casualties on the night of 3 June were named James Stuart (2872692 and 2878825). This tragic coincidence now sees them resting side by side in the War Cemetery at Longueval, surrounded by twenty-three of the comrades who also died in this action.

On 5 June dawn broke to the sounds of battle with the whine and crump of artillery shells, the thump of mortar bombs, the rattle and crack of small-arms fire. A strong force of German infantry attacked the position held by Second Lieutenant Ran Ogilvie and this was supported by machine guns and mortars. Private Willie Bremner, the number one of the Bren-gun team of Ogilvie's platoon, was wounded in the chest and sent back for aid and so Piper David Robbie took over his position and was supported by Ran Ogilvie as his number two and they continued to engage the enemy. An enemy machine gun was causing them a lot of trouble and on instinct Ran picked up Willie Bremner's rifle and, being a qualified marksman, shot and killed the two machine gunners. His satisfaction at having dealt with that situation was short-lived when Piper Robbie collapsed at his side, killed with a bullet through his forehead. Another man who died that day was Eddie Dick. He had had a premonition of his premature demise when, a few months earlier, he wrote home to his friend, Jean Bennett, 'my hopes are very low as regards coming through alive, but you can lay some dandelions [for me] on the war memorial …'. Eddie's body was never recovered and he is commemorated on the Dunkirk Memorial.

Meanwhile the 4th and 6th Gordons, who had remained with the rest of the British force, were being evacuated at Dunkirk. The 6th Gordons moved from their position in the Bray dunes, a few miles along the coast north-east of Dunkirk, under the cover of darkness. They ran the gauntlet of a constant artillery bombardment as they marched straight to the harbour and boarded two Royal Navy destroyers, which set sail for Dover at 6.00 am on 1 June. The 4th Battalion also embarked on two destroyers some twenty hours later and both battalions made it safely to Dover. Several of these men were subsequently posted to the 2nd Battalion in Singapore, including James Scott, Robert Anderson, Peter Taylor, Alan Greig and William Mackie. They had successfully avoided capture for the moment but when Singapore capitulated to the Japanese on 15 February 1942 all that changed and theirs was a very different experience to those who fell into German hands.

Although their evacuation had gone fairly smoothly, prior to this they had seen some intense fighting with their combined losses, during their time in France, being nine killed, twenty-nine wounded and 175 missing. When the German offensive began, on 10 May, the 6th Battalion, now part of 2 Infantry Brigade, was ordered to advance into Belgium to take up defensive positions on the Dyle Canal, near Corbeek. The 4th Battalion, a machine-gun unit, was initially deployed defending the airfields of Ronchin and Lesquin, as a precaution against an attack by German paratroopers seeking to gain control of these strategic positions.

On 16 May the 6th Battalion positions received a heavy pasting from German artillery and Stuka dive bombers but luckily there were no fatalities. Ironically they did suffer losses when withdrawing that evening with three men killed, five wounded and Private George Thomson posted missing. His family were notified and had an anxious wait for almost three months until they were notified that he had been captured and was a prisoner of war at Stalag XXA (Thorn), Poland. A general withdrawal of the brigade was ordered which took the 6th Gordons through the city of Brussels where they were surprised to see many of the inhabitants calmly going about their normal business. However, as they proceeded beyond the city the roads were clogged with refugees heading for Paris and the south. The large columns of military vehicles only exacerbated the problem.

The Allies' situation became precarious with the Germans slicing through the Ardennes and heading for the coast, effectively cutting the British off from their Channel supply bases and splitting the combined British and French force. There was an urgent need to avoid encirclement and the BEF fell back westwards, the 6th Gordons covering much of this journey on foot in unaccustomed hot weather. The men were exhausted. When the earlier losses of vehicles meant there was insufficient motorized transport for all the Gordons to travel from the River Bresle defensive line to their new positions on the River Dendre, seventy men commandeered abandoned bicycles to continue their journey.

Meanwhile the 4th Battalion employed their machine guns to cover the withdrawal from the Bresle and had taken up a position near Assche, west of Brussels. Their situation was hampered by a lack of radios and all communications had to be by despatch rider, which was far from ideal. With their superior numbers, the Germans were pressing hard and when the order was given to withdraw, one company which had been detached, lost touch with the adjacent unit and, unable to disengage from the enemy, was surrounded. Captain W. Holmes waited to guide his men to safety but the enemy reached his position. He shot one German and, under pursuing gunfire, made his escape through enemy-held country, returning to his own lines by swimming the river. All the bridges had been blown to delay the enemy advance. He was awarded the Military Cross for his bravery and determination. On the same day Corporal David McPhee, a despatch rider, volunteered to try and get through to an isolated platoon but found himself encircled. Under the cover of darkness he successfully travelled twenty-five miles through enemy-held territory to return to his own lines and, like Captain Holmes, this involved swimming the river. He was also rewarded for his courageous action with the Military Medal. The seventy-eight isolated men had no option but to surrender.

On 20 May the Germans reached the coast, having advanced some 200 miles in just seven days. On this date the 4th and 6th Gordons found themselves in positions on the River Escaut, separated by only a few miles. The forward positions saw the brunt of the German pressure with systematic artillery fire making their situation dangerous. There were also clashes with enemy patrols and Lieutenant Harry Shand was wounded and captured in one of these actions. A valiant effort by another patrol to rescue him was unsuccessful. The evacuation plan through Dunkirk was now well in hand and on 28 May the 6th Battalion was ordered to travel directly to the coast at Bray Dunes, just north of Dunkirk and saw no further action.

One Gordon Highlander who was a senior officer with the BEF but who was not serving with the Regiment at this time was Brigadier Dougie Usher.

After handing over command of the 1st Battalion three months earlier he became responsible for logistical support of the BEF. However, as the Germans threatened to encircle the British at Dunkirk he was given command of a mixed unit to defend part of the Dunkirk perimeter. This mixed force of men, created from the remnants of a variety of units, was named Usher Force. On 23 May Brigadier Usher, and his aide, Major Jeffries, were being driven by Private William Carle, an experienced Gordon Highlander with eight years' service. Near Bergues, just six miles from the port area of Dunkirk, the road was being heavily bombed by the enemy and their journey was brought to an abrupt halt. The route was blocked by abandoned lorries as their drivers had just dumped their vehicles and were taking shelter in the roadside ditches. While the two officers got out to remonstrate with the drivers to get them back into their vehicles and clear the road, William Carle took the initiative and drove several lorries in turn to clear a passage for Brigadier Usher's car. William Carle's actions were an example to the others and he showed a total disregard for his own safety in order to secure a quick passage for his superiors. Not surprisingly, Brigadier Usher commended Carle for his bravery and he was subsequently awarded the Military Medal.

By 23 May the 4th Battalion's machine guns were being employed widely in defensive positions around Lille, at Lannoy, then pulling back to the Mauvaux area north of Lille. Two days later the Battalion was ordered to join 4th Division defending the line of the Comines–Ypres Canal between Comines and Houthem, which straddles the French-Belgian frontier. This line was of vital importance to the security of the sector and on the evening of 26 May the infantry, who were established in that vicinity with the purpose of taking over the tasks previously performed by the machine guns, were taking heavy enemy fire and decided to withdraw without orders. Lance Corporal W. Morgan, who was in command of a section of guns, while his section commander was absent carrying out reconnaissance, realized the dangers and assumed command of the sector. He rallied the infantry soldiers and so prevented a break in the British line. A similar situation developed near Moeres, where A Company was covering the eastern approaches on the Dunkirk–Furnes Canal. The casualty situation in A Company meant it was necessary to form a composite machine-gun platoon from two platoons which had suffered badly. On the night of 27/28 May their position become isolated when the infantry withdrew, leaving them in a dangerous position near Wytschaete. After almost three weeks of combat the men were becoming anxious and nervous, realizing their backs were to the sea. Morale was in a precarious state but the two most experienced men from each of the original platoons, Privates R. Campbell and R. Armour, kept a cool head and worked together to steady the men and kept up their spirits during the night. This ensured they remained in position until morning when, to everyone's relief, they were given the order to withdraw. Lieutenant Colonel Grant Taylor, the Commanding Officer of the 4th Battalion, recommended both privates for the Military Medal for their accomplishment at Wytschaete and throughout this dangerous period but, when passed up the chain of command, the award was downgraded to a Mention in Despatches.

On 27 May Private F. Goodwin, a despatch rider, was conveying messages along roads which were being heavily shelled on the line of the Ypres–Comines Canal. After delivering his last message he was blown off his motorcycle by a shell and his machine was so badly wrecked it was useless. Goodwin then elected to stay with that platoon and operated a Bren gun until the platoon withdrew to HQ Company where he obtained another motorcycle and continued his duties as a despatch rider. In recognition of his fine example to others he was recommended for the Distinguished Conduct Medal but again higher authority deemed a reduction of the award to the Military Medal, still recognition of his significant bravery. In a similar action, Private I Barnett, who was a runner at the company HQ, carried an important message to his platoon to withdraw on 31 May. In spite of continual enemy fire, on his return journey he voluntarily delayed to repair the breaks in the telephone line and was also awarded the Military Medal for his courage.

It was on the night of 28/29 May that the actions of Lieutenant (Quartermaster) Douglas J. Palmer (a Great War veteran commissioned in 1937, after five years' service as the 4th Battalion's Regimental Sergeant Major) sealed his award of the Military Cross and immediate promotion to captain for gallantry in the field. This exemplified the importance of logistical support to the front line, keeping the men supplied with equipment and rations which was essential for the maintenance of morale. It also illustrated that those providing this support were also subject to great danger. His citation, signed by the Commanding Officer of the Battalion, read:

Since the outbreak of war this officer has performed invaluable service for the unit. During the recent period of active operations, he has shown courage and resource of a very high order and as a result of his initiative and energy, the unit never went short of rations, even at times when these could only be procured and delivered to the [forward] Companies at considerable personal risk. In particular on the night of the 28/29th May, Lieutenant Palmer led the ration vehicles up to Company positions under heavy shellfire and returned to wagon lines with all his vehicles intact. His cheerful, loyal and gallant attitude at all times was a fine example to all.

The 4th Battalion's final move before evacuation was to Malo les Bains on the northern outskirts of Dunkirk where they suffered shells exploding all around their position. In spite of this, they were soon able to move along the beach and out along the Mole. Harry Foster was waiting his turn to embark but the shout went up 'wounded!' to which priority was given, so Harry had to wait for the next ship. As he watched the ship he had been about to board pull out to sea it was bombed by a German plane and it sank very quickly. Harry could hardly believe his luck and considered he had a guardian angel watching over him that day. His luck held as he was soon able to embark for England on another Royal Navy destroyer.

During the Great War, serving as a young lieutenant with the 1st Battalion Gordon Highlanders, Brigadier Dougie Usher had been captured on 27 August 1914, at le Cateau, northern France. The commanding officer failed to receive a message to withdraw which left them isolated and surrounded. He became a prisoner of war at Torgau PoW Camp, between Berlin and Leipzig. For him there was a sense of *déjà vu* but he had no desire to suffer the same fate again. Fortunately, he and his unit were relieved and made their way into Dunkirk where they were able to get away, arriving back in Britain on 1 June. In addition to Brigadier Usher, Major Douglas Gordon, another Gordon Highlander, assisted in the higher echelons of The British Expeditionary Force (BEF). He was the military assistant to the Chief of the Imperial General Staff (General the Viscount Gort VC KCB CBE DSO MVO MC) from 1938. When Lord Gort was appointed Commander in Chief of the BEF he acted as his personal assistant and was largely responsible for the detailed and successful arrangements for the visit of King George VI to the British forces in France in December 1939. Major Gordon was killed in action on 4 June 1940. In recognition of his service, he was posthumously appointed an Officer of the Most Excellent Order of the British Empire (OBE) which was published in the *London Gazette* exactly a month after his death.

Meanwhile, at Abbeville, the success of the French attack on 4 June was considered imperative to protect Paris and prevent the Germans from crossing the Somme. Two earlier attempts had failed to dislodge the Germans and the operation on the 4th involved the Gordon Highlanders taking a full part. The French artillery was ill prepared for the attack and had little reconnaissance information. The British were only a little more organized, having a Lysander spotter plane at their disposal but it had no radio so could only drop messages. Such was the degree of preparedness to meet a well-organized, disciplined and well-equipped enemy. The attack began at 3.30am with an Allied bombardment of German positions and the 1st Battalion Gordon Highlanders progressed well, executing a carefully worked out plan of attack and achieving the first objective, at the cost of eighteen killed and over twenty wounded. Among the dead was B Company's commander, Major D.W. Gordon, who was caught by a burst of machine-gun fire, but the attack was pressed on when Lieutenant Dennistoun Sword swiftly took command. They had succeeded in killing many more Germans and had taken some prisoners and were keen to continue to press home their attack but instead were ordered to withdraw, conceding all the ground taken. They were extremely frustrated by this situation but soon discovered the rest of the actions had not gone so well. The 5th Battalion, which was charged with supplying covering fire to the French advance through Moyenneville, also suffered a number of casualties. Among these were Privates David Spink and George Eddie who were killed near the Behan-Moyenneville road. Davie Spink had left his trench trying to observe the movements of some German soldiers advancing on their position and was caught in the open by an artillery bombardment. David Thom looked out from the safety of his trench and saw David Spink's rifle propped up against a tree but there was no sign of his friend. He crawled out to see what had happened and found him lying over a barbed-wire fence, mortally wounded by a shell splinter which had pierced his left temple. Although he was still alive when David Thom reached him, Davie Spink died within minutes in David Thom's arms. George Eddie, who was in the adjacent trench, was caught in the same bombardment which brought down a tree that fell into his trench, killing him outright. These two young men, aged just twenty and twenty-one, lived within a mile of each other in the centre of Peterhead, Aberdeenshire. They had been at school together, trained in the militia together and died together. They now lie buried next to each other in the churchyard at Réalcamp, a small French hamlet where theirs are the only British graves. In essence, the French armour had been decimated in their frontal attack on German positions and there was no alternative to the withdrawal of the entire division. The fate of the British 51st (Highland) Division was now entirely bound up with the French and this was emphasized when the Germans mounted a massive offensive the following day.

During that morning the 1st Battalion was outflanked by advancing enemy forces and there was an urgent necessity to organize a withdrawal with Lieutenant Basil Brooke's Bren-gun carriers fighting a rearguard action to cover this. Captain Donald Alexander was wounded by mortar fire and Lance Corporal Groves and Private Alan Knight did their best to carry him to safety but he ordered them to leave him and save themselves. He fell into enemy hands but died later that day. Also wounded that same day was Second Lieutenant Charles Barker but he was more fortunate and was successfully evacuated back to England for medical treatment.

The enemy were closing fast but initially the 5th Battalion, in the village of Huchenville, four miles south-west of Abbeville, was not in the path of the German advance. However when B Company was sent forward to Mareuil-Caubert to relieve a company of the Queen's Own Cameron Highlanders, it became involved in its defence to the extent that neither could withdraw and were surrounded and forced to surrender. There were many close encounters with the enemy and Lieutenant A.D. Ritchie won the Military Cross for his work commanding a platoon of Bren-gun carriers which successfully covered the withdrawal. However not everyone was so fortunate. Regimental Sergeant Major James Leel was travelling in a vehicle which took a wrong turn and ran straight into the position of a German anti-tank gun; the RSM was killed.

The withdrawal was completed and new positions taken up where they dug in, followed by another organized withdrawal, which was to be the pattern for the succeeding days. The situation was deteriorating rapidly with the French faring badly on every front and the plan was to fall back on le Havre for evacuation by the Royal Navy back to Britain. Some units were evacuated, as part of Ark Force, its name taken from the French village of Arques–la–Bataille where it was formed, but the Gordons were not amongst these. Their objective was to cover the division's withdrawal to le Havre but German armour had reached the coast at Veullettes-sur-Mer and closed off the road to le Havre but Ark Force did manage to embark and get away. These events also had a profound effect on a draft of reinforcements, sent from the Depot in Aberdeen, under the command of Lieutenant Ian Monteith. Monteith was a school friend of Ran Ogilvie at Ampleforth and, having been originally posted to the Depot, felt he was missing the action and was keen to link up with his friend again. Ian Monteith was a son of the Regiment, his father being Major Basil Monteith, Baron of Carstairs and Cranley, whose older son, George, had been killed in the Great War fighting with the 3rd Battalion. The cutting off of le Havre not only prevented the remainder of the Division from reaching the port, it also prevented the reinforcements from joining the Gordons at St Valéry so they had to re-embark and return to Aberdeen, avoiding the fate of the 51st (Highland) Division. Ian Monteith would have to wait for his chance to have a crack at the Germans but this came in 1942 when, serving with the 5th/7th Gordon Highlanders, he was posted to North Africa, as part of the 'phoenix' 51st (Highland) Division.

The situation was changing rapidly and the Germans were pressing forward and were caught badly by the Bren guns of the 5th Battalion, losing many men. The reply was, however, swift and an artillery bombardment killed three men and wounded several others. Piper George McLennan was among a group of men who were in a ditch on the other side of the road from Harry Tobin (2878125), taking cover from enemy machine-gun fire which was pinning them all down. They crawled along the ditch, then bolted for a safer position, watched and encouraged by Major Rupert Christie and RSM A. Noble. As each man made his move the German machine gunners gave them a burst but fortunately none were being hit. When George's turn came he got up and ran about twenty yards and dropped to regain his breath. When he moved again he felt as though a sledgehammer had hit his ankle and from across the road he heard a shout go up that 'Mac has been killed' but at least he was alive to hear this. A bullet had struck the buckle of his gaiter, tore through the other side, scorching the boot and then through his other trouser leg. George thought it was not too serious, but it was very painful and he managed to crawl the remaining distance to safety. As the Battalion withdrew a truck stopped to pick up injured men and only then did Harry Tobin notice his trousers had a neat hole in them where the bullet had passed through. George was picked up by Corporal Peter Noble, who saw him sitting disabled at the roadside and helped him into his truck and took care of him. Next day, when examined by the Medical Officer, (Captain George I. Davidson) it was confirmed the ankle was broken and George was told he would have to go to hospital. George protested vigorously and was finally allowed to stay with the Battalion as they were on their way home; at this time there was no doubt in their minds they would soon be evacuated from France.

Evacuation of the wounded across the open ground was difficult but Lance Corporal Tom Borthwick acted courageously by ferrying these men back to the field dressing station in his truck, endangering his own life in the process. After retreating in early hours of darkness some Gordons were able to snatch a few hours' sleep in a wood outside Dieppe. Private Philip McCarron was ordered by his corporal to change places with the Bren gunners which probably saved his life. The Germans attacked with mortar bombs and, although blown off his feet and knocked unconscious by a blast, he was not seriously hurt. However, the rest of the section were not so fortunate with the Bren gunners having caught the full force of the attack with two men dead and the rest wounded, one of whom lost an arm. Things were obviously going badly and, with shelling becoming increasingly close, all non–essential kit was dumped so as not to hinder their withdrawal. Such was the confusion of the situation that men were becoming detached from their units and no one knew what had become of them. After James Reynolds was killed he was hurriedly buried behind the Mairie at Blosseville but the location of his grave was lost so that he has no known grave and after the war he was commemorated on the Dunkirk Memorial. In addition, it was reported to and recorded by Major Bruce that Thomas Mercer and Robert J. Hinds had been killed in action but luckily they had just been wounded.

On 11 June 1940 the Gordons were in convoy and proceeded along the main Dieppe road but progress was slow as the road was crowded with vehicles. It was sobering to discover part of the reason for the hold–up was a burning ammunition trailer, the result of the constant attention they had been receiving all day from the Luftwaffe's Stukas. George McLennan remembered passing this blazing truck, the air punctuated with intermittent explosions with bullets flying everywhere. With Dieppe harbour now blocked and the road to le Havre in the hands of the Germans, the fate of the 51st (Highland) Division was sealed, with everything resting on an evacuation by sea through St Valéry-en-Caux. This was far from ideal as the town occupied only a narrow cleft in the 300-feet-high chalk cliff coastline. Furthermore, the small tidal harbour was inaccessible to vessels at low tide but, with little other option available, General Fortune ordered that the Division fall back and form a defensive ring around the town. The remnants of the Highlanders took up positions on the flanks with the French holding the centre. The 1st Gordons took up a position around St Riquier-le-Plains, just two to three miles to the south-west of St Valéry, whilst the 5th Battalion was ordered to hold the area around the village of St Pierre-le-Viger, approximately eight miles to the south-east of the town. The Gordons had dug into their positions and were satisfied they were relatively well concealed but were frustrated to see French soldiers wandering aimlessly around into open country. In mid-afternoon there was heavy shelling of the 5th Gordons' positions but welcome news was received that the embarkation was likely to take place that evening. In the early evening enemy machine-gun fire began to harass the Battalion Headquarters but this was successfully engaged and destroyed but, ominously, German tanks were seen moving across their front, at a distance of approximately a mile, too far away to fire on.

That afternoon the weather deteriorated and it poured with rain. In order for some of the men to take an improvised meal break, Philip McCarron and another man were ordered to take up position to guard the road and issued with an anti-tank rifle and two bullets. Fortunately no tank came down the road and he and his comrade were thankful to be relieved when it was time for their meal. There was, however, a short time later, a concentrated tank attack, supported by aircraft, on the main St Valéry road which was in the area being held by 1st Gordons who were caught up in this. Despite heavy casualties the enemy failed to break through. The men were exhausted, having been in action almost continuously for five weeks, were running low on ammunition and had not eaten a proper meal for some time. Lieutenant Brian Hay was in command of the transport and, despite heavy shelling of the roads, he had spent much time maintaining contact with HQ. He had managed to get his transport to the outskirts of St Valéry when his progress was halted by the road being completely blocked by two overturned and burning French vehicles. He took charge of the situation and ordered his men and a number of stragglers who were in the vicinity to form an improvised defensive position until he could receive further orders or the evacuation situation became clearer. His position was approached by a French officer, accompanied by two Germans who brought a surrender demand from the enemy. They wondered at first if this Frenchman was a fifth columnist impersonating a French officer but the French Brigade Liaison Officer checked his papers and was satisfied he was genuine. Brian Hay had no thought of surrender and it is recorded that in giving the Frenchman his uncompromising reply he finished by barking, 'take that to your General'.

As darkness began to fall, a car, coming from the direction of St Valéry and under fire all the way, screeched to a halt at Ran Ogilvie's position and out stepped Lieutenant Johnny Rhodes. He had orders from the company commander to ascertain their situation and advise that their evacuation was likely to take place that night. He then left under heavy fire. At dawn next day they were surprised as the same car re-appeared, riddled with bullet holes. Again, out stepped the irrepressible Johnny Rhodes with a message that they should fight their way into St Valéry-en-Caux. As they tried to withdraw into the town they came under fire from all sides with the heaviest fire coming from the direction of St Valéry. However, on the way there disaster struck. Things started well enough when they came across two serviceable trucks with their drivers who had no orders, so Ran commandeered their services and headed into the town. When they came over a blind summit they were confronted by a German panzer directly in their path with another at the side, both aiming straight at them. Ran ordered the driver to press on and rush the tanks in a desperate attempt to get through, but they were fired upon by the tank's machine gun and brought to a grinding halt with the driver being badly wounded. The Gordons did, however, manage to jump out into the roadside ditch but this offered little cover. With only small arms at their disposal and two tanks only fifty yards away Ran Ogilvie made the inevitable decision to surrender and yelled 'cease fire'. He then got out of the ditch with his hands held high, his handkerchief in one hand and holding the barrel of his captured Luger pistol in the other. He surrendered to the nearest tank commander who calmly took the Luger, applied the safety catch and put it in his pocket. Ran then had a nerve-racking moment when he remembered that he had been told that if captured with a German weapon he was likely to be summarily shot so his relief was palpable when he was merely led away into captivity.

Around midnight, news was received that the French commander in St Valéry had decided to capitulate which was a shock but there had been an air of defeatism in the French for some time, with their government abandoning Paris for Bordeaux the previous day. Around 3.00am, a message was received by the 5th Battalion to withdraw into St Valéry but in the chaotic situation the Division found itself it was deemed sensible to have this checked and Second Lieutenant C.B. Hughes was sent to 153 Brigade HQ at Blosseville to confirm it. On his return, orders were issued to destroy all secret papers, non-carried weapons and transport vehicles, with the exception of the Bren-gun carriers and the CO's car. The Battalion began withdrawing into the town at 4.30am with Bren-gun carriers acting as rearguard. Their CO went forward to the embarkation point and found there were no ships and that beaches and town were under fire from cliffs to the north and south. He also discovered that the French Divisional HQ had capitulated. A thick fog had descended on the coast and it was impossible for the Navy to approach the little harbour, so the evacuation had to be delayed. Some destroyers, together with some ancillary vessels, were just off the coast but were being attacked by aircraft and fired upon by the German guns on the cliffs. By the time the weather cleared it was too late to evacuate men from the town. There was still a hope that they could be successfully evacuated but many men, including experienced soldiers such as Colour Sergeant Alex Moir, feared this was an increasingly slender prospect. A group of men, which included Privates Malcom Mackintosh, H. McCloy and James Watt, were desperate to get to the coast and hoped to get away but found they were on top of the 300-foot sheer cliffs which stretched on either side of St Valéry as far as the eye could see. In despair they started tying their rifle slings together to make a makeshift rope to lower themselves down the cliff but this proved impractical and Malcolm Mackintosh fell to his death before they accepted this. Some men made their way to nearby Veules-les-Roses where there was another little harbour. The Royal Navy destroyer HMS *Codrington* managed to put some parties ashore here and, despite heavy machine-gun fire, some men were lucky enough to embark and escape. This was not however, the fate of Private Alex Simpson, who died in this area and now lies buried in Veules-les-Roses Communal Cemetery. The tug *Fair Play* was towing some small vessels and approached the beach west of St Valéry just after midnight; some beach parties were landed but came under intense fire immediately and four boats were sunk.

PSM Charlie Fullerton managed to get through to St Valéry with his men, by moving cross country and slipping through enemy lines. He got to the pier by daybreak but found it was being raked by enemy machine-gun fire and since they had been up all night they retired to a house and had something to eat. Trying to find out what he should do he approached a major of the Royal Army Service Corps (RASC) who said they were trying to make a last stand in the hope the ships would still be able to get in if the weather improved. Charlie Fullerton took two men with Bren guns and climbed a hill to the west of the town and dealt with the machine guns and then returned to rendezvous with the rest of his men on the beach. The tragic sight that greeted them was one of utter chaos with soldiers of various units lying dead and dying. Charlie gave the order, 'every man for himself' but found that his men all continued to follow him. They walked along the beach under the cover of the cliff and passed some French soldiers sheltering in caves. Continuing eastwards they saw two ships, one beached with the other lying only some 300 yards offshore. Making for these they attracted the attention of a German machine-gun post, ahead of the ships, so tried to get up the cliffs. There was no cover so, under a hail of bullets, they ran to the beached vessel and climbed on board to find it full of wounded together with a number of French women and children. The Captain would not allow him to fire the ship's gun for fear of retaliation by the German tanks, which were on the cliffs above them. Just then the Germans opened up with armour-piercing shells, causing absolute chaos. Charlie took control of the situation and stood on a box and shouted that he would shoot any man who attempted to get out before the women and children were safely off the ship. The women were then hauled up on to the top deck and able to get clear and all of the French, who had been sheltering on the vessel, raised their hands and shouting 'Kamerad'. The Germans were throwing grenades down the cliff which was too much, so Charlie and Corporal Bill Grant slipped over the side. They started to swim for the other ship when it took a direct hit from a shell and was blown out of the water so they headed back to the shore where a group of Germans, armed with sub-machine guns, were waiting for them.

They were allowed to put on their boots and then marched off to an assembly area on top of the cliffs. On the way through the town, where the lower part and seafront was in ruins with burning buildings all around, they passed General Fortune. Platoon Sergeant Major Fullerton gave the 'eyes right' command as the party passed him to show that despite them being forced to surrender to the enemy's superior numbers and equipment they were not disheartened. For 51st (Highland) Division the fight for France was over, at least until the 'phoenix' could rise from the ashes, re-formed from 9th (Highland) Division. The men surrendering that day could not have known that the names of their units would live on and continue to play a vital role in the war.

A few miles inland, at Manneville-ès-Plains, an officer gave the news that they were surrounded by enemy tanks, announced that General Fortune had surrendered to General Erwin Rommel's 7th Panzer Division and gave the command, 'everyman for himself', adding 'good luck!' Alex Watt (2875918) was with Jack Davie, a friend also from Bucksburn, Aberdeen, who had just returned to active service following an operation to remove his appendix. They decided to make for St Valéry with the hope of finding a boat. On their way they came to a brick-built shed in an orchard where they found some of the pipers discussing what to do next. This shed was more or less filled with five pipers and Despatch Rider George Rennie, who were brewing up some food so Alex and Jack, together with Sammy Robertson and Jim McDonald sat outside, their backs resting against the wall. They started to eat some of their hard-tack biscuits when, suddenly, there was a loud bang, as a mortar shell went through the roof of the shed and exploded inside. A cloud of dust billowed out from the building quickly followed by Bill Maitland and James (Curly) Allan who stumbled out and fell to the ground wounded. While Sammy and Jim, who were both first aiders, rushed to help the wounded the Germans were moving in. Lance Corporal George Watson tried to help Curly, helping him into another barn and dressed his wounds. Captain Christie ordered George to get Curly to a doctor and he got a door to act as a stretcher. Unfortunately it was too late as a group of eight Germans, armed with sub-machine guns, surprised them in the barn and they had to surrender. While this was all going on, Alex and Jack took off across some fields but Bill Maitland found himself looking up at a German standing over him with a pistol pointing at his head. This German spoke good English and helped Bill on to a tank which ferried him some distance up a hill where he received some medical treatment.

Alex and Jack made their way across country towards the sea where they encountered a large group of French soldiers who were waving white flags and it was noticeable they had prepared well for their surrender as they were all carrying suitcases full of food and spare clothing to sustain them in their expected journey into captivity. Soon afterwards they met up with a large body of 5th Gordons in a sunken lane. It was clear to all that there was no escape and an NCO instructed them all to destroy their weapons to prevent them falling into enemy hands. Alex Watt (2875918) initially had a feeling of disbelief then annoyance. As a battalion signaller he had had no active combat role but had still been required to carry his rifle with him at all times. He had carried it faithfully since September 1939, cleaned and oiled it regularly but, despite being a very good shot, he never had any opportunity to use it and now he had to dismantle his rifle by removing the bolt and throw it away. Even if the Germans could find and collect all the rifles and bolts they would have to match each bolt to its own rifle for it to be of any use. As the men were contemplating their future their fate was sealed. Two German tanks appeared on the bank above them and with machine guns pointing directly at them a German officer shouted 'Hände hoch!' (hands up). Despite the seriousness of the situation, Alex couldn't help suppressing a snigger, seeing himself and his comrades with their hands raised, something he had only ever seen in films. They were all stunned.

During the past month, when the fighting had been intense, they had always realized there was a possibility that they could be killed or wounded, but never thought they would become prisoners of war. However, now that it was all over and for the time being they were still alive there was a feeling of bewilderment and the anxiety of what the Germans would do with them, but there was also a sort of relief that it was all over. Bill Reaper, although not with Alex Watt and the others, had almost exactly the same experience. He was with B Company of the 5th Battalion when they had heard a bugle call from the village signalling 'lay down your arms' although he had not known what this meant. They too were in a sunken road, which was a feature of this chalk country, when suddenly six grey tanks burst through the hedge above them and Bill saw a German, in the distinctive black uniform of panzer troops, waving a grenade in each hand who proclaimed, almost in comic book fashion, 'the war for you is over Tommy!' A number of Gordons had surprising direct encounters with German soldiers when they were captured. Private Bill Ewen was a truck driver with the 1st Gordons and when he arrived at St Valéry, as ordered, he helped destroy his and one other remaining truck which had taken them there, the others being destroyed the day before. They almost made it to the beach when they were fired on from the cliff opposite and they were forced to retreat back into the town. Eventually it was clear their situation was hopeless and they surrendered to some Germans who told them to throw away their weapons. One German said to Bill, in good English, 'well Jock, wish to hell it was all finished'.

They were led to a field with a truck in each corner, each with a machine gun mounted on a platform. This was a collecting area where there were thousands of British and French soldiers who had already been rounded up. Bill Maitland was also taken to this collecting point and he met up with Sammy Robertson, Jimmy McDonald, Alex Watt (2875918) and the others. They told him that Patrick (known as Peter) Stewart, Duncan Reid, Johnny McLennan and George Rennie had all been killed. In addition, Curly Allan's foot was smashed and he was in hospital. Bill was declared fit enough to be able to march into captivity, but at this point neither he nor the others fully understood what this would entail. Sammy was also able to tell Bill and Alex that George and the pipers had all been killed instantly with little disfigurement. They had been killed by the shock wave of the blast, enhanced in the confined space of the building. Ironically, by containing the blast inside the building, to devastating effect for those inside, the strength of the wall saved Alex and the others on the outside. This was a sad day for two other pipers. Gordon Reid (2880758) was told of the death of his brother Duncan and George McLennan told his brother Johnny had died in the same incident. The McLennan brothers were the sons of Pipe Major G.S. McLennan, the most famous piper of the Regiment. Also killed near Manneville-ès-Plains, this same day, was Corporal Bill Neilson, the Regimental Tailor. His death was particularly tragic. Not only did he leave behind a very young family but Bill's two older brothers, Charles and Rolland, had both been killed in France during the Great War. Like Bill, they had been NCOs serving with the 5th Battalion Gordon Highlanders, Rolland's gallantry being recognized with a Mention in Despatches and the award of the Meritorious Service Medal. Both men had been good footballers, having played for a time with Aberdeen FC (The Dons) before their lives were cut short.

George McLennan and the other wounded had been ordered to make their way down to the beach where they were being gathered together and were still being informed they would be evacuated by a Royal Navy destroyer. As they neared the seafront they found the road impassable due to the enemy machine-gun fire, which had already claimed the lives of a number of men, whose bodies they could see lying around the square, so they took shelter in a garage. When the surrender was confirmed the wounded were escorted into captivity and there was a rumour that the Nazis were not taking prisoners and they would all be shot. George took the precaution of keeping a grenade in his greatcoat pocket so that he could give them something to think about if and when he was shot. Fortunately this was misinformation and they were spoken to, in good English, by a German NCO who directed them to the German aid post. Going up the hill out of the town, they encountered SS tanks and the leading tank attempted to run them down. Their escort shouted a warning to throw themselves on the banks, which saved them but one man had his toes crushed in the process. In the field at the top of this road, tanks were re-fuelling with petrol and replenishing their ammunition and paid very little attention to this band of wounded. Then one of these SS men, whom George described as either mad or having lost a good friend, forced some of the wounded up against the tanks, saying that they were 'useless, wounded swine who had been bayoneting German wounded and would all be shot', rekindling the original rumour. This Nazi had a Schmeisser machine pistol, and was red-haired. With his thick pebble glasses, he looked the horror that he was. He had really got himself worked up to killing and the crews of the tanks hastily got out of the line of possible fire but the day was saved by an ordinary German *unteroffiziere* (corporal), who, on seeing this situation, had the courage to draw his pistol, press it against the SS man and told the wounded to get away quickly. They needed no second telling and moved as quickly as possible, helping each other along. They reached an RAP which was being used for both British and German wounded and it was here that George again met up with Captain George I. Davidson, his Battalion Medical Officer. He was working with a German medical officer dressing the wounded as they came in and, on seeing George, exclaimed 'You *!***!* fool! If you had gone on the ambulance when you were hit, you could have been out of this'. George could only agree and accept his fate. One man struggling to come to terms with his fate was Archie Jeal, a Great War veteran. He was wounded badly and lying in a field alone and unable to move. For some considerable time he lay there helpless until, luckily, he was found by some Germans and taken to hospital.

PSM Robert Clubbs and his men destroyed their rifles after their company commander, Captain Nelson Keith, came to Clubbs around 10.00am on the morning of 12 June and told him there was no point on fighting on individually and to cease fire and rendezvous behind his position. Clubbs and his men were in a small wood, so he gathered them together and told them to break up their rifles, bury their ammunition and destroy all paybooks and papers. Before they marched out, PSM Clubbs told his men that, although they had surrendered, they should not be downhearted and they should try to escape, if possible. They then joined the rest of the 5th Battalion, who were already formed up in the field surrounded by German tanks armed with machine guns.

Some men were able to slip away without falling into German hands. One was Private Walter Philips of the 6th Battalion who had been transferred to the 5th, so instead of being evacuated with his comrades at Dunkirk he found he was cornered at St Valéry, although at this point he knew nothing about the miracle of Dunkirk. He got as far south as Caen and had met up with some RASC men. Their luck ran out on 16 June, after being at liberty for only four days, when they were captured as they attempted to escape by boat. Walter Philips was not outdone yet and vowed to escape again if an opportunity arose. He then joined his comrades being marched north into captivity. A few Gordon Highlanders were more successful in their attempts to evade capture. Jim Moggach and his cousin Sandy Kydd managed to find a boat and stayed out of sight, covering themselves with bolsters, while it floated down river to the sea, where fortunately they were picked up by a friendly ship. Jim's mother had received the standard War Office letter advising her that her son was posted missing on 12 June 1940, but she did not have to wait long to find out he was safe. After arriving back in the UK he went straight to his family home, in Aberdeen, before reporting to Seaton Camp, the Regimental HQ, to tell her in person that he was safe. She was not surprised, therefore, when, a few days later, she got a letter from the Infantry Records office telling her he had returned to the Regiment on 17 July 1940. Captain Leslie Hulls had previous experience of escaping from the enemy in the Great War. Captain Hulls was no ordinary man and was wounded in July 1917 and returned to the UK via Archangel in August 1917 after serving as a lieutenant with the

Royal Naval Armoured Car Service during the Russian retreat from Galicia, Poland. He transferred to the army in January 1918 and, while serving with the Machine Gun Corps, was awarded the Military Cross for escaping from enemy imprisonment in May 1918. Although originally commissioned into the Gordon Highlanders in 1915, he entered the Royal Naval Volunteer Reserve in January 1916, so it was fitting that he escaped directly from France in the company of another naval officer, Commander Robert Elkins. They sailed from Lion-sur-Mer, ten miles due north of Caen, on the night of 23 June 1940 and, as a consequence, Captain Hulls was awarded a Bar to his Military Cross. The award of a Military Cross in both World Wars for an escape on both occasions is probably a unique occurrence. Leslie Hulls remains enigmatic to this day as the Ministry of Defence has 'locked' his file for 75 years until 2020.

At the assembly point the Germans separated the British and the French and the officers from the other ranks. Once this was arranged the officers were taken away in motorized transport. Prior to this the prisoners were instructed to deposit all their equipment on the ground and the Germans started to search this, looking for weapons, such as knives or grenades. Some Germans also used this opportunity to steal valuables, such as watches and rings, from their prisoners, although some of these items were willingly traded for bread or a piece of sausage. Ran Ogilvie lost his treasured silver stag's head Gordon's badge from his glengarry when it was demanded by the German officer in charge of the troops guarding them. They then were marched off with the shrewd ones retrieving their mess kit and coats. Alex Watt (2875918) noticed their company sergeant major still had his kilt and remarked that it would probably fetch a few loaves but, on hearing this, the CSM quickly put it out of sight. However, many of the men of HQ Company had already lost a lot of their spare boots and uniform as it had been in their kitbags in one of the trucks. When the order was given to destroy the trucks by setting fire to them all of this personal kit was lost. After being rounded up with the others, Sergeant John Duncan was already thinking about how he could slip away and behaved in such a way that the guards thought he was drunk so they kept him in a corner of the field. At about midnight he managed to slip away unnoticed and went to stay with people he knew at Saint Gilles de Cretot, some twenty-four miles south of St Valéry, where he had previously been billeted. His freedom was relatively short lived when he was recaptured just over a year later, on 11

September 1941. He then spent an anxious time over the next three months locked up in a political prison in Rouen until his story that he was an evading British soldier was accepted by the Gestapo and he was transferred to Stalag VIIIB (Teschen/Lamsdorf).

The Germans appeared anxious to move their prisoners away from the coast as quickly as possible, so thousands of men, including around 1,500 Gordon Highlanders, began the long weary trek into captivity that afternoon, but many more followed the next day. They marched five abreast with the French in front accompanied by German guards on foot, on bicycles and on motorcycles. In addition, approximately every hundred yards was a lorry, with a machine gun mounted on the cab roof, which frequently forced the men on with its bumper. Anyone straggling was hit with a stick or kicked to induce him to keep up. Friends stayed together and the many brothers searched out their kin to help each other in these trying circumstances. Maurice MacLean couldn't find his brother Hugh, who was an ambulance driver serving with the Royal Army Service Corps, so became anxious for news of him. He kept asking Service Corps personnel if they knew anything and eventually met a group who said they had seen his ambulance bombed and burned outside St Valéry but they knew nothing of Hugh's fate. It was another nine months before he learned that he was one of the few who had managed to get down the cliffs, using a rifle-sling rope, and escaped back to Britain by boat. Brothers Jack and Billie Hutcheon stayed together every step the way with Billie helping Jack who was already suffering physically. The first day they marched for twenty miles to Yvetot where they spent the night under guard, in the grounds of a château. The first priority for most of the men was food but the Germans, who were not prepared for the large number of British and French prisoners in their hands, had little to offer them. Some men were lucky enough to get a piece of bread or some watery bean soup but most went hungry. The next concern was rest. Most had been travelling and fighting for almost forty-eight hours without any sleep and were mentally and physically exhausted. The first night was spent in an open field with no protection from the elements. The lucky ones with great coats and groundsheets, which could also double up as a cape during the rain, could sleep in relative comfort. Exhaustion overtook the pangs of hunger and they slept as though unconscious. The day after the surrender was Private Robert Milne's 22nd birthday, certainly not a very happy one. In the vicinity of the battle there were corpses and discarded equipment lying around so pragmatism trumped squeamish feelings and the opportunity seized upon to make up for their own lack of personal kit. It was some days before regular food was available. It was a bad day for all the men but one soldier was hardly a man. This was Private Gordon Holmes, who, as a young burly youth, managed to enlist into the Gordon Highlanders at the Bridge of Don Barracks in Aberdeen in March 1939 by lying about his age. When captured at St Valéry he had not yet had his 16th birthday, which he ultimately celebrated in a German prisoner of war camp.

The Germans asked for men with farming experience to volunteer to carry out some work locally. Realizing this could delay his movement to Germany and imprisonment, Alex Moir, a sergeant of the 1st Battalion, put himself forward. Alex didn't have a farming background but was determined to escape, so he seized the excuse to stay in France a while longer as he believed this was his best option to escape. This party was detailed to return to St Valéry to round up the numerous stray French army horses and bury the dead. This was also a golden opportunity to acquire some food from deserted houses, and farms. By pooling their ill-gotten gains, they, at least, were able to produce a passable meal. The reality of the situation was now unmistakable. Individual resourcefulness was essential to ensure survival, obtain food and, if possible, escape. With some 1,500 Gordon Highlanders in enemy hands, the responses to this situation they now found themselves in were almost as varied as human nature itself.

Chapter 3

The Long Weary Trail to the East

As the days passed the routine was the same with the German guards harrying the long columns of PoWs. These men became increasingly dirty and sweaty from the lack of facilities to wash. They were also hungry and tired with the relentless marches of twenty miles or more each day coupled with spending each night exposed to the elements and lucky if they were fed a watery soup. Some of the TA men recalled the 1938 route march in the Ballater area when the weather had been awful and they were close to breaking point. This proved a good character builder and helped them go on but this period marked a low point in their morale. The lack of information about the wider position was troubling. The Germans kept telling them the war was lost which raised the prospect of them being held prisoner indefinitely, possibly never seeing their families again. This all preyed on their minds with all their hopes and expectations of victory dashed. During their progress northwards French civilians tried to help them as they passed through the many small towns and villages. Women would throw bread into the column or put out pails of water or milk for the men to drink. The Germans were not pleased with this and, although they had little food for the prisoners themselves, many mean-minded Nazi guards would ride along on their bicycles and kick over the pails to spill the contents. Anyone giving food to a prisoner could be severely dealt with and physically beaten by these guards. Despite this, some women bravely rushed out to press bread or other pieces of food into the hands of the grateful men who wolfed down these gifts with relish. A villager threw a crust of bread towards Jim McInnes, so he gratefully stopped and bent down to pick it up and was shot in the hand. One morning a woman gave Private Maurice MacLean an egg but he was unsure if it was raw or cooked so he carried it carefully all day. That night he was able to make a small fire to boil it, only to find that 'Madame' had, very sensibly, already cooked it. Nevertheless Maurice and a friend enjoyed this rare treat. At a later stop he went one better by boiling up some nettles in his steel helmet to make a thick soup which may not have been tremendously nourishing but was a comfort.

Driven on by their insatiable hunger the men tried to obtain food in any way they could. Alex Auld ran into a butcher's shop and slapped all the French money he had down on the counter and grabbed some sausages and ran back out into the street. Alex hadn't noticed all of the sausages were linked together so, as he ran off, a string of sausages was trailing after him. Unfortunately, he ran straight into arms of two German guards who stopped him and consequently he lost his sausages, his money and incurred the wrath of both the guards and the butcher. The only other available food was in the fields they passed. The prisoners spread into the adjoining fields, pulling up anything which was edible such as potatoes, cabbages and turnips. There were generally no facilities for cooking these so indigestion and diarrhoea often followed, adding more misery to the marchers. Water was also a priority and drinking water from streams or stagnant ponds was a serious risk to heath with dysentery often the result. The incursions into the fields were not without risk as the guards were inclined to shoot anyone they thought was attempting to escape. The French farmers were also very angry about the loss of their crops and livelihood and so started to guard their fields. Word went ahead of the column and soon the farmers stood guard prepared to defend their property as the column passed, like a swarm of locusts stripping the countryside of anything edible.

At times like these some men sought solace in any way they could. Charles Morrison (2881803) was a God-fearing man and as he left home his father gave him his own *Soldier's Bible* which he had kept treasured from his service in the Great War. Charles knew its contents well and turned to it often. Corporal Bill Grant realized, too late, that he had lost his bible in the chaos and confusion at St Valéry. A few days after the soldiers had been marched away into captivity a curious young French boy found a mud-spattered bible in a deserted slit trench on the outskirts of St Valéry. He opened the cover to find the inscription Corporal W. S. Grant, D Company, 5th Battalion Gordon Highlanders and slipped it into his pocket. Sixty-four years later, that boy, now an old man living in Brittany, approached some British holidaymakers, Ann and Geoff Berry of Solihull in the West Midlands, and asked them to help him re-unite the bible with its owner. Back home they made an appeal through newspapers circulating in Scotland and the bible was reunited with the Grant family but unfortunately this was some time after Bill's death. Robert Hastie had his bible with him all through his captivity and when liberated he wrote down the names and addresses of the close friends he had made in Stalag XXB (Marienburg) one of whom was J.M. McDonald (2882830) whom he was with from day one at the PoW camp. Maurice MacLean, the son of a Church of Scotland minister, was also very familiar with the scriptures and was studying theology at St Andrews University. Before joining the Gordon Highlanders he had started officer training but was unable to complete the course due to an injury to his foot. During his time as a PoW he was called upon several times to conduct services and the funerals of some of his fellow PoWs. Corporal Peter Noble had not been as fortunate as some others and was pleased to receive the gift of a bible in June 1943 through the auspices of The Ecumenical Commission of the Chaplaincy Service to Prisoners of War based in Geneva. Peter made sure this did not go astray and wrote his name and number on the inside of the front cover and it was approved for him to keep with the official Stalag VIIIB stamp. He looked after this bible for his entire life and over seventy years later his daughter, knowing how much he had treasured it, decided to donate it to the safekeeping of the Gordon Highlanders' Museum.

The route the columns of prisoners of war followed took them through Forges les Eaux, Aumale, Amiens, Villers Bocage, Doullens, St Pol, Béthune, Lille and into Belgium at Tournai. Meanwhile, the Germans pressed on with their conquest of France and marched into Paris on 14 June and flew the Nazi swastika from the Eiffel Tower. The French government had already fled the city and were in Bordeaux where a defeatist attitude took hold. When the head of the French government, Great War hero Marshal Philippe Pétain, announced on 17 June that France would seek an armistice the German guards were elated and started to poke fun at their British captives. Gregor Macdonald, a Cameron Highlander, recorded an amusing incident which was reproduced in the book *The Impossible Odds* where Gregor's story was published in an edited form by Bill Innes. He recalled that in one small town, possibly Amiens, the Germans had set up a platform in the main square where there was a man strutting around dressed as the former British Prime Minister Neville Chamberlain, complete with morning jacket, striped trousers, top hat and rolled umbrella. The column was halted for the performance with the guards laughing and shouting 'so will you hang out your washing on the Siegfried Line now Schottlander?!' As the uproar died down the tables were turned on the Germans when, in a clear voice in Doric, which could only have been a Gordon Highlander, shouted out 'Dis is feel loon nae ken we hiv got Churchill noo?!' (Does this stupid boy not know that we have Churchill now?) It was now the British who were laughing and the Germans, who had no idea what the Gordon had shouted, realized their joke had fallen flat. This was one brief light moment in the otherwise general sense of despair, which was accentuated by the confident swagger and smart appearance of the Germans, compared to the bedraggled appearance of the British soldiers who looked like a bunch of tramps.

As the days and weeks passed the Germans became more organized and food became more regular but still in meagre quantities and often revolting, such as bread already green with mould. While most nights were still spent in the open there was an occasion at Doullens where they spent the night in a deep quarry giving some protection from the elements and what seemed like luxury was experienced in Béthune, where they slept under the seats of the football stadium. The guards also became less nervous and more relaxed and they were all now on foot with only a few lorries to carry men who were acknowledged temporarily unfit to march. Those who were more ill, such as Private James McNair, left the column and remained at Renaix. He had become fevered through developing a chill after spending nights in the open and getting wet through as he had neither a greatcoat nor cape for protection against inclement weather. Alex Watt (2875918) was suffering from blistered feet. His boots were completely worn out by the time they reached St Pol, having marched over 120 miles in eleven days. A sympathetic guard noticed him hobbling and said his first aider would look at it to prevent an infection setting in, so his sores were cleaned and dressed. Later he was taken to a school converted to a hospital in Lille where he was allowed to walk freely in the grounds and speak to local children at the gate. The guard kept a watchful eye but was totally relaxed about their contact. These children offered to take his name and address and pass a message to his family to say he was safe and, although Alex had no idea how this was achieved, a letter was received at his home.

The men knew it was their duty to escape and the lectures on the subject, which had been given by their officers at the start of the campaign, had been ringing in their ears ever since the initial shock of capture had passed. The Gordons had been stationed in this part of northern France, near the Belgian border, in the early part of the war so knew the country well from exercises, route marches and their various billets in the areas of Béthune and Lille. In addition they had made a favourable impression on the local population who were sympathetically disposed towards them. At this time a private in the British Army was being paid approximately 100 French francs per week, so had money to spend and some made friendly contacts with the staff of local shops and bars. David Thom was among a group of 5th Battalion men who were regulars at the Hotel Suisse which was run by a woman who had two children. He became a great favourite of the proprietor as he often sat in a corner of the bar with her children and tried to teach them English, improving his French at the same time. He would regularly drop into the hotel and the frying pan went on right away with Madame making him a pancake the circumference of the pan. He considered this a great delight as it was sprinkled with sugar and washed down with a glass of beer. In this way cordial relationships were fostered with the local residents and further developed through concerts by the military band and displays by the Drums and Pipes 'beating retreat'. As the column passed through this area the Gordons knew that there was the possibility of help from local people. In addition, the guards seemed less vigilant since they were beginning to tire, also having to march about twenty miles every day in exceptionally warm weather, although they at least were properly fed and had ample water to drink. For most escaping was considered too risky an enterprise, hunger and fatigue dulling their minds. The occasional sight of men being summarily shot in vain attempts to break away also convinced many it was foolhardy to try. For some others the very lack of food and water and the vindictive behaviour meted out by some of the guards drove them to think of nothing else but escaping and so they were constantly looking for an opportunity to get away. Around seventy Gordon Highlanders successfully made breaks for freedom in the days and weeks shortly after their capture.

Most of those who attempted an escape were accompanied by a friend or relative and their gamble had to be taken wisely or fatal consequences were possible. Brothers Jim and Bill Ewen escaped together, as did Robert (Bunny) Shearer and his older brother Willie. Willie's bid for freedom did not last long as he had new boots and his feet were badly blistered so, after a short time, he decided he just couldn't go on. Bunny volunteered to give himself up also but Willie insisted that he must go on, which was propitious. While Willie was to spend the next five years in a PoW camp, Bunny made it back to the UK by the end of October. Captain David Morren did not try to escape with a relative but saw a chance to seek help from a long distant relation. While marching north into Belgium he saw a shop with his family name emblazoned above the door and he knew that some of his forefathers had settled in Belgium. The column of PoWs was sparsely guarded at this point so he seized his chance and ran into the shop. He explained to the shopkeeper that he thought they were distantly related and begged for his help by hiding him until it was safe to escape. Unfortunately, the Belgian branch of the Morren family would not co-operate and David Morren was forced to re-join the column. Luckily his excursion had not been noticed by the guards. Bobby Dunbar (2879107), Stanley Westland and Alex Harper had a friendship made when they enlisted into the 1st Battalion at the same time and had been together through their training and deployment, their army numbers separated by only a few digits. In a similar way, the simple fact that the homes of Archie Neill, Andy Pow and Joe Ross were all within two miles of each other, in East Lothian, meant that they had developed a bond and trusted each other. In general the mode of escape was simple. They watched the guards, examined the surrounding countryside and looked for some cover to conceal their getaway. The majority of the escapes were made by dodging out of the marching column in the sixty-mile stretch between Doullens and Béthune. Platoon Sergeants Keiller and Fullerton merely jumped into some bushes when the column stopped for its first rest of the day after they had marched for about three hours. They stayed in hiding until darkness fell as there was a lot of traffic on the road. Jimmy Beattie and Bill Donald, who became friends when they had trained together, were also determined to escape. Jimmy suggested a bend in the road up ahead of them where there was thick hedging running at right angles away from the road. As they reached the bend, where the guards behind could not see them and the guards in front had their backs to them, they ran down the side road, their dash for freedom being obscured by the roadside hedge. They later made significant progress south on stolen bicycles. Bill Masson escaped by jumping through an open door of a house while the column was passing through Oisement. On 19 June, between Doullens and St Pol, Corporal Walter Young, together with Privates Tom Kelly and Bernard Gray, noticed that during a five-minute halt the PoWs crowding round a well trying to get a drink of water inadvertently created a screen to a hedge behind the well. They got to the back of this crowd and slipped behind the hedge and lay quietly to let the column get away. Others employed a more planned approach. Sergeant Robert Clubbs had noticed that the guards invariably turned to look at the markers on roadside graves to see if anyone they knew was buried there. At Flexicourt, some twenty miles north of Abbeville, they came upon about twenty graves by the roadside, so, while the guards were distracted, concentrating their attention on the graves, he dived into the hedge and waited until the column passed. Bobby Dunbar (2879107) and his friends told the guard they had to stop to answer the call of nature and were surprised when he agreed they could go behind some houses and didn't escort them. Here they broke in to a house and hid until the column passed.

As a result of serious wounds, some of the men captured at St Valéry were not fit to march into captivity. These men were generally treated well by the Germans and taken to a hospital, which was often a converted building as the need for medical attention for men, on both sides, was far greater than the local infrastructure could provide. George Gall received wounds in both his leg and arm and was taken to a hospital at St Pol. James Cromar, who was wounded on 11 June, was taken by ambulance to a hospital in Lille. After treatment he was later taken to Alost, Belgium, to convalesce. Security here was not very strict and he was able to abscond and escaped to Brussels where he met up with Tom Farquhar, a friend from his own battalion. Stanley Westland remained at large in the Béthune area, where he had befriended a French woman. They boldly visited the hospital in Béthune where a number of British soldiers were being treated and took food to them. In addition they managed to smuggle civilian clothes in for Corporal Gill, of the Lancashire Fusiliers, who subsequently escaped and eventually managed to get back to the UK through Spain and Gibraltar. Albert Paterson ended up in hospital after initially escaping from the marching column, on 24 June, near Doullens. He was living and working on a farm for a month but, on 24 July, he was betrayed by some French peasants and recaptured. While imprisoned Albert developed dysentery and was sent to the military hospital in Compiègne. Here he met Lieutenant Lion, a young French medical officer, who offered to help him escape. On 2 January 1941 Lieutenant Lion was as good as his word and took Albert to Paris by train. They went directly to the American Embassy but received no assistance, so Lion introduced him to an English girl who sheltered him in Paris for a month until other arrangements could be made. Lieutenant Lion eventually returned and took Albert by train to Dijon, where they hoped to cross over the Demarcation Line into Vichy France (the Unoccupied Zone) but were arrested by the French police. Lieutenant Lion remained very calm in the circumstances and coolly told the police officer that Albert was a French prisoner of war who was both deaf and dumb and as such had been released by the Germans. He further explained that he was taking him to the Unoccupied Zone hoping to find him some work. They were released but returned to Paris as Lieutenant Lion thought it inadvisable to cross the Demarcation Line at that time. However, Albert did eventually make it through Spain and Gibraltar and returned to the UK, reaching Glasgow only six months later, courtesy of the Royal Navy. Bill Donald and Jimmy Beattie successfully pedalled their way south to the Demarcation Line and entered an inn where a Spanish barmaid was initially friendly but shortly afterwards betrayed them to the Germans. They were taken to a prison near Bourges where they were the only British detainees. Here they were set to work sorting out piles of refugees' clothing, discarding the useless material which was taken by truck to a dump near the Vichy border. Their escape route was obvious and, after bribing the driver, they hid in the truck and were dropped off within striking distance of the Demarcation Line which they were able to cross while the Border Guard was distracted dealing with a passing car. However, their liberty didn't last long as they were again arrested and taken to Fort St Jean and later transferred to St Hippolyte du Fort but they were able to get away again. They entered Spain but were detained by the Spanish police in Seville and again in Saragossa. Eventually, after the intervention of the British consul, they were released for repatriation and allowed to travel to Gibraltar in the summer of 1941. However, after managing to travel across the whole of occupied and Vichy France and several terrible spells in horrible prisons, in both France and Spain, Jimmy was hurt badly in an accident in British Gibraltar. They both came home to Scotland but Jimmy's army days were over as he was discharged from the Army in July 1942 as being medically unfit for further military service.

Illness could present a means of repatriation as a Medical Commission, set up under the terms of the Hague Convention, examined some prisoners and declared them unfit for further military service and so they were repatriated through a neutral country. Andrew Methven was examined by such a medical commission in the summer of 1941, having spent five months interned at Marseilles. He was declared unfit and given a visa for Spain, where he was sent to Gibraltar for repatriation, arriving in Gourock on 14 January 1941. He was discharged from the Army eight months later.

For the men who escaped, the first priority was to obtain civilian clothes and get out of their uniforms. This was also a dilemma. Whilst their uniforms instantly gave them away they did also offer the protection of the Geneva Convention and they were less likely to be treated as spies. However, in the circumstances, where there were Germans almost everywhere, escape would have been impossible in uniform. After slipping out of the column of marching PoWs near le Bassec, on 22 June, Alex Moir, acting alone, reached the coast at Hardelot Plage. He tried to acquire a boat but couldn't find one although he did find a very heavy German presence guarding the coastline. Sneaking along the esplanade, trying to slip past some machine-gun posts, he was spotted and challenged. He was still in uniform and, with other Germans levelling their rifles at him, he had no option but to surrender again. Alex was taken to a French army barracks which the Germans were using as a hospital for both French and British wounded. He found some of his guards quite friendly towards him, including an Austrian who claimed to have a girlfriend in Newcastle on Tyne. Alex Moir did not stay a prisoner long and managed to get away again, this time remaining free long enough to get to Marseilles but was recaptured and interned in Fort St Jean. In considering their options, most would-be escapers opted to change into civilian clothing, which was often generously provided by local people. Once they were less conspicuous the obvious thing to do was to head for the coast in the hope of finding a boat to get back to Britain. This often proved the undoing of many escapers. Charles Leighton, who could speak a little French, walked with Alan Knight to a small coastal village near Montreuil where they had been told there were small boats. They were able to watch the coast but it was being continually patrolled so they abandoned their attempt. A short time afterwards, as they were walking along the road between Bruay and Béthune, they were stopped by a German patrol which apprehended them as they had spotted their British Army boots. Three other Gordons (Michael Donnelly, John Carroll and John Macaulay) were luckier when they encountered some Germans. After escaping from the column of marching prisoners they were walking along the cliffs at Hardelot near Boulogne when they were tripped up by a telephone wire strung along the ground. Three Germans emerged from a small hut a short distance away and challenged them as they were in an area forbidden to civilians. Private Macaulay managed to convince them they were Belgians looking for work and, after a reprimand, they were allowed to carry on their way.

After their escape Sergeants Fullerton and Keiller were in their khaki uniforms for several days when they found an empty house on the outskirts of Amiens. This was seen as a golden opportunity and they promptly broke in and stole some civilian clothes. This was just as well as, shortly afterwards, they were stopped crossing the railway line at Blangy-sur-Bresle by Germans with fixed bayonets. Charlie Fullerton spoke French and told the guards he was on his way to see his mother at le Tréport and they were allowed to go on. Near Eu they approached an isolated house and asked for help and were taken in and given food and shelter for three nights. A bicycle was available and Charlie used this to reconnoitre the coast but found that the small fishing boats were all smashed and in any event, there was a chain of mines across the entrance of le Tréport harbour. Their French host found them another bicycle and they decided to cycle south with the aid of a map and the present of some food for their journey. Unfortunately Sergeant Keiller's bicycle broke after only seventy miles, so he decided to retrace his steps and was recaptured.

Once free, it often proved very difficult for men to stay at large in northern France where the Germans were present in large numbers. The chances of a successful escape were already slim but without the generosity and daring assistance provided by ordinary civilians it would have been hopeless. The extent of the help they could offer varied enormously from the simple act of providing food and clothes to concealing men for long periods and even arranging false papers for them. Lance Corporals Alex Hardie and Alex Robertson escaped with Private Robert Copland and another man by slipping out of the line on 19 June as they passed a wood near Doullens. Soon after their escape they met a French woman who gave them civilian clothes and a little map of France and advised them to avoid large towns. They made for the Channel coast, walking by day and lying low at night and during this time they were provided with food and shelter from a number of farmers along the way. They reached the coast at Fort Mahon, about twenty-five miles northwest of Abbeville, only to find the village occupied by German troops. They were sheltered by an English woman who hid them in a disused house and provided them with food. They realized that escape was impossible from there so, with the gift of 100 francs each, they returned inland. At Amiens they decided to separate as they thought their group of four was too conspicuous. However, all four were recaptured, although Copland and Hardie did manage to cross the River Cher, using a rowing boat they found. They were arrested trying to buy bread in a shop in Châteauroux, in central France. The River Cher was part of the Demarcation Line between the Occupied and Unoccupied Zone (Vichy France), which had been created as part of the Armistice agreement between France and Germany. This agreement left the northern and western parts of France, including Paris, under German occupation but allowed the south-eastern third of the country to be governed by the French government, who were now based in the small spa town of Vichy in central France. This location was chosen because it had many hotels so could easily house the many civil servants and various ministries of the puppet administration.

After separating from Keiller, Charlie Fullerton made it to Paris just before the night curfew at 10 o'clock. He discreetly approached some people and asked for accommodation but it was only after taking the risk of revealing to a French woman, at the Suez Hotel, that he was an escaping British soldier that she took him in and gave him a room. There was, however, a big surprise for Charlie when he discovered that the hotel was full of German officers. The next day the proprietor of the hotel took him on the Metro to the American Consulate who sent him to the Salvation Army hostel where there were another eight British escapers. Charlie Fullerton made friends with Lance Corporal Lee Warner, of the Queen's Own Royal West Kent Regiment, and they decided to team up to try to escape together through Spain to Gibraltar. So far, things were looking very positive for Charlie.

Some other Gordons were fortunate enough to come across sympathetic local people who were organizing resistance to the German occupation of their country and endeavouring to assist evading British servicemen. Among these were Jim Cromar, Tom Farquhar, William J. Clark (793156), Leonard Andrews, Bobby Dunbar (2879107) and Herbert Mitchell. Bert Mitchell was in Cysoing where Privates Tom Kelly, Bill Ewen, J. McGarva and CQMS Robert (Bunny) Shearer were also in hiding. Bert worked on farms there and in Holland and was subsequently smuggled into Amsterdam. However, when his capture was inevitable, he gave himself up and was put to work in the cookhouse of a local prison. A year later he was mistaken for a German and drafted for service on the Russian front. He had great difficulty in identifying himself as a British soldier but, after some severe treatment at the hands of the Gestapo, he was sent to Oflag VIB (Warburg, Westphalia) PoW Camp in 1942. Bobby Dunbar's (2879107) experience illustrates the courage and audacity of the French civilians who sheltered him. He was hiding in plain sight, having been given a job as a waiter in Auchel, a small mining town of around 10,000 people just eight miles south-west of Béthune. However, after three months of freedom, he was denounced to the authorities by a Polish woman. He claimed to be a demobilized French soldier and that he did not speak English. His false papers failed to stand up to a thorough inspection so he was arrested, taken to Lille and interrogated by the Gestapo. This was an ordeal where he was given the 'third degree' and treated very roughly but he refused to answer questions put to him in English, pretending he didn't understand. After a period of prolonged interrogation he became disorientated and confused and when suddenly commanded in English to 'stand up' he complied and the game was up. He was tried for attempted sabotage but fortunately acquitted as this charge carried the death penalty. He was found guilty on the lesser charge of escaping for which he received a sentence of four months solitary confinement in Stuttgart gaol. If an escaping British serviceman fell into the hands of the Gestapo his treatment could be very harrowing. John Grassick also fell into their clutches when he had escaped from prisons in Abbeville and Amiens and subsequently recaptured. Here the Gestapo took charge of him and he was sent to the infamous Fort Romainville, on the outskirts of Paris which was used to hold and interrogate Resistance men and women and also as a transit camp for Jews destined for the extermination camps of Auschwitz, Buchenwald and Dachau. Fortunately he was spared and served time in Brussels gaol before finally ending up in Stalag 344 (Lamsdorf). Corporal James Macdonald escaped from the marching column just three days after the surrender but was recaptured after a month. The disadvantage of breaking away from the rest of your unit alone was the lack of support from comrades. This was brought home to James when he was taken to Stalag 210 in Alsace Lorraine. He was moved again, arriving at Stalag VB on 26 December 1940 (his 22nd birthday) where he remained for just over two months at Heuberg, near to Stetten, southern Germany. This was a special disciplinary camp built at altitude on a rocky plateau where he could see the line of the Swiss Alps, and freedom, frustratingly so near yet so far away. In this camp he was isolated. There were no other Gordons in the camps and he didn't know any of the other PoWs or which, if any, he could trust.

Meanwhile the PoWs marched on through Belgium, bypassing Brussels via Ninove and Aalst then on to Lockeren and Sint Niklaas before entering Holland. In these countries the local population were also generous to the prisoners, throwing fruit and bread to them. At the beginning of July, they finally reached the end of their march, at Dordrecht, on the River Scheldt, where they were herded onto large coal barges. As they climbed on board they were each handed half a loaf of bread and told it had to last three days. They were directed into the holds where there was a thick layer of coal dust but they had to make the best of this until the vessel got underway. The Scheldt connects with the Rhine through a network of canals and they were now bound for Wesel on the Germany-Netherlands border, where they arrived after three days and nights. Little did anyone suspect then that Wesel was to be the scene of a bloody battle in March 1945 when British and American forces successfully crossed the Rhine near the town, which was almost totally obliterated during the action. Other barges arrived at Hemer, all stopping in the area around Dortmund. The journey by barge was crowded, dirty and uncomfortable. It was during such a journey, on 29 June, that Lieutenant Ran Ogilvie celebrated his 20th birthday. The PoWs were allowed up on deck to use the toilet. This was an improvised wooden frame projecting over the sides of the vessel with a canvas screen which was loose at the base. When there was a gust of wind there was an interesting consequence, giving the people on the banks of the river a marvellous view of the bare backsides!

Their journey was far from over and the next leg was to be by train. After a short stay in Dortmund they were loaded into cattle trucks. About seventy men were crammed into each car, which was designed for only forty, so overcrowding was worse than on the barge. Again a ration of one loaf of bread was issued to every third man so it was imperative that each trio kept track of their man with the bread. This was a horrific journey of over 500 miles across Europe to PoW camps in Germany and Poland. This journey took three days because their trains were given a low priority. Later, during his time as a

PoW, Second Lieutenant Ran Ogilvie drew a map of his movements from the time he arrived in France and including his route into captivity. He entitled his drawing, 'Seeing Germany – "Cattle" Class (with apologies to the cattle)', which gives an illustration of how he felt about his treatment.

Arriving at their destinations the prisoners were weak, filthy and lousy, with their uniforms in rags. Many found it difficult to comply with the requirement to march the final few miles to their prison camp. Germany and its occupied territories were divided into Military Districts (Wehrkreise), each of which was assigned a Roman numeral corresponding to a particular Wehrkreise with a letter added to distinguish a particular camp. In addition another letter added to identify a main camp (Hauptlager H) or a sub-camp (Zweiglager Z). The officers' camps were designated Oflags, abbreviated from the German Offizierslager and many of the officers of the Gordon Highlanders went to Oflags IXA/H (Spangenburg) and IXA/Z (Rotenburg Fulda). The other ranks were dispersed to camps in Poland and Germany designated Stalags, an abbreviation of 'Kriegsgefangenen Mannschafts Stammlager'. With two battalions of Gordon Highlanders captured at St Valéry-en-Caux, plus small numbers from the 4th and 6th Battalions, there were several hundreds of them to be accommodated along with the thousands from other British and French units. Considering only the Gordons, around 600 were held in Stalag XXA (Thorn) and Stalag XXB (Marienburg), some 400 at Stalag 344 (Lamsdorf) and a smaller number at Stalag XXID (Posen), all in Poland. A further 200 men were sent to Stalag IXC (Mühlhausen - Bad Sulza), with many non-commissioned officers sent to Stalag 383 (Hohenfels), Germany. When they arrived at their designated PoW Camp they were processed by the German authorities. They were allowed to wash, a great luxury, then had all their body hair shaved off, were deloused and either given new clothes, often ill-fitting and uncomfortable uniforms of soldiers of other nationalities or, if they were lucky, their own uniforms after these had been passed through a steam compartment to kill the lice. They were photographed, fingerprinted and given a PoW number, which replaced their British Army service number and was used in all matters relating to them, such as registering them with the Red Cross, and for all correspondence with their families and friends. Their personal items were returned to them and Albert (Spud) Robertson found to his surprise that, as a result of the steam disinfection process, his membership card for the Royal Antediluvian Order of Buffaloes, a fraternal organization similar to the Freemasons but completely open in its dealings, had shrunk to a fraction of its original size but was still completely legible. In effect it was a perfect miniature version of the original. Personal items such as family photographs were stamped with the camp number to show they had been authorized and it was an offence to hold anything not registered.

Thousands of British servicemen were now incarcerated and would play no further part in the war but there were still hundreds free in France and Belgium, including a significant number of Gordon Highlanders. Their freedom depended largely on the courage of French and Belgian nationals who risked their own lives to help these men evade capture and return to Britain to re-join the war effort. Some of the assistance was through seemingly random acts of kindness or defiance against the new regime; others were from members of organized groups, hell-bent on making life as difficult as possible for the occupiers of their country. Shortly after France had surrendered the Germans realized that there were escapees and evaders being sheltered by the local population. In an effort to counter this, in October 1940, they ruthlessly decreed that any civilian caught harbouring an enemy serviceman would receive the death sentence and that their family members could also be shot or imprisoned. The evading soldiers and airmen were aware of this, so were immensely grateful for these brave civilians who chose to resist, refusing to accept that their country was to remain under Nazi control. Bill Stuart had managed to get away from the column of men marching northwards into captivity. While resting he hid in a Great War cemetery where he was noticed by a young boy who spoke to Bill and took him home. Apparently the boy's father was British and was employed by the Imperial War Graves Commission to maintain the cemetery but at the outbreak of war had returned to Britain, leaving his wife and child. His wife was sympathetic to Bill's situation and fed him and also agreed to write a letter to Bill's mother back in Aberdeen, telling her he was alive and well, which was not without risk. Bill moved on, so as not to endanger the family and was recaptured shortly afterwards. He spent some time in a civil prison before being handed over to the German military authorities.

Since the coast was being heavily guarded, the possibility of getting a boat and making the short passage across the English Channel was impossible, so the only alternative was to go south to Spain, a neutral country, and hopefully reach British Gibraltar. This was no easy feat, having to cross 800 miles of hostile country to reach the Spanish frontier, where the Pyrenees were a formidable natural barrier. In addition, although a neutral country, Spain was no friend of Britain and the pro-German fascist regime was unlikely to be sympathetic towards any British serviceman discovered travelling through the country illegally.

For a few, these adventures were fairly trouble free but for most there were extraordinary adventures and close shaves involving the police and border guards on both sides of the French-Spanish frontier. Corporal Walter Young, a seasoned Regular soldier with twelve years' service, was initially quite despondent as he marched into captivity but into his second week marching through northern France he saw an open gate to a farm which seemed to him to be symbolic and an invitation to escape. Fortunately, this was on a sharp bend in the road so it was obscured from the view of guards behind and in front of him. On impulse he dashed through the gate and was spontaneously followed by Privates Tom Kelly and Bernard Gray, both Gordon Highlanders. They dived into a small shed near the gate to get out of sight and lay still until the column passed. This was a very uncomfortable couple of hours as they had chosen to dive into a pigsty and the stench was almost unbearable. Once on the move, through open countryside, Walter's mood changed and his spirits soared to be a free man again. Along the way they approached small farms and begged for food. After a few days they were offered food and shelter at a farm near Doullens in return for work. However, the farmer exploited their position, working them hard but not feeding them properly and when they asked for some wages he threatened to turn them in to the authorities. They decided this situation was not desirable so they stole some bicycles and rode off early one morning. The large alsatian at the farm started barking loudly as they left but it was silenced by the bribe of a piece of ham, which they had also appropriated from the farmer in lieu of wages. Once on their way they encountered a number of Germans and Gray became nervous, so they decided to split up. Walter Young grew increasingly confident and bluffed his way through a number of checkpoints by telling the Germans he was a Belgian refugee, which they seemed happy to accept. He continued south, after a short stay in Cysoing, where he tried to meet up again with Tom Kelly who was, like a number of Gordons, hiding and working on farms locally, all thanks to the friendships made during the Regiment's time in the area prior to the start of hostilities.

Walter reached the border of the Unoccupied Zone near Loches at the end of July and, by simply following the valley of the River Rhone, made straight for Marseilles. Just outside Marseilles he was stopped by two gendarmes and asked for his papers. He claimed he was a shipwrecked Czech sailor which is why he had lost his papers and he was looking for work until he could find a ship. The gendarmes didn't accept his story but allowed him to retrace his steps. Fortunately, he found a way to bypass this particular obstacle, so making it safely to the cosmopolitan metropolis of Marseilles, France's largest and busiest port, where there was hope of getting away on board a ship. With no money for accommodation, Walter fell asleep near the harbour area where he was found by some other gendarmes and arrested. After admitting he was an escaped British soldier he was interned in Fort St Jean. Walter's experiences were shared by a number of Gordon Highlanders but few had such an uncomplicated passage to Marseilles. Some had a good command of the French language and were familiar with the country but few had had the advantages of Corporal George Hignett. He had been called up as a reservist on the outbreak of the war but, prior to this, had been working as a gardener for the Imperial War Graves Commission at Longueval, in an area crowded with the graves of the men who fell on the Somme in 1916. He had French friends there who could assist him and he was already familiar with the language and way of life in France. He made his way south and, although arrested and imprisoned for four months in southern France, managed to get across the Spanish frontier and was eventually repatriated through Gibraltar, arriving at Gourock, on the Firth of Clyde, in February 1941. Private John Edgar, who had escaped with him, also managed to return safely to Britain but not until five months later. Edgar returned to military service but left the Gordon Highlanders and transferred into the Argyll and Sutherland Highlanders.

To reach Marseilles was no small accomplishment, having to navigate through hundreds of miles of unfriendly territory where there were many checkpoints. Their route generally involved passing through, or around, Paris, where there was a heavy enemy presence, although it was easier to blend into the crowd in a large city. The next goal was to cross the 'Ligne de Démarcation' into the Unoccupied Zone, where, it was hoped, there would be more favourable treatment by the authorities, in what was nominally an autonomous state. However, the border between the two zones was tightly controlled and it was no easy matter to cross without the correct permits. Walter Young was not the first British soldier to make it to Marseilles but he was the first Gordon Highlander. Like many of his Regiment he was tantalizingly close to reaching Spain and then Gibraltar but being held interned by the French, the very people he had come to help defend their country against the Germans, was a bitter blow. Walter vowed not to give in but he realized his predicament was far from ideal and prepared himself for a long period of detention in Fort St Jean. Some others negotiated their way into Vichy France by various devious means. Private John Henderson (2883894) openly crossed the bridge at Moulins, which marked the border, by carrying a bale of hay on his back and was not challenged by the guard, who took him for a French peasant farmer. Sergeant Robert Clubbs was assisted across by two small boys throwing stones into the River Cher at Menneton, which attracted the attention of the sentry on the bridge, while Clubbs swam across unnoticed farther downstream. Private Andrew McPhillips resorted to bribing the French guard at Courcay to allow him to cross. Bribery also played a part when Corporals William Burnett, Malcolm Straughan and Lance Corporal Neil Rae were detained at the crossing, near Châteauroux, while they were being guided south on the train from Paris. Their false papers were not in order but they managed to continue their escape when they gave some railway employees 50 francs each to put them on another train, eventually all making it safely to Glasgow in 1941. Malcolm Straughan re-joined the reformed 1st Battalion Gordon Highlanders and after D Day was at St Valéry with the reformed 'phoenix' 51st (Highland) Division when the town was liberated in September 1944. Later, during fierce fighting in Holland in February 1945, when the Highland Division was engaged in Operation VERITABLE, Malcolm, acting as the company sergeant major, displayed great valour. At Heyen, on 13 February, his company was heavily counter-attacked by German infantry supported by two self-propelled guns. The Germans had some initial success, infiltrating the British position. Malcolm saw ten Germans behind his position and, with total disregard for his own safety, grabbed a Bren gun, rushed into the open and engaged them, killing a number and forcing the remainder to flee. This single action rallied the rest of his men and the counter-attack was halted. Later, however, the Germans renewed their attack and as ammunition was running critically low Malcolm went round the company positions to re-supply the men, which necessitated him darting across open ground, again with little regard for his own safety. He was immediately awarded the Military Medal to mark his bravery that day.

The men with the best chance of a successful escape were those who were fortunate enough to meet up with members of the Resistance who were assisting Allied soldiers and airmen to escape so they could re-join the war effort, the highest priority being given to aircrew. One such organization was the Comète Line, based in Belgium. Their first successful escaper was Gordon Highlander James Cromar who made it to Gibraltar and retuned to Britain in October 1941, just six weeks after leaving Brussels. Tom Farquhar and James Cromar were both in Brussels, being sheltered by the Belgians operating this escape line. When an escape party was being assembled they cut cards to decide who should get the last remaining place. Tom lost and had to stay behind and wait for his opportunity. James Cromar was guided all the way by a Belgian guide, using the rail network and false papers. They travelled through Paris and Bordeaux and on to Saint-Jean-de-Luz, on the Atlantic coast, which was the route generally preferred by the Comète Line. This was only five miles from the Spanish frontier, which they crossed on foot with the help of a gang of smugglers who were in league with the Belgians. Cromar made his way to San Sebastian and on to Bilbao where he was able to contact the British Consul, who arranged his repatriation through Gibraltar. When Tom Farquhar's turn came he was guided by a young Belgian whose aim was to join up with the Free Belgian Army in Britain. They also had false papers and travelled by train, through Paris and headed for Bourges, on the Demarcation Line, which they crossed on foot, then on to Perpignan, from where they were to cross into Spain, only ten miles away. However, his guide was arrested and although Tom tried to get to the frontier himself the roads were too well guarded and, inevitably, with no money or support, he too was arrested and was imprisoned in St Hippolyte du Fort, near Nîmes. Other Gordons who were helped by this line were Leonard Andrews and William J. Clark (793156), both of whom made it safely back to the UK.

Another successful escape line, referred to only as 'the Organization' by the Gordons who were assisted by it, was the Pat O'Leary Line. Those Gordons included Walter Philips, Archie Neill, Joe Ross and Andrew Pow who made it safely across the frontier into Spain but in a document inspection on the train to Barcelona, only Walter Philips and Archie Neill's papers held up to scrutiny and, after a short spell in Madrid, they were soon back in the UK via Gibraltar. However, Andrew Pow and Joe Ross were arrested. After questioning and internment in Barcelona, they were then imprisoned in Miranda del Ebro concentration camp but, after nine long weeks they were released for repatriation through Gibraltar.

James Smith (2882348) was another Gordon who had been hiding in the Lille area, working on farms. He had survived some close shaves when he was almost recaptured, so grabbed the chance when he was offered the opportunity to be transported to Spain with forged papers provided by 'the Organization'. However, his expectations that being helped by an escape organization would be more secure than evading recapture on his own resources proved wholly inaccurate. His party, together with their French guide, were all arrested crossing the Demarcation Line. When they were being transferred from Nîmes to St Hippolyte du Fort for internment, James Smith managed to get away again and successfully returned to Lille to warn the Organization that their group had been compromised. The return journey was a selfless heroic effort, since he could have remained in the south of France where he had a better chance of escaping himself. It was also not without cost as, after swimming across the River Somme on his way north, he became very ill. He was, however, given new identity papers and was successfully delivered to Marseilles at the second attempt.

Tom Farquhar's recapture was the start of a fairly remarkable time, seeing him being moved from prison camp to prison camp. After five months he was moved from St Hippolyte to Fort de la Revere, la Turbie, in the Alps near Nice where the views to the Cote d'Azur were stunning. This prompted Tom to send a picture postcard to his sister, Mabel, in Keith, Banffshire, telling her the picture was the view he saw every day. He went on to say, 'looks pretty nice and of course we can manage to look all around as we are pretty high up'.

Tom had already met up with Tom Kelly, who had also been at St Hippolyte and they were still together when they were moved again, in September 1942, to Camp Chambaran, Isère, near Grenoble. This was more comfortable than the fort but their time there was somewhat limited. This prison camp was in the Italian Occupied Zone of France, so when the Allies commenced Operation TORCH, invading French North-west Africa in November 1942 both the Italians and the Germans moved to occupy the whole of Vichy France. They also decided to move their prisoners of war, nervous that the substantial Vichy forces in North Africa would join the Allies and so threaten southern France. A previous attempted mass breakout from this prison also made it appear to the Fascist authorities that it was not very secure. In December 1942 the two Toms were on the move again and a fleet of vehicles arrived to transport the prisoners the eighty miles through the mountains to the railway station at Modane, on the Italian border. They boarded a train which took them via Turin to Modena and arrived at the little town of Carpi in the Po valley and were marched to Italian PoW camp – Campo No. 73 (Concentranento di Prigioneri di Guerra). Here they met up with Private William Davidson, another 5th Battalion Gordon Highlander, who had also been captured at St Valéry and had escaped, on 2 July with Private Alexander MacQueen (also 5th Gordons) at Ninove, Belgium. Both had been recaptured at Sancoins and taken to Fort St Jean, Marseilles. MacQueen had escaped and made it into Spain from where he was repatriated to Britain in July 1941. Their arrival in northern Italy was, however, not the end of their travels courtesy of the Axis powers. In September 1943, when Italy capitulated and Germany occupied the country, they were moved again to Stalag VIIA, Moosburg, Bavaria.

At St Hippolyte du Fort, and Fort St Jean, British PoWs were generally allowed out during the day so long as they were back for the evening roll-call. While the USA remained neutral, until December 1941, British internees were looked after by the American consulate. Treatment in the forts was fairly relaxed but the food was terrible, so it was fortunate that the Americans gave them a small monthly allowance, which meant they could supplement their rations. Daily parole also gave the opportunity to explore Marseilles and its port, looking for a passage on a ship or hoping to make contact with someone who could help them escape. This was not a vain hope. Assistance was not far away, if only it could be identified, but those who would come to their aid were naturally cautious in order to protect themselves. The city had many enemy collaborators and the Vichy authorities were also under pressure from the Germans to clamp down on anyone seeking to help Allied servicemen escape.

Probably the most celebrated benefactor assisting escaped British servicemen was the Reverend Donald Caskie, a Church of Scotland Minister, originally from the Hebridean island of Islay. He had been the Minister of the Scots Kirk in Paris, before the fall of France. The Reverend Caskie set up the Seaman's Mission in Marseilles, which was the perfect cover for his clandestine activities, for which he was dubbed 'The Tartan Pimpernel', the title he subsequently used for his autobiography which was published after the war. Donald Caskie had many opportunities to assist escaping servicemen, especially those who had been recaptured in Vichy France and interned in the various prisons in the Marseilles area. He was the visiting padre to the Forts, St Hippolyte, St Jean and de la Revere and was a close collaborator in the activities of the Pat O'Leary escape line. Although there were around twenty-five Gordon Highlanders interned in these forts who met Donald Caskie, in his role as a padre, he directly influenced the fate of at least eight Gordon Highlanders. These were Company Sergeant Major Alex Moir, Platoon Sergeant Major Charlie Fullerton, Corporal Walter Young and Privates Robert Copland, Tom Kelly, Michael Donnelly, Francis Mumme and James Smith.

These Gordons came into contact with Caskie in a variety of ways. While at Fort St Jean, Alex Moir was selected by Donald Caskie to sail with some Polish soldiers to Gibraltar but their ship was searched by the police before it sailed from Marseilles and Alex had to jump over the side and swim across the harbour to avoid being caught. He did eventually cross into Spain and made it back to the UK via Gibraltar, for which he was decorated with the Military Medal. He returned to the Regiment and served with the 5th/7th Battalion Gordon Highlanders in North Africa. Unfortunately, this was one campaign too far for this brave soldier. He was killed on 3 November 1942 in the Battle of El Alamein. Charlie Fullerton was outside the American Consulate in Marseilles when he first met Donald Caskie, who took him to the Victoria Hotel where he stayed for three days. Charlie then approached the American Consul who assisted by providing a paper confirming he was a British subject. Subsequently, with Corporal Wilfred Jamieson and another man, he crossed into Spain. Walter Young also met the Reverend Caskie while he was interned at Fort St Jean and through him, and the auspices of the Church of Scotland, was able to send his first letter home to tell his family he was alive and well. Walter also made good his escape from France and sailed into the Firth of Clyde in December 1940. Robert Copland was fully aware of the significance of the Reverend Caskie's clandestine operations from the Seaman's Mission as, when he was given an opportunity to escape and take one other man with him, he went directly to the Mission to enquire if anyone was willing to join him.

Tom Kelly and Michael Donnelly were also serial escapers and when at Fort de la Revere were involved in the mass breakout organized by the Pat O'Leary escape line, in which Donald Caskie is believed to have played an important part. On one of his visits to Fort de la Revere he noticed a large drain emerging downslope from the prison. He passed this information on to the Resistance who investigated the internal drainage of the fort and passed on the plans so that the prisoners could tunnel into it. They used the only implements they had available, knives, forks and spoons. Both Donnelly and Kelly were among the fifty-eight men who successfully escaped but the operation was too large and only the first twenty-five to reach the rendezvous point were given further instructions which resulted in them successfully returning to the UK. Michael Donnelly was among those. The remaining thirty-three, who included Tom Kelly, were hiding in a monastery when it was raided by Vichy gendarmes and they were recaptured. Francis Mumme was the last of Caskie's close contacts to make it back to Blighty, although his story is contentious.

When Private James Smith (2882348) returned to Marseilles he was persuaded not to return to the UK immediately but to use his proven ability, good command of French and resourcefulness for the good of the Organization. He courageously agreed and, under the alias Jean Dubois, made six return trips to Lille and helped over twenty Allied servicemen and other refugees escape to safety. He was not the only British soldier involved in these clandestine operations and worked with a number of other people, co-ordinated to some degree by British Intelligence agents on the ground, with the Reverend Donald Caskie assisting when he could. James was known to Harold Cole, a sergeant in the Royal Engineers, and Francis Mumme. Mumme, a 1st Battalion Gordon Highlander, was operating under the pseudonym 'Emar' and was a go-between between the Resistance movement and escaped British servicemen in Lille and later in guiding them to the Spanish frontier. In many ways his role was similar to James Smith's. After the war, Mumme's involvement with a woman in Lille created the suspicion that he was a double agent. This woman was Christine Gorman whose British father, a civilian, was understood to have been interned in Germany during the war. It was believed she was betraying escaped British servicemen, who were in hiding in Lille, to an officer in the Gestapo, with whom she was having an affair. She claimed her only motive was the promise of the release of her father through the Gestapo officer's intervention. In April 1941, after Mumme heard that the Gestapo had called at his former address enquiring about him and arrested some people there, he fled to Marseilles as he felt his position in Lille was perilous. This proved accurate as, soon after his departure, the Gestapo attempted to arrest another family he had been staying with but luckily they got away. The whole organization became compromised and Cole was implicated as being a double agent. James Smith was arrested while escorting a group of servicemen south in late August 1941. He was taking them to Marseilles when they were all arrested in a document check on the train at Orléans. It subsequently transpired that one of their party, who was posing as a Norwegian pilot, was in fact a German. James Smith was brutally interrogated by the Gestapo but refused to talk and was not recognized as a prisoner of war and so was sent to a series of civil prisons and was fortunate to survive until liberated by American forces at Untermassfeld in April 1945. Francis Mumme was arrested at Perpignan in June 1941 and questioned by the Vichy security police but escaped and crossed into Spain where he was again arrested by the Spanish police but escaped again and reached the British Consulate in Barcelona, who arranged for him to be repatriated through Gibraltar. He arrived at Gourock in January 1942. Both Francis Mumme and James Smith (2882348) were awarded the Military Medal.

Harold Cole was captured in Germany by the British in June 1945 and in an interrogation by MI5 he denounced both Francis Mumme and Christine Gorman as being Gestapo agents while portraying himself as a loyal to the crown. However, Mumme was investigated by British Military Intelligence who concluded there was no evidence against him, Christine Gorman was tried by the French after the war and sentenced to hard labour for life. Cole escaped from the Paris detention barracks in November 1945 but was shot dead, in January 1946, resisting arrest.

All the escapers who spent time in the internment camps in southern France or in Spain suffered horrendous situations, where the food was bad, hygiene terrible and disease and vermin abounded. They were often put into mixed cells with cut-throat criminals and other undesirables. The two worst prisons were undoubtedly the fort at St Cyprien, France, on the Mediterranean coast, just twenty miles north of the Spanish frontier, and Miranda del Ebro in northern Spain. St Cyprien was really filthy, with open latrines, swarms of flies spreading disease and other vermin such as rats and lice. Dysentery was rampant and there was an outbreak of typhoid causing the deaths of many of the inmates. Fortunately this camp was closed in October 1940 but not before Sergeant William Masson, Platoon Sergeant Major Robert Clubbs and Private C. McIvor had endured these terrible conditions. Miranda de Ebro housed many International Brigade republican prisoners who had been on the losing side during the Spanish Civil War. General Franco's Spanish regime cared little what became of these men and so conditions there were horrific. British prisoners were forced to do hard manual labour and those who were too weak to keep up with the pace required by the guards were lashed with thongs and sticks. Charlie Fullerton complained to the Commandant with little success, so he wrote to the British Ambassador in Madrid. A representative of the embassy travelled to the prison to investigate and was horrified at the situation he found there. He arranged for Charlie's release, together with another fourteen British soldiers. They were taken to Madrid and then, under the protection of a naval attaché, they were repatriated through Gibraltar, reaching Londonderry on the Royal Navy destroyer, HMS *Velox* in September 1940. Lieutenant Colonel Alick Buchanan-Smith recommended that Charlie be awarded the Distinguished Conduct Medal for his valour in the face of the enemy onslaught during May 1940 and his subsequent escape. However, this was not accepted and he was awarded the Military Medal. He was subsequently commissioned as a second lieutenant into the 9th Battalion Gordon Highlanders with whom he went to the Far East.

With all the ingenuity displayed by those Gordons described above it is hard to believe there could be even more incredible exploits by men determined to escape. Bill Ewen met a Frenchman in the Maire's house at Leauville who knew of three British pilots in hiding in the area who planned to steal three German bombers and fly six men each back to Britain. This plan came to nothing when it was discovered the planes were only refuelled immediately pre-flight so that any night attempt to purloin a plane would result in it taking off with insufficient fuel to reach friendly territory. Although most attempts to reach Gibraltar focused on crossing through Spain there were some attempts to escape by sea. In January 1941 Lance Corporal Leslie Wilson and Private John Henderson (2883894), who were interned at Fort St Jean, tried to put into practice their plan to sail the 250 miles to Barcelona and then journey overland through Spain to Gibraltar. Unfortunately, bad weather prevented them launching a small motor-boat they were attempting to steal in the village of Saintes-Maries-de-la-Mer, in the Camargue, and they were apprehended and sent to Avignon gaol. Andrew McPhillips tried to stow away on a ship bound from Marseilles to North Africa but he was discovered and arrested before the ship left port. He was given a six months' sentence in gaol for breaking his parole from Fort St Jean but, fortunately, following the intervention of the American Consul, he served less than half of his sentence. However, sailing on a large ship to North Africa was to prove a winning strategy for three Gordons. All three, Leslie Wilson, Robert Copland and Walter Young, sailed to Algeria and then travelled by train to Casablanca, Morocco, but they made their escape bids independently of each other.

All three were held in Fort St Jean which, although being used to intern Allied servicemen, was principally a depot for the French Foreign Legion. Under the French-German Armistice agreement the Legion was to be disbanded, so there was a flow of men being sent from the fort to the Legion's barracks in Casablanca for demobilization. Some of these men were not keen on being returned to North Africa and preferred to stay in France. Walter Young met a Frenchman who wished to desert and return home, so was keen to trade his uniform and papers for civilian clothes. This was full of risk for both men but Walter decided that it was worthwhile. Another British soldier made a similar arrangement, so they agreed to stick together as with two of them they felt a little more confident. Mixing with the legionnaires, they marched to the docks and sailed to Oran. They had taken some civilian clothes with them in their packs so, after disembarking from the ship and passing through customs with the legionnaires, they changed and discarded the uniforms. This was a little premature as they had hoped to get assistance from the American Consul but he was unavailable. They had, therefore, little alternative but to board the train which was bound for Casablanca with the demobilizing men but, as they had discarded their uniforms, they had to continually dodge the ticket inspector, which would not have been necessary if they had looked as if they were part of the Legion. However, all went well and they reached Casablanca on 13 September 1940. Luckily they made contact with a British agent who gave them the details of a ship which was in the harbour at Casablanca and would take them when it sailed. The problem was that they would have to get into the port which was sealed and closely guarded. Under cover of darkness they scaled a wall and, keeping in the shadows, crept past the sentries, crawling on their hands and knees, and successfully scrambled aboard the ship. They were concealed under the floor of a cabin and so were undetected when the harbour authorities came aboard to search the ship prior to its departure. After two days at sea they rendezvoused with a British destroyer which took them to Gibraltar and, on 14 December 1940, almost exactly six months after the surrender at St Valéry-en-Caux, Walter sailed into the Firth of Clyde.

Robert Copland followed a similar plan to Walter Young but the Foreign Legion contact he made in Fort St Jean was an American, who told him that he was due to be part of a group of legionnaires leaving soon for Casablanca by ship. Copland went to the harbour and got into a conversation with a French sailor from the ship who told him he had a brother with General de Gaulle in Britain and he too wanted to join the Free French forces. This sailor managed to obtain two passes for the ship which allowed him and another to board with the demobilizing legionnaires. It was agreed that the sailor would desert when they reached North Africa and they would help each other to reach Britain. Robert Copland went to Donald Caskie's Seaman's Mission and offered the British servicemen in hiding there the chance to accompany him, which was snapped up by Private Stan Jones of the South Lancashire Regiment. When the time came to board the ship things went well as some legionnaires were wearing civilian clothes, so they did not look odd. They mixed with the crowd but dared not speak in case they gave themselves away. Their sailor friend was able to get food for them during the crossing and they docked in Oran, which was a bit of a surprise as they had assumed they were going to sail directly to Casablanca. The next problem was that all the draft marched into the barracks and so the trio of escapers had to follow. Here they had a stroke of good luck. Robert Copland met an Englishman who was a demobilizing corporal from a French armoured unit who managed to get passes for them to leave the barracks. With their little band now numbering four with the addition of the corporal, they left the barracks that evening, mingling with a group who were travelling to Casablanca by train where they arrived on 6 November 1940. After receiving a gift of money from the American Consulate, they took a train to Rabat hoping to cross into the Spanish protectorate just north of there, but they were arrested and sent back to Casablanca where they were tried by a military court. They were lucky that the judge appeared to be sympathetically disposed towards them and only levied a fine for crossing into Morocco without proper papers. This fine was paid by the US Consul who also arranged for them to stay in a hotel in the city, which is where they remained for over twelve months. Their comfortable situation was brought to a sudden end when one night their hotel was raided and they were arrested and in March 1942 they were taken to Laghouat internment camp in Algeria. This was a remote location, some 300 miles south of Algiers, at an oasis in the Sahara Desert which had all the elements of a Beau Gest film set. Their treatment here was not too bad and there were already some British and Commonwealth servicemen interned there. Once they were accepted by the other inmates, they discovered that there was already a group who were busy tunnelling their way out of the camp. Copland and Jones both joined in the tunnelling effort but as new boys they were not included in the twenty-nine strong escape party which exited through the tunnel on 6 June 1942. Places were allocated on the basis of the amount of work put in excavating the tunnel, which stretched for almost 100 metres and had begun four months before they arrived. In any event the escape was a failure and all the fugitives were recaptured. There had been heavy rain overnight and the guards simply followed their footprints in the wet sand which would normally have been erased by the wind. However, freedom was not long in coming for all the prisoners as the camp was liberated by American forces in November 1942, shortly after the landings in Morocco and Algeria as part of Operation TORCH. Robert Copland was soon in Gibraltar and sailed up the Firth of Clyde, to Greenock, on 23 November 1942.

The third Gordon Highlander who took this most circuitous of routes home, a journey of over 5,000 miles, was Leslie Wilson. His approach was more direct and he acted entirely alone. He stowed away aboard a cargo ship, hiding among some timber stowed on the deck. When the ship docked in Algiers he left the ship and walked into the town without anyone asking for his papers. He took the train to Oran where a representative of the American Consulate gave him money and a British identity card. After spending some time in Oran, he took the train to Casablanca where he again went to the American Consulate for assistance, which was readily given. He was given more money and put up in the Hotel de la Victoire, where, to his great surprise, he encountered

Robert Copland of his own battalion. It appeared Copland was not ready to continue his escape and appeared content to remain in Casablanca whereas Leslie Wilson was keen to progress his escape. He took a bus to the Spanish Protectorate but was arrested and imprisoned. Leslie proved a hard man to incarcerate and escaped no fewer than nine times from German and Vichy forces. Perhaps the most desperate of these was after his imprisonment in Fez where he met up with a French airman. The two were handcuffed together for the train journey to the concentration camp at Missour, on the north-western edge of the Sahara. As the train travelled slowly through a tunnel they jumped off and made for the border of Spanish Morocco but were caught by Arabs who handed them over to the police. He spent Christmas day 1941 in solitary confinement in a prison in the remote northern Moroccan town of Guercif, from where he was sent to Missour where he spent six months. Another escape from there earned him a sentence of seven months' imprisonment, where he remained until the Allies invaded French North-west Africa in November 1942 which, like Robert Copland, led to his liberation. However, he did not go back to Britain immediately but worked for the US Army as an interpreter for a short time. He was then flown to Gibraltar and taken by the Royal Navy to Plymouth, arriving there on Boxing Day 1942. In recognition of his gallant and distinguished service he was awarded the Military Medal.

Opening of the Gordon Barracks in September 1935. The parade, crossing the bridge over the River Don, Aberdeen. (*Courtesy of the Gordon Highlanders Museum*)

'*Champ*', the 1st Battalion's mascot, with Private Arthur Smith and the Battalion boys. (*Courtesy of Gordon Highlanders Museum*)

5th Battalion TA Camp, Drumlithie, 1938. Harry Tobin with his arm on truck with Alex Watt sitting in front of him. (*Courtesy of Henry Tobin*)

The 1st Battalion display their mechanization, Redford Barracks, Edinburgh 1938. (*Courtesy of Kath Hope*)

Edward Dick of the 1st Battalion Bren Gun Carrier Platoon, Aldershot 1939. (*Courtesy of Gordon Highlanders Museum*)

1st Battalion Despatch Riders, Aldershot 1939. Left to Right: G. Simpson; W. Inglis; P. Kemp. (*Courtesy of John Inglis*)

A Company, 5th Battalion marching off to war – leaving Bucksburn, September 1939. (*Courtesy of Gordon Highlanders Museum*)

HQ Company, 5th Battalion marching off to war – leaving Bucksburn, September 1939. Jack Caldwell extreme right. (*Courtesy of Moira Mapely*)

Granite pillar commemorating the ceremonial kilt burning by the 5th Battalion in 1939. (*Author's Collection*)

The Durward Brothers. William (Died a Japanese PoW); James (PoW Stalag 383); Arthur (PoW Stalag IXC). (*Courtesy of Arthur Durward*)

The first group of 'Militiamen' arrive at Gordon Barracks, Aberdeen, 15 July 1939. (Harry Milne, front row 3rd from left and Albert King back row 2nd from right). (*Courtesy of Francis Knowles*)

Embroidered novelty postcard, sent by Gordon Reid (2880758) from France, March 1940. (*Courtesy of Gordon Reid Jnr.*)

Général Fagalle inspects Guard of Honour at Béthune, 25 February 1940. (*Courtesy of Gordon Highlanders Museum*)

5th Battalion Pipe Band, 1939. (*Courtesy of Ron Robertson*)

PoW Identity Tags: 528 George McLennan, Stalag 344; 16487 Harry Milne Stalag XXA. (*Courtesy of Hamish McLennan and Francis Knowles*)

PoWs loading sand into 20 ton rail trucks at Lappin Sand Quarry, Steinwerk, Danzigland, September 1940 (The Cross identifies Bill Maitland with barrow on narrow wooden plank). (*Courtesy of Gordon Highlanders Museum*)

PoW Group with German guards and civilian overseers at Lappin sand quarry, Steinwerk, Danzigland, September 1940. (*Courtesy of Bill Maitland*)

Left and below: PoW burial service, Stalag IXC (Mühlhausen – Bad Sulza). (*Courtesy of Stan Robertson & Arthur Durward*)

Arrival of junior British officers at Fort VIII Stalag XXID reprisal camp, March 1941. (*Courtesy of Gordon Highlanders Museum*)

Roll call and inspection at Bleicherode salt mine (Stalag IXC) 1942. (*Courtesy of Roy King*)

Gordons in PoW work group at Nordhausen salt mine (Stalag IXC) Back Row: Harry Tobin 1st left; Bill Jamieson 3rd left. Note Gordon Highlanders cap badge being displayed in the centre. (*Courtesy of Henry Tobin*)

2 Reichsmark note (*Lagergeld*) was used to pay PoWs for their work. (*Courtesy of Gordon Highlanders Museum*)

James Murray at sugar beet factory. (*Courtesy of Gordon Highlanders Museum*)

Four propaganda photos taken at Stalag IXC. Different PoWs but same instruments which they couldn't play. (*Courtesy of Henry Tobin*)

'Wigwam Band' rehearsal at Stalag IXC (Trumpeter – Albert King). (*Courtesy of Albert King*)

The cast of the Christmas pantomime take a bow at Stalag IXC. Bill Jamieson in sombrero on extreme right. (*Courtesy of Valerie Fraser*)

Stage show at Stalag IXC. Ralph England, ukulele; Albert King, trumpet. (*Courtesy of Roy King*)

The Camp newspaper from Stalag 383 (Hohenfels). (*Courtesy of Gordon Highlanders Museum*)

Football match at Stalag IXC. (*Courtesy of Roy King*)

Scotland vs England football match. Stalag 383 on 23 April 1944. (*Courtesy of David Potter*)

Boxing practice at Stalag IXC. (*Courtesy of Roy King*)

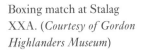

Boxing match at Stalag XXA. (*Courtesy of Gordon Highlanders Museum*)

Left: boxing certificate awarded to Private Rodney Knowles at Lamsdorf. (*Courtesy of Abby MacDonald*)

Right: Lamsdorf PoW football knockout competition card. (*Courtesy of the Gordon Highlanders Museum*)

PoW Pipe Band, Stalag 383 (Hohenfels). (*Courtesy of Lewis Gibbon*)

The Pipe Band, Oflag VII B. (*Courtesy of Gordon Highlanders Museum*)

The Hutcheon family record their BBC Christmas broadcast to the nation in 1941. (*Courtesy of Cecil Hutcheon*)

BUT I ASSURE YOU, MY DEAR CHAP — I REALLY <u>AM</u> FATHER CHRISTMAS!

Christmas cards produced in the PoW camps. Left: sent by Captain J. Shankley; Right sent by Captain Duncan Campbell. (*Courtesy of the Gordon Highlanders Museum*)

American General Wade Haislip presents the 5th Battalion drum. (*Courtesy of Gordon Highlanders Museum*)

Brigadier J.R. Sinclair hands the drum to Corporal Willie Sim. (*Courtesy of Gordon Highlanders Museum*)

The Drums & Pipes of the Gordon Highlanders, with Guard of Honour, march off the Königsplatz, Munich. (*Courtesy of Gordon Highlanders Museum*)

Gordon Highlanders' graves at Manneville-ès-Plains. Front Row: William Neilson; Back Row: Peter Stewart; R. A. Lyth (RASC); George Rennie; Johnny McLennan; Duncan Reid. (*Author's Collection*)

George McLennan at Manneville-ès-Plains. Visiting the grave of his brother, Johnny. (*Courtesy of Hamish McLennan*)

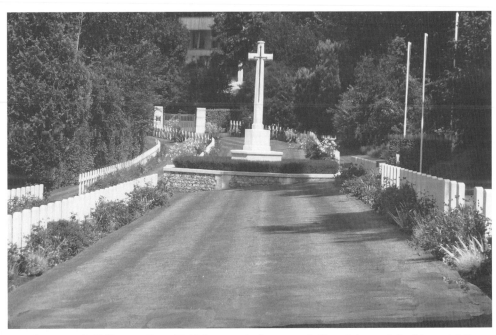

War Cemetery, St Valéry-en-Caux. British graves in foreground. French beyond the Memorial Cross. The Memorial Gates are in the distance. (*Author's Collection*)

Beach and cliffs at St Valéry-en-Caux. (*Author's Collection*)

51st (Highland) Division Monument, St Valéry-en-Caux, Overlooking the harbour. (*Author's Collection*)

French dignitaries honour the British soldier's graves at Manneville-ès-Plains. Nancy Wilson looks on while visiting the grave of her father (Patrick Stewart). (*Courtesy of Nancy Wilson*)

Chapter 4

Stalagites – Life in the PoW Camps

It was not long before the Germans started to make their prisoners earn their keep and all physically fit men, below the rank of sergeant, were required to work. Under Article 49 of the Geneva Convention, senior NCOs and officers could not be compelled to work but some NCOs chose to work to escape the mind-stultifying life in the main camp. Alternatively, others busied themselves in camp administration for the benefit of the other prisoners, such as organizing the distribution of Red Cross parcels. The work camps or *Kriegsgefangenenarbeitskommando* or more simply *Arbeitskommando* (AbKdo) were sub-camps for prisoners working on farms, forestry, building sites, road construction and in a variety of factories, quarries and mines. Dangerous work, or the manufacture of war materials aiding the German war effort, was supposed to be excluded from the work programmes but this restriction was often disregarded by the Nazis. One blatant example of this was experienced by Bobby Shand, who was among a small group of men, all unmarried, chosen to dig out unexploded bombs at Erfurt. These Arbeitskommandos could often be some considerable distance from the main camp and so the men were generally billeted at their workplace, although the main camp was still responsible for the PoWs' welfare and security. Although there were always guards present at these sub-camps, the discipline was less strict and there were opportunities to trade with the local population for extra food and cigarettes. Although the work was often very physically demanding, there were other incentives, such as female company and even the increased chance of escape.

A common occupation for PoWs was working on the land and in associated agricultural industries. Sugar beet was grown extensively in Poland and there were large factories to process the crop into sugar. For many Gordon Highlanders, many of whom were from the rich agricultural areas of the North East of Scotland, farming was in the blood and many of the 1st Battalion Regulars had been farm labourers prior to enlistment. It was somewhat ironic, therefore, that many had enlisted into the army to get away from the drudgery and poor wages that characterized farm work but were now forced to work on the land for a pittance, often in extremes of temperature far removed from anything experienced back home. Others were quite at home on the land tending livestock and often developed a rapport with the farmer and his family, which generally led to better conditions and more plentiful food. For example, a close bond developed at Ault Janischau, a farm designated as a working camp in the area of Stalag XXB (Marienburg), between three Gordon Highlanders (David Greig, Walter Cooper and John Jack) and the Kiep family. After the war, Frau Kiep wrote to David Greig asking for his help. She detailed the changed situation for them under the Russian occupation and requested he and his Gordon comrades write to her confirming they were treated fairly by the family while PoWs working at their farm. This was to show the Russian authorities they had been sympathetic to the Allies. In addition, she asked if they could send some coffee and other goods. The three Gordons were sympathetically disposed to this family who had not only treated them well but protected them from investigation by the feared Gestapo or the SS. The Gordons agreed to reply to her as though they had all been good friends which, of course, they were not since their relationship was just an accommodation of convenience for the PoWs.

On the smaller farms PoWs would sometimes be trusted to work alone, travelling freely around the local area to their various jobs. Some farms were however much larger and run more like country estates. After about seven weeks, the Germans started to ask what trade the men had. Corporal Jimmy Nicol was a blacksmith in civilian life so he was put in charge of a blacksmith's shop. He considered this was an ideal job for him as he knew what he was doing and he could keep nice and warm during the harsh Polish winters. The farm was huge, several square miles in size, and officially designated Stammlager XXB AbKdo 72.

A German colonel owned this farm and treated the PoWs reasonably well, bringing them British cigarettes when he returned home on leave. The farm boss was a Russian who had been captured by the Germans in the Great War but stayed in Germany and became a naturalized German citizen. He listened to his wireless in the evenings and when he had news of the Allies' progress he passed the information on, swearing them to secrecy as he would have been in a lot of trouble if the authorities found out. There were Polish resistance fighters hiding in the forest near the farm and they would often provide the PoWs with extra food such as a chicken thrust through the window. There was generally plenty of food on the farm and a dairy farm and large creamery were also located alongside. This processed milk from lots of other farms in the surrounding area. Although Jimmy considered this life just bearable, he found out the hard way that he had to 'toe the line'. When he did get into trouble, arguing with a guard, he was sent back to the main camp and given six weeks' solitary confinement, where nobody spoke to him and his food (bread and water only) was just slid under the door. He worried that after his sentence he could be sent anywhere, rather than back to the farm, and his worst fears were realized when he was sent to a salt mine. Fortunately, after only three weeks of this, he was sent back to his original blacksmith's job at the farm and he knew he had had a narrow escape.

Bill Reaper was labouring on a construction site when the Germans called for volunteers to assist with the harvest. Bill, who grew up on a farm in Aberdeenshire, volunteered. He was billeted with twenty other men who all slept in the loft while two guards slept downstairs. Bill worked in a flour mill in Hohenstein, in the Danzig area, where his job was to look after the horses used to deliver the flour around the local area. A guard escorted him to the mill each morning and collected him again in the evening, with the miller being responsible for him all day. He was very happy here as the miller and his family were kind to him, allowing him to eat his meals with them, gave him new boots and underwear and the miller's wife even did his laundry for him. The family applied to keep him as their permanent worker but after three months, much to Bill's disappointment, he was returned to the construction site.

Many Gordon Highlanders were employed seasonally in sugar beet harvesting and processing. These root vegetables were generally grown around Marienburg (with Gordons pressed into service at Reichenau and Praust) and Lamsdorf, (with Gordons working at Ratibor and Ottmachau). The harvest normally began around September and ended as late as January. Lifting the crop was hard back-breaking work, exacerbated when carried on in extreme cold with deep snow covering the crop. The conversion of the beets into processed sugar took place in large specialist factories, taking the harvest from a wide area. These also employed many PoWs. This was physically demanding too, and the concentration of the sugary liquid to produce the syrup and the final step to granulated sugar was very hot work, but a welcome contrast to the ambient temperature of the harsh Polish winters. The availability of sugar was also a welcome addition to their diet. This activity was an important industry for the Germans as the import of cane sugar was severely restricted by the Royal Navy's blockade.

A number of Gordon Highlanders held in Stalag IXC (Mühlhausen) were employed in the agriculture-associated activity of horticulture. This was in a seed factory at Erfurt, some thirty miles away from the PoW camp headquarters and located in the centre of Germany. Erfurt was in a very fertile area which was an important centre for market gardening and seed production. The work involved growing vegetables and flowers to harvest the seeds, rather than the direct production of food. The seeds were then processed and packed for distribution to places all over Germany. The work was not as arduous as some tasks and generally considered pleasant in the summer months, but the digging and preparation of the ground in the spring was tiring and the cold weather in the winter months was disliked intensely as the PoWs were rarely properly dressed for the freezing temperatures. The main outdoor task at this time involved protecting the plants in cold frames with straw matting, which was removed during the day when the sun was out and replaced before darkness fell.

Working comfortably indoors, Tom Duncan engaged in some sabotage in the seed factory by mixing up the seeds so that they were packaged wrongly and consequently the orders sent off to farmers and growers were incorrect, inflicting a small swipe at the enemy. Although only causing inconvenience and perhaps a reduced crop yield, it was an important boost to morale, just giving them the belief that they were not completely powerless. The operations at this seed factory were substantial and a lot of PoWs were employed there. Dave McDonald worked on a machine packaging seed but he didn't like this and asked if he could have an outdoor job, so he was detailed to work with a tractor driver doing deliveries which he preferred. There was a certain degree of kudos in this role as they often gave women workers a ride to the factory and the PoWs had chocolate and cocoa from their Red Cross parcels to induce the women to submit more readily to their advances. The factory was large and, in Dave's own words, 'there were many places to hide'. However, the penalties if caught having intimate relations with a German woman were serious and large posters, four feet high, two feet wide, with a thick black border proclaimed, 'DEATH if caught with a woman'.

One Gordon Highlander who did have a date with death here was Bob Ingram, from Aberdeen. His demise was nothing to do with the fairer sex but he failed in an attempt to escape in November 1943 and was shot. He was extremely unlucky to suffer such a fate where normally he would have been recaptured and returned to the camp. Bob received a posthumous Mention in Despatches after the war. In contrast, William Milne (2884045) had escaped from another AbKdo in Erfurt the previous year and was at large for four days as he tried to make it to Switzerland. The difference here was that, when recaptured, he was handed over to the civil police and on return to the camp the punishment was solitary confinement for twenty-one days on bread and water. Normally the Germans were keen to publicize their fair and respectful treatment of the PoWs and Albert King, Sandy Gammack and Arthur Durward all had photos of, and possibly attended, the funeral of Corporal Fredrick Collison of the Royal Engineers. He died in February 1943 and was buried with full military honours, with the German guards firing a volley of shots over his grave and British PoWs laying wreaths.

There were not many deaths of Gordon Highlanders while prisoners of the Germans. Although there were some tragic acts of senseless killing during escape attempts, or through the callous actions of some unpredictable Nazis guards, in cases of illness or injury, medical treatment was generally administered promptly. This was not always successful, however. Almost immediately after arriving at Stalag XXA (Thorn) Poland, at the end of July 1940, Jack Hutcheon became ill with what he described as 'his rheumatics' (rheumatism) affecting his legs. He was admitted to the camp hospital in Fort XXIV and as a result of this became separated from his brothers, Archie and Billy, who were soon sent out from the main camp on working parties to farms in the area. Jack's problem with his legs was probably brought about, or seriously aggravated, by the weeks of marching through northern France, Belgium and Holland, being forced to sleep in the open, exposed to the elements, and given insufficient food. After his initial stay in hospital, which lasted several weeks until mid-October, he was only well for a short time. Unfortunately, his condition deteriorated quickly and he was back in hospital. He was unable to recover and died on

18 March 1941, only nine months after his capture at St Valéry. His wife's first knowledge of his death came in a personal letter from Lance Corporal Leonard Chapman of the Royal Army Service Corps who was a PoW orderly in the camp hospital. He was in charge of the PoWs working in the hospital and, realizing Jack's poor physical state, gave him a small job so that he would only have to do light work. He also tried to keep Jack on in hospital when he was declared fit for general work but was over-ruled. In his letter to Mary Hutcheon, he explained that he had promised Jack he would write to her after his death. He informed Mary that he was with Jack when he died, reassuring her he died peacefully. Private George Shepherd also died at Stalag XXA. The cause of his death was pneumonia and heart failure, passing away on 27 April 1943. He was initially buried in a local cemetery near Graudenz and Captain Gordon Duff, from Oflag VIIB (Eischstätt) took the funeral service. George had been wounded in the arm when he was captured but he wrote home to his wife, Violet, re-assuring her he was alright. It must have come as a shock to her when, over two years later, she was notified he had died from a totally different cause. It is clear that the authorities accorded a great deal of consideration and sympathy to George's family following his death with an account of the funeral arrangements, obtained from the camp's 'Man of Confidence', communicated to Violet Shepherd by the Red Cross. This letter also gave details of where he was buried, informing her, re-assuringly, that his grave had been marked by a simple wooden cross and properly recorded. She also received a letter of condolence from 12 Downing Street written by her local MP, William Whitely. Violet Shepherd also received a widow's pension of seventeen shillings and sixpence per week (75 pence). The highest ranking Gordon Highlander to die in German captivity was Brigadier George Burney, the 153 Brigade Commander, who died after a short illness in a hospital in Munich on 7 November 1940, aged 51. Five officers, from Oflag VIIC (Laufen), were allowed to travel to his funeral. He now lies buried in Durnbach War Cemetery, Bayern, Germany. Similarly another group of officers was allowed to attend the funeral of Lieutenant David Crichton, who died unexpectedly at Freising, a hospital camp serving Stalag VIIA (Moosburg). He died on 29 August 1941, aged 34. In December of the same year, the 1st Battalion's Medical Officer, Captain Norman Altham, of the Royal Army Medical Corps, died of typhus while at Lamsdorf.

Working on construction sites has always been a risky business but under the insouciant conditions of safety applied for PoWs their risk was increased. In July 1941 Alex Watt (2875918) had a serious accident while working on a building site. This was the result of a somewhat foolhardy operation, riding down a makeshift railway on a bogey with three other PoWs. As the brake man his responsibility was to control the speed of their descent by applying a wooden stake to the ground, so slowing the bogey down. Unfortunately, he had an equipment malfunction when his stake snapped. The bogey gathered speed and the others leapt off, leaving Alex who came to a crashing halt and spilled out of the bogey, breaking his ankle. He was taken to the military hospital in Thorn where he was looked after by PoW orderlies and German doctors. They treated him along with German soldiers who had been wounded in the newly commenced Operation BARBAROSSA, Germany's invasion of Russian-occupied Poland and beyond. Alex made a full recovery but was hospitalized for several months, as the first attempt to reset his broken ankle was unsuccessful. This meant he had to endure the pain of having the bone broken again to have it reset it properly. It was a strange coincidence that Alex's fiancée, Alice, also broke her leg at almost the same time. She fell down some stairs when working for the Land Army at Craibstone Estate, just outside Aberdeen.

Perhaps the job hated most by the Gordon Highlanders was mining. With the majority of the Gordons hailing from North-East Scotland, where there has never been any tradition of mining, this type of work was that to which they had the greatest aversion. In part this was because of the alien nature of this work but also because it was universally known to be dangerous and dirty. Salt mining was principally organized at Bad Sulza, the location of the Headquarters of Stalag IXC (Mühlhausen). Gordons worked in a number of these salt mines, including Bleicherode, Kraja, Unterbreizbach and Dorndorf, the latter being a potassium mine. In general they worked an eight-hour shift for six days. At the end of their shift the civilian miners and the PoWs were provided with hot showers, which were essential to avoid salt rash due to the astringent nature of the salt on the skin. Working conditions in these mines were really bad with many men suffering accidents or illness which often resulted in them having to be hospitalized. Bobby Shand and his three friends, George (Dod) Dunn, Walter (Wattie) Skinner and Charlie Birnie, stuck together, which they had done from the time of their capture at St Valéry. When they arrived at Stalag

IXC they registered together, being allocated PoW numbers 171 for Bobby, 172 for Wattie and 176 for Charlie. When the time came for them to be sent to Kraja salt mine they again volunteered to stay together but were dismayed to learn that, just prior to their arrival, three British PoWs had died when there was a roof fall underground. The conditions in the mine were very taxing. They had to walk a considerable distance to the working face, stooping all the way, due to the low roof of the tunnel, with only the dim glow from the carbide lamps they carried to light their way. In addition it was hot, every small cut stung from the ingress of salt and their eyes and mouths were constantly dry. Following an accident in the mine, James Donald injured his leg and was sent to Obermassfeld Hospital (Reserve-Lazaret IX-C(a)), which was operated by nine British doctors aided by over forty PoW orderlies, under the supervision of a German military doctor. He was in hospital for two months and had returned to work for only two weeks when another accident saw him back in hospital for another six weeks. After nearly three years working in the salt mine the toll on his health was such that he was again hospitalized with problems with his heart and trouble with his nerves from the strain of working underground in dangerous conditions. On discharge from hospital he was transferred to the seed factory in Erfurt which was less demanding work. Harry Tobin was also hospitalized and was a patient at Obermassfeld where he was told that about a month before his arrival, Douglas Bader, the Battle of Britain Spitfire 'ace', had also been a patient. He was given a group photo showing staff and some patients with the legless man, seated in the centre of the front row. Harry believed this photo was given to him by the Germans as they wanted to boast that they had held such a prominent person in captivity. The effects of long-term working in the salt mines sometimes persisted after liberation. Bruce Milton contracted typhus at Stalag IXC, due to the unhygienic and insanitary conditions of his work camp, and this also had an effect on his health long after the war was over. Alex Thow's health was affected to such a degree that he died in Aberdeen, just six months after his liberation. Kenneth Mackenzie did not live long enough to see his home again. He died of an abscess on a lung while in hospital at Reserve Lazaret-Hauptlagerett-Bayreuth on 2 April 1945, just a short time before he would have been liberated. Although also seriously ill, Fred Wedderburn was more fortunate. He was at a camp in Germany, suffering from dysentery and pneumonia, after the 600-mile trek from Lamsdorf, when he was liberated. Later he described this as 'the greatest day of his life'; so he felt motivated to rise from his sick bed and greet his American saviours.

The unsatisfactory working conditions in these mines led to conflict with the mine administration and Bobby Shand was sentenced to work in a stone quarry as a punishment. Here conditions were even harsher and some PoWs deliberately injured themselves to escape. Work in these quarries, particularly during the winter months, was dreadfully hard. The PoWs were breaking rocks and a quota system was in operation. Thirty wagons had to be filled every day by a party of two. If this was not achieved by the end of the normal working day they were forced to continue until their quota was met. Although the sentence was for three months this was often extended. The hopelessness of their position spurred many Gordon Highlanders to try to escape. Corporal Hamish Gow and Private George Robb made a clean escape from the salt mine at Menterode but they were recaptured three days later, whilst trying to get aboard a railway goods wagon. They were taken back to the main camp and given twenty-one days' solitary confinement with only bread and water. This was not the end of their sentence as they were then sent to Rhomhild stone quarry as a further punishment, where George was injured. He was taken to Obermassfeld Lazeret where he told a senior British doctor about conditions in the quarry. The doctor's position enabled him to inform the Red Cross, who eventually intervened on the PoWs' behalf. Alexander Gray also made an unsuccessful attempt to escape and used the railway to get away. However, in the darkness he had no idea where the goods train he boarded was bound and found himself in Warsaw. It was bitterly cold and he developed frostbite and was recaptured, with the same inevitable consequence that he was sent to work in a stone quarry. George Gall made no fewer than three escape attempts from Bleicherode, the first two by simply cutting the wire and getting away. He walked for ten days before recapture by the civil police. On his third attempt he managed to get much further by boarding a goods train bound for Holland but was recaptured after a week on the run.

An equally large number of Gordon Highlanders worked mining coal rather than salt. This was organized through one of Germany's largest prisoner of war camps for Allied servicemen at Lamsdorf (Stalag VIIIB/344) but the town has been renamed and is now called Łambinowice, Poland. There were several coal mines in this area but the Gordons were concentrated at Hindenburg (AbKdo

E603), Klausberg (AbKdo E51) and Oehringen Grube, between Gleiwitz and Kattowitz. Most of the men employed in this activity were engaged in it for almost the whole of their time in captivity. The PoWs worked with professional Polish miners with the PoWs doing the more arduous work, such as shovelling coal into coal tubs on rails or fetching pit props and moving coal tubs. The working conditions in these mines were unpleasant and unsafe, the mines were wet with water everywhere in the working areas and their lighting was carbide lamps. Occasionally a blast would blow out the light of the carbide lamp and the only thing to do was to wait in the inky darkness until a civilian miner came along to relight the lamp. This was one of the few occasions when it was possible for the PoW to shirk work. Since it was clear that the production of coal was of great assistance to the German war effort, some men tried to sabotage the output from the mines. James Davidson (2881743) sabotaged the coal conveyors, halting production for a time and Albert Donald destroyed tools but there was limited opportunity for causing serious disruption as they did not wish to endanger fellow PoWs working in the mine.

The Germans had a strange system of vetting men to ensure they were fit to work underground. They were given an X-ray and if this was clear they were then required to provide a stool sample. Maurice Maclean was given the all clear following his X-ray but due to the paltry rations and sluggish bowels he was unable to provide the all-important sample. This was frustrating as winter was on them and Maurice needed to get underground where it was much warmer than the bitterly cold mine yard, where he was forced to work until he was pronounced fit for work underground. One night he was awoken by a fellow PoW who presented him with a small package with newspaper used for the wrapping. Unwrapping this he was astonished to find it contained one of the man's stools! This gift was an effort to be helpful to Maurice so he accepted graciously. Next day he submitted the sample and was duly declared fit to work down the mine.

The precautionary approach in selecting men seemed at odds with the general safety ethic applied to PoWs. Accidents and sickness were not uncommon as the damp conditions led to rheumatism and sciatica, whilst James Gray suffered enlarged and septic tonsils due to the coal dust in the air and Albert Donald blamed the conditions for a skin disease which troubled him for two years. More serious injuries also occurred. Donald Graham suffered from shock and a broken leg after an explosion underground, at the Hindenburg mine, triggered a rock fall causing him to be in hospital for five months. A similar fate befell William Reith, who was also hospitalized for three months when his wounds turned septic. While he was working as a coalminer, Albert (Spud) Robertson kept a diary and made several references to his friend's injuries, such as Sergeant Stan Houghton, of the Queen's Own Royal West Kent Regiment, who died from the effects of a poisoned foot and Archie Hepburn being hospitalized with a swollen knee. Archie Hepburn was Spud's long-term friend, both having served as drummers in the 5th Battalion Pipe Band for many years before the war. The two friends had managed to stick together throughout the journey from St Valéry to Lamsdorf. They registered together when they arrived at the camp so their PoW numbers were consecutive and they worked together in the same coal mine near Krakow, Poland. Archie was hospitalized for four weeks with his knee and Spud himself was admitted to hospital after an injury which required his foot to be put in plaster. It was not uncommon for good friends or relatives to try and stay together and help each other in times of need. John Davidson was glad of his brother's help and concern when he contracted diphtheria in 1941 and was ill for three months. Two years later the damp conditions of the mine contributed to his developing pneumonia. These brothers, James Davidson (2882072) and John Davidson, both worked at Klausberg coal mine and also had consecutive PoW numbers, as did conscript militiamen Alex Reid (2883069) and Stephen Hadden, who were photographed standing next to one another in their passing out parade photo, taken after they had completed their basic training at Gordon Barracks, Bridge of Don, Aberdeen, in February 1940, just four months before they were captured. The friendships formed during those weeks of intense military training, followed immediately afterwards by the stress of dangerous combat, forged such a strong bond that the same passing out parade photograph shows Frank Wilson and Angus Keith standing together and they subsequently registered together at Stalag 344 (Lamsdorf), and were allocated consecutive PoW numbers.

The dangers of being a prisoner of war at Lamsdorf were not just limited to the nature of the work the men were required to do. The guards controlled their fate in many ways and sometimes it didn't take much provocation of a Nazi guard for dire consequences to result. Early on the morning of 17 December

1941 Private George Strachan arrived to take his place in the line-up of a small group of men who were about to go to work in the mine at Klausberg. As he arrived, he was smoking a cigarette but it was forbidden to fall in while smoking although only half of the work detail had reported for duty at this point. The guard on duty shouted 'zigaretten aus' and, without giving George any chance to obey, he immediately flew at him and knocked the cigarette from his mouth. In surprise, George instinctively put up his hands to defend himself. Unfortunately, the guard chose to treat this as a threatening gesture and reacted by drawing his bayonet. He lunged at George and drove him back against a wall, from where George staggered forward clutching his side. The guard then put away his bayonet, concealing the fact that he had used the weapon. He then shouted to the feldwebel (the German sergeant who was in charge of the work party), that George Strachan had struck him, adding 'shoot him like a dog', whereupon Feldwebel Rolle drew his pistol, ran over, and shot George at close range. George fell to the ground and died shortly afterwards, just a week before Christmas and two weeks short of his 22nd birthday. All of this happened in full view of the other fourteen PoWs who had already assembled and they were quickly marched off to work. Statements were taken from the witnesses by the Allied Officers Board in May 1945, at Moosburg, but it is not known if Feldwebel Rolle, who carried out the murder, was prosecuted for this war crime. George Strachan now lies buried in Krakow Rakowicki Cemetery, Poland, together with two other Gordon Highlanders, George Murray, who died in the camp hospital in May 1944, and William Howells, who was killed by friendly fire during an Allied bombing raid in August 1944. Spud Robertson first recorded the occurrence of air raids by Allied planes over Poland in his diary in August 1942. These raids presented as great a danger to the PoWs as the Germans. Spud noted that when the air raid warning sounded there was great excitement in the camp as the raids appeared to be fairly close, as they could clearly hear the noise of the planes and the explosions of the bombs.

Many Gordon Highlanders were employed in a variety of quarries. While some of these were designated punishment camps, there were others working to extract material for the numerous construction and road-building projects. Although the mental strain of being underground was not a factor, these were dangerous sites, with the work physically very demanding. James Davidson (2882072) was injured by a rock fall in a quarry at Godolin, Poland, and was unable to work for five months. At Lappin, which was an Arbeitskommando controlled through Stalag XXB (Marienburg), a long steep hill was being exploited for the sand. Piper Bill Maitland, a survivor of the mortar bomb attack at Manneville-ès-Plains and Gordon Reid (2880758), the brother of Duncan Reid, one of the pipers killed there, were sent to work here in August 1940. A railway track ran along the base of the hill and the PoWs dug into the hill to fill wheel-barrows which they then pushed along a narrow plank to fill the trucks parked in a loop line close to the steep slope, just off the main line. Every day each man had to dig out at least twenty tons of sand, filling a metal mineral wagon. During the summer this was exhausting hot and dusty work but at the end of the day they were allowed to swim in the adjacent lake to cool down and get clean. However, in the winter, with temperatures well below freezing, they had to use heavy hammers and pick axes just to break the surface of the ground before they could excavate the sand. At this time of year swimming was also impossible as the lake was frozen. This work was too physically demanding for Gordon Reid and, after fifteen months, he was transferred to Willenburg and then to a farm.

The large numbers of prisoners of war being used by German industry in Poland and eastern Germany meant that the accommodation was of a temporary nature and not of a very high standard, or comfort. Men were locked up at night, so in small work sites there was no access to toilets or washing facilities during this time. There were, however, some lighter moments amidst the hard work and danger. At one coal mine, where Dawson Henderson was working, the PoWs' quarters had proper latrines which were in a wooden enclosure with several seating places over a pit, into which the human waste flowed by passing down a concrete slope into a large tank. These were considered above the average standard and were kept clean, but there was one drawback to the design which became strikingly apparent during the cold Polish winter. This was that the effluent froze on the slope and this was not considered pleasant or hygienic. After some discussion, someone had the bright idea that the waste calcium carbide from their miners' lamps, which was tipped into a large bucket each night on their return to camp, could be emptied into the latrines. The theory advanced for this was that the reaction of the calcium carbide with water produced heat and so the effect would be that the ice would melt and the environment would be sweeter as a result. Unfortunately, nobody stopped to think about the product of the reaction which was acetylene gas, which was what burned to produce the light in their lamps. Another failing was not to make all the prisoners aware of this wheeze. One night, as he answered the call of nature, an unfortunate PoW tossed his glowing cigarette butt into the latrine. The effect was immediate: the acetylene gas being given off exploded, excrement flew everywhere and the latrines burned down, not to mention the shock received by the unwitting perpetrator.

Erfurt was a hub of PoW activity with many Gordon Highlanders being employed in this area. One other large employer was a shoe factory, while other Gordon PoWs were employed in a wine factory and in various construction and road making projects in the area. This large concentration of prisoners allowed for the men to organize and engage in numerous sporting and amateur dramatic productions. These activities were photographed by the Germans who passed the pictures, printed on postcard format paper, to the PoWs in the hope that they would be sent back to Britain and illustrate how well their prisoners were being treated. This extended to men posing in groups with instruments they could not play. Harry Tobin had a series of consecutively numbered photos of completely different groups of PoWs in Stalag IXC, all posing with the same two piano accordions and a concertina. Harry is shown holding one of the piano accordions but he couldn't play a note so it must have been somewhat of a puzzle to his family back home when this photo arrived in the post. The implications were that their loved one had been receiving music lessons while a prisoner, rather than that they were in fact slaving down a mine or in a quarry. Naturally, the PoWs were happy to receive these photos to send home as it showed they were alive and healthy but they couldn't disclose the fake poses as this would have fallen foul of the censor. But it was not all pretend. Some PoWs, like Albert King and Ralph England, were proficient musicians and played in bands that performed concerts or supported musicals, to entertain and boost the morale of their fellow PoWs. Albert played the trumpet and performed with a number of bands including the 'Wigwam Band' and 'Robbie's Rialto Swingers'. Both ensembles supported the shows in the *Rialto Club*, where the centrepiece of the stage was a mock-up of a ship's bow, emblazoned with the name the *Lady Blighty*. Ralph played his ukulele and was pictured for posterity in a show entitled 'London Calling'. The variety of shows was extensive, with make-up and costumes being used to make things look as realistic as possible. Bill Jamieson was shown appearing in a pantomime and in this and other productions, men posed in a variety of roles including as credible female characters, Victorian sailors, African natives, cowboys and Indians. These performances were all held within the camp and photographed by the Germans and many men had a large collection of these photos. The musical instruments were mostly provided courtesy of the Red Cross but the costumes and props were all created with fantastic ingenuity from materials scrounged or stolen from around the camp.

Photos were also taken of groups of PoWs at their places of work but rarely with German guards or at work. One of the few examples of this is a photograph of a group of PoWs, including Bill Maitland and Gordon Reid (2880758), at the Sandhill at Lappin. The German guards, complete with rifles slung over their shoulders, and the civilian charge-hands all look relaxed and appeared happy to pose along with the PoWs. Regimental insignia was generally discouraged but in a number of group photographs of Gordon Highlanders they are shown proudly wearing their cap badges pinned to their chests. In one case, in a photo of ten Gordons at Nordhausen salt mine, which includes Harry Tobin and Bill Jamieson, a gleaming Gordon Highlanders' cap badge is attached to a leaf-shaped piece of cloth and held up to show it off. This was a clear message to their folks back home that they were with comrades and sticking together.

There were several means whereby men teamed up together to help each other when they were in trouble, sick or to share resources. One obvious means was sticking with people they knew well so that the men with relatives in the same camp, or from the same town or platoon, would often form alliances for mutual benefit. Within the ranks of the Gordon Highlander PoWs there were very many family ties. The Regiment recruited almost exclusively from the North East of Scotland so it was natural that many men would be related. Often brothers would enlist together, particularly in the 4th, 5th and 6th Territorial Army battalions. This was the case with Charles and Edward Irvine, James and Arthur Durward, Robert and William Park, William and Robert Shearer, twins Leslie and Thomas Gray and Charles and Peter McPherson. There were at least thirty-seven brothers serving together, with numerous other blood relationships, for example Sandy Kydd and Jim Moggach were cousins, as were Tom Farquhar and Bill McLean. In addition men such as Andrew Duncan and Robert Smith from Aberdeen were neighbours, as were George Anderson and

Victor Shearer from New Pitsligo. In fact seven other Gordon Highlanders in the PoW camps were from this small village in north Aberdeenshire. This pattern was repeated all across the region. For example, over thirty Gordon PoWs came from the small provincial town of Fraserburgh, including Sergeants James Burgess and Alex Watt (2871083) who both lived in Cross Street, only five doors apart. Both were former Regulars who had served in India with the 1st Battalion and were both prominent members of Fraserburgh Football Club. Others were workmates, such as men from Bucksburn who worked in the large Stoneywood and Mugiemoss paper mills. In addition some formal clubs were formed, such as the Lamsdorf Loons and the Edinburgh and District Club, all with Gordon Highlanders among the membership. These clubs were formed to give mutual support to each of the members and to share resources and news from home.

The Lamsdorf Loons Club was formed secretly, on 21 October 1943, in Barrack Room 16A of Stalag 344 (Lamsdorf) with the members, all from the North East of Scotland, choosing the alliterative club title from the camp name and the Doric term 'loon' meaning boy. At its height, the club had around fifty members, the majority being Gordon Highlanders, who met and entertained each other with stories and songs, with Bill Barclay playing his mandolin accompanied by George Forsyth on his guitar. One of the founder members of the Loons was Thomas Gray, who was with the 6th Battalion and captured at Hem in Northern France just over a week before the Battalion, including his twin brother Leslie, was evacuated through Dunkirk. In an unlikely coincidence, Lesley joined Thomas in Lamsdorf almost four years later. He was captured on the Anzio bridgehead, Italy. Lesley also joined 'the Loons', as did William Fyfe who arrived at Lamsdorf with him. William Fyfe was also from the small village of Aberlour, Banffshire, as the Gray twins, famous for the single malt whisky distilled in the village and salmon fishing on the River Spey.

The other main leisure activity available to the PoWs was sport. Football, athletics and boxing were all popular, for both spectators and participants. As with the musical instruments the Red Cross often provided the necessary sports equipment. An interest and participation in sporting activities, particularly team sports, helped many men handle their long-term imprisonment. The old football rivalry of the home nations was also recreated with Scotland versus

England being a special fixture for the Gordons. At Stalag 383 (Hohenfels) this event was heralded by the two teams marching on to the football pitch led by five kilted pipers. Boxing matches also drew large crowds and even German officers and guards enjoyed these events. At Lamsdorf Rodney Knowles was matched to fight a German guard who had been an international champion before the war. Knowles was taking a terrible beating and had been knocked to the canvas several times. The seconds in his corner were concerned about him and told him to stay down the next time he was floored by the German's punch. He refused saying 'no German will keep me down'. Although the inevitable happened and Knowles lost the bout, the camp commandant presented him with a certificate for his courage and refusal to give in. The Edinburgh and District Club was based in Stalag 383 and organized highland games which were well supported. The camp, which held mainly NCOs, had several pipe majors, including Pipe Majors MacLeod and Mitchellson of the Gordon Highlanders. Sergeant David Shore, who was the secretary of Edinburgh Club, wrote to various organizations in Scotland and received funds and bagpipes to start a pipe band. This was not only seen as a booster for the morale of the many Scots PoWs but it kept up the level of skill in playing the pipes. One of the philanthropic organizations which supported PoWs was the British Prisoners of War Books and Games Fund. They tried to meet the specific requests made to them by individual PoWs, including the supply of bagpipes. Sergeant Charles Grant (2876445) had a more modest request and received the much more portable and much less raucous mouth organ. Andrew Third was grateful to receive books on ancient history, travel and biographies, which helped him take his mind off the work he hated in a salt mine at Stalag IXC. On a lighter-hearted note, Drummer Harold MacFarquhar, in Stalag XXB, was delighted to receive the gift of books on music, while his fellow inmate there, Sergeant Tommy McLeod, received books on his favourite literary genre of crime. Douglas Davidson was surprised and delighted to receive a parcel of nine books through Miss Christine Knowles of this organization. A more unusual pastime was chosen by William Anderson who obtained worn-out woollen garments from other prisoners and with a toothbrush, which he managed to adapt and fashion into a hook, crocheted a woollen blanket. Sandy Gammack received a gift from F. Flemming, who was keen on handicrafts. In one example he asked a large number of the PoWs at Stalag IXC to sign a handkerchief which he then stitched, following the writing exactly. The result was an embroidered handkerchief which was a unique memento.

Mail was universally considered to be a salvation. It was not until September or later, three months after the surrender, that families learned the fates of their men. Alex Watt's (2875918) mother received an official letter informing her that he was a PoW on 4 September 1940 but it took longer to exchange personal correspondence, all adding to the anxiety. Each man could write one letter and four postcards per month. The postcards, which were in a pre-printed format, allowed room for only a short message, which had to pass through the German censor before despatch. The families back in Britain also had the opportunity of keeping in touch with their relatives with letters and parcels. The Red Cross arranged for the mail to be transferred to and from the PoWs through a neutral country, such as Portugal or Sweden. In addition, the Red Cross packed and delivered food parcels to the PoWs which were paid for by donations, often raised by local committees. These Red Cross parcels were invaluable to the PoWs as they provided a much needed supplement to the meagre rations being issued by the Germans. In addition, particularly as the war progressed, they contained items such as British cigarettes, soap and chocolate, which were considered by the German and Polish civilians as luxury goods. As such these became a kind of currency, invaluable in trading with local people or, sometimes, to bribe guards. Ran Ogilvie listed the contents of both British and Canadian Red Cross parcels showing these were really generous gifts. On average, these contained three tins of meat or fish, jam or marmalade, packs of margarine or butter, powdered or condensed milk, cheese, biscuits, sugar, chocolate, tea and or cocoa, dried fruit and soap. In addition there was an issue of two ounces (50 grams) of tobacco and fifty cigarettes each week.

One other arrangement which was a great boon to the PoWs was a scheme to adopt a PoW. Charles Morrison was a beneficiary of this when the staff of S.T. Law, a shoe shop in Aberdeen which he had links to pre-war, adopted him and sent him parcels of cigarettes. Similarly Edward Marr was adopted by the Aberdeen University Ladies Club at their AGM in 1942. They agreed to donate 10 shillings (50p) per week for him, which was extremely generous as the average agricultural worker's wage was only around £2 per week at the time, although this was often supplemented with free potatoes, turnips, and oatmeal produced on the farm. The Ladies Club was also very active in other ways, making bandages and knitting garments to send out to the PoWs via the Red Cross. At their meeting on 25 June 1945 it was recorded that during the war, in addition to donating £138, the ladies had provided much material support, including 2,300 bandages, 258 knitted pullovers, 80 pairs of bed socks and 108 handkerchiefs. Since the disaster at St Valéry had affected the north of Scotland disproportionately, it is not surprising that newspapers circulating in the area took up the cause of the PoWs. On 8 November 1940 the *Huntly Express*, the local newspaper serving the area of Aberdeenshire where the Gordon Highlanders Regiment was first raised by the 5th Duke of Gordon in 1794, highlighted that some 2,000 officers and men from the North East of Scotland were prisoners of war. The newspaper further explained that the British Red Cross Society was the only authorized channel through which parcels of food and clothing could be sent to these men. It publicized an appeal for funds for this purpose being made for the counties of Aberdeen, Banff, Kincardine, Orkney and Shetland on behalf of the Scottish Branch of the Red Cross under the convenorship of Lord Hay of Seaton. Lord Hay, formerly Major Malcolm V. Hay of the Gordon Highlanders, was well placed to lead this appeal as he himself had been a prisoner of war. He was captured by the Germans in northern France in the first month of the Great War, on 27 August 1914, after receiving a serious head wound the previous day in the battle of le Cateau. He was held captive until 17 February 1915 when he was part of a prisoner exchange and, on return to the UK, was immediately admitted to the Queen Alexandra's Military Hospital in London. In addition, his own son, Lieutenant Brian Hay, was a prisoner of war who had been serving with 1st Battalion Gordon Highlanders. One example of how arrangements were made to collect money for this fund was a local organization set up in the Huntly area to encourage the formation of groups of people willing to combine to adopt one or more prisoners. This was a well-supported initiative being made for the counties of Aberdeen, Banff, Kincardine, Orkney and Shetland with the *Huntly Express* listing numerous donations from a wide range of sources. These included a variety of local businesses and clubs, such as Huntly Laundry and Gartly Women's Guild, as well as various individuals. In addition, from this small rural area, which is likely to be representative of the region as a whole, many PoWs were adopted, including four by Huntly Townswomen's Guild and one by the staff of Huntly Gordon Secondary School, as just a few examples.

On a larger scale a variety concert was organized in the Capitol Theatre in Aberdeen in December 1940; the cast comprised young Gordon Highlanders and local young women who sang and danced. One particular song, entitled *O Ma Shelter* sung by local star Jack Angel was specifically written for the show and the sheet music was sold in aid of the fund. A subsequent concert, appropriately entitled *Stalag Party* was held in August 1941, the programme including an appeal from Lord Hay for regular donations to pay for the Red Cross parcels being sent out to the stalags.

Such was the importance of the mail the men received from their families and friends that some men, including Albert King and Drummer Albert (Spud) Robertson kept a log of the letters received and often noting the news they contained, together with listing photos and the contents of parcels received. Spud was a prisoner held in Stalag VIIIB (Teschen) whilst his brother, George, also a Gordon Highlander captured at St Valéry-en-Caux, was being held in Stalag XXB (Marienburg). In what must be an extremely rare piece of inter-PoW camp correspondence, Spud received a postcard from George on 9 July 1942 asking how he was and chastising him for not keeping in touch. (Spud's son, Ron Robertson, still has this postcard.) In addition Spud corresponded with his young son, Billy, who was just about to leave school but was keen to tell his father how busy he was doing casual work, such as 'tattie pickin'' (harvesting potatoes). He also mentioned that he had caught a rabbit and took it home to his granny as a birthday present, which was very welcome as butcher's meat was strictly rationed. The prisoners who had young families were always keen to communicate with their offspring. Corporal David Greig did his best to customize his standard-issue PoW postcard by using coloured crayons to enhance his Christmas greetings and a ninth birthday wish, which ended 'nine big kisses, Dad'. He illustrated his Christmas card with two radio masts broadcasting his message to his daughter Isobel. This was almost prophetic as about eighteen months later, in the summer of 1944, another 5th Battalion Gordon Highlander, a prisoner at Lamsdorf, was able to make an actual broadcast to his family back in Fraserburgh, Aberdeenshire, just a few short miles from Fetterangus, where Isobel Greig lived. Corporal Alex Dickie was able to send a radio message to his daughter Alicia to wish her many happy returns on her ninth birthday. There had been a previous announcement on German radio that this was going to take place and, understandably, Alicia and her mother were both excited and delighted to hear the sound of Alex's voice after a gap of four years.

Another unusual and remarkable episode occurred in the run-up to Christmas 1941. The Hutcheon family were approached by the BBC about recording a broadcast for their *Home Forum* series, which the family hoped would be heard by prisoners of war in Germany. It was understood that PoWs were allowed to listen to certain entertainment broadcasts and it was expected this might include the *Absent Friends* broadcasts. The programme was recorded at their home, School Croft, Balmedie, just north of Aberdeen. It took the form of a fireside chat among all of the family members, reminiscing about Christmas the previous year when all the family, including Jack, now deceased, and brothers Archie and Bill, now prisoners of war working on a farm in Silesia, had sat down together for their Christmas meal. This programme was broadcast on Christmas day 1941. After the broadcast Mrs Christina Hutcheon was visited and interviewed by a reporter from the local newspaper. When he arrived Mrs Hutcheon senior was looking wistfully out across the cold grey North Sea which was plainly visible from her home. After the initial pleasantries Christina said 'They are somewhere out there'. The reporter commented that her family were giving much for the country and she bravely replied, 'it is war, we can do no other'.

Gordon Reid (2880758), a piper and poet, was moved to put the sentiments of most of his fellow PoWs into verse. Such was the resonance of this poem that Bill Maitland, a fellow 5th Battalion Gordon Highlander who, after the war was the Pipe Major and founding member of the Bucksburn and District Pipe Band, copied it and kept a copy for over seventy years. His poem is entitled *The Postman*.

Every day we look for him
With longing in our hearts,
The man who brings us news of home
And also Stalag marks.

He rides a bike of yellow hue
A true and trusty steed
And on a very special day
He brings 'The Camp' to read.

He never seems to hurry
But gets here just the same
And if there is any mail for us
We almost go insane

Let's hope they never call him up
Or take him off his job
And that his mailbag gets so big
He has to hire a cab

For that is all we live for
News of folk at home
And if the mail comes after
You'll never hear us moan

So do your stuff old postman
And do not let us down
And when you die and leave this earth
You'll surely get your crown.

The reference to *The Camp* was to a newsletter for PoWs and their families. In the December 1941 issue Bill Maitland had his drawing of a pipe major printed together with a verse in Doric exalting pipers through history.

Dear friends and pipes a',
I'd like to say a word or twa,
Tae praise the piper and pipers braw,
(Tae some they're diels),
But may they land be spared tae blaw,
Strathspeys and reels.

Tae Soords or Fling, Schottische or Reel,
There's naething made can dae sae weel,
Whaur tunes are played wi' proper zeal,
And perfect beat,

They mak' the dancers think they feel,
Springs on their feet.

The pipers blaws wi' arduous sough,
(He'd think the job was unco teugh),
As young and old wi noisy hooch,
And dizzy whirl,
Aye feel their speeds nae fest eneuch,
At ilka birl.

Trace back the Empire's growth wi' care,
In peace or war the pipes were there,
Tae cheer the soul to do or dare,
And aye win through,
Lat's drink a toast tae ilka player.
Wi mountain dew.

The nature of the correspondence between the PoWs and home was not always just family news. Major George W. (Tony) Bruce maintained a link with the Commercial Bank of Scotland Ltd, which was holding the funds of the 5th Battalion Gordon Highlanders. In October 1940, while in Oflag VII C/H (Laufen), he wrote to the bank asking them to transfer funds from the Westminster Bank in Farnborough, where the Battalion had been stationed prior to them joining the BEF in France. He asked that certain debts be paid with the remainder to be held on deposit. The bank's agent obviously knew Tony Bruce well and signed off his reply

> I trust that all our friends are in good health and in good heart and now receiving parcels from this side. I see many of your old friends at our usual midday meeting place and all are pleased to know you are well. With kindest regards and best wishes for 1941.

There was also a poignant postscript: 'The Colours are in fine trim and ready for use.'

The bank wrote again in February 1941 confirming the transfer of Battalion funds to War Stock, which was attracting a more favourable rate of interest, and there was a reference to this being 'all in consultation with our friend A.D.B.S', a reference to Brigadier Alick Drummond Buchanan-Smith, who had left France in 1940 due to illness. Tony Bruce was also contacted directly by the International Committee of the Red Cross asking for information on Private Malcolm McIntosh, who was a casualty at St Valéry. In another unusual case Captain Colin Dennistoun Sword studied for a law degree while at Oflags VIB (Warburg) and VIIB (Eischstätt). Before he joined the Gordon Highlanders as a Supplementary Reserve officer in 1936 he had been admitted to Lincoln's Inn, one of four Inns of Court in London to which barristers in England and Wales belong and where they are called to the Bar. After being seriously wounded, he was captured at St Valéry and spent the first part of his captivity in hospital. He was the son of a solicitor and after his distance learning was called to the Bar in absentia in 1944. One unusual aspect of his progression to the Bar was that there was a requirement, by the Inns of Court, for aspirant barristers to eat a certain number of dinners within the Inn itself, which, for Captain Dennistoun Sword, was clearly impossible. However, his wife, whom he had married in 1939 just prior to going to France with the 1st Battalion, acted as his proxy and enjoyed the dinners in his place. He was not the only studious officer at Eischstätt. Captain James Shankley, a 5th Battalion Territorial Army officer who worked as a quantity surveyor for Aberdeen City's Architect's Department in his civilian life, studied for and passed the Institution of Structural Engineers graduate exam in 1943.

Christmas was a time of year when the PoWs looked forward to mail and greetings cards. These were hand-drawn in the camps to send home and the camp artists did their best to add a touch of humour. One particular example, sent in 1941, by Captain J. Shankley, from Oflag VIB (Warburg) to his old commanding officer, Alick Buchanan-Smith, was a simple pen-and-ink line drawing showing a figure, dressed as Santa Claus and carrying a sack of parcels, climbing out over the camp perimeter fence. He was being challenged from the corner watchtower by a German guard and the caption gives the would-be escapee's response to the guard, 'But I assure you, my dear chap - I really AM Father Christmas'. Another, sent in 1941 from Stalag IXC (Mühlhausen) by Private George Shepherd to his wife Violet, showed Father Christmas with a sack brimming over with Red Cross Parcels. Another style of card was sent by Captain Duncan Campbell from Oflag VIIA (Marnau). This was a beautifully pencilled scene of the camp entrance portraying the distinctive old bell tower with two PoWs in the foreground, one wearing a kilt. The twist was that the border of the whole scene was a wreath of barbed wire which also formed the words 'Oflag VII CH' across the top and 'Christmas Greetings 1940' along the bottom of the picture.

Christmas was a time when every effort was made to celebrate in style. Some of the contents of Red Cross parcels were hoarded to make a better than average meal. Although alcohol was officially forbidden, the ingenuity of some men managed to get round this, especially as a number of men from Speyside had experience working in the numerous malt whisky distilleries for which the area is famous. At a farm near Danzig, Jack Caldwell and his friends set about making some schnapps and fashioned a makeshift still from pieces of copper pipe pilfered from an old steam engine. Using potato peelings and some baker's yeast, which they obtained by bribing a guard, they successfully made some passable liquor which they bottled for storage. They kept this hidden and were fortunate that a search of their billet failed to reveal their hoard, which was placed around the bucket that formed their dry toilet. This was a close call as one of the guards had actually used this during the search. The Scottish tradition is to celebrate Hogmanay and New Year with a dram of whisky but it rarely stops at just one, which can lead to unpredictable consequences. Charlie Irvine mentioned that he and some friends decided to distil some alcohol, using potato peelings as their base, but not many of them liked the resultant drink so Charlie's brother Eddie drank their share. The result was that he became so drunk that he went up to the perimeter fence and started swearing at the German sentries. Fortunately, Charlie was able to get him back into their hut before the sentries reacted adversely.

While the other ranks were forced to work the officers were excused from this. In one respect this made for an easy life but most complained about the boredom of doing nothing every day, with little opportunity to see outside their camp and with limited interaction with anyone other than each other or their guards. There were various activities undertaken to fill their days. Sometimes these were cherished projects which had, perhaps, been a long-term dream but time or opportunity had prevented this previously. Now time was something the officers had plenty of so Major Rupert Christie used this time to compile a Russian-German dictionary. In 1923-24 he had spent twelve months in Riga, Latvia, learning Russian while on special duties for the War Office and had gained a linguist qualification. In another example of a man's desire to keep his intellectual capacities fit, Captain David Morren asked his wife to send him some books on science and agriculture which he used to give lectures to other prisoners, having set up an education circle in Oflag OVIIB (Eischstätt). Lieutenant Ran Ogilvie, who created and cultivated his own vegetable patch, looked forward to the fruits of his labours. He commented after the war that Captain Morren's lectures were a great help in keeping him sane during his captivity. Captain Stuart Aylmer studied fruit farming and lepidoptera and was taught Norwegian, to interpreter standard, by some Norwegian PoWs. Bridge was also widely played, with some games going on for years. Some large debts were accumulated but, magnanimously, these were all cancelled on liberation.

Captain David Morren was a very resourceful man. His father died when he was around 12 years old but his mother continued to run the family granite works in Aberdeen. He attended Robert Gordon's College and studied medicine at Aberdeen University. While there he was an outstanding athlete, gaining a blue in heavy field events. However, he did not finish his studies and decided to go into farming. He took the tenancy of a farm at Glenlivet but was also a keen musician. Oflag VIIB (Eischstätt), where he was a prisoner, had a fully functioning pipe band with David Morren as their drum major. His musical ability was obviously important in this but it was equally important for him to present the correct image. In order to create the correct uniform some improvisation was necessary. The hair for his sporran was created using string from Red Cross parcels and the mantle was cast after melting down cigarette tins. The pipe band represented a cementing of the Gordons with the other Highland regiments who were present in the camp. The group comprised of Captain David Morren plus Lieutenants G. Cruickshank and S.D. Rae from the Gordon Highlanders, together with three officers each from the Seaforth Highlanders, the Cameron Highlanders, Argyll and Sutherland Highlanders and four other individuals. They included Brigadier Southam, of the 48th Highlanders of Canada, which was the first regiment to affiliate themselves with the Gordon Highlanders, the oldest affiliation in the British Army. Brigadier Southam was the band president and is believed to have been the highest ranking officer captured in the ill-fated Dieppe Raid in August 1942. The pipe band was the pride of the camp and 'Beating Retreat' was an event of great meaning to many of the 1,500 PoWs in that camp who hailed from Britain, Australia, New Zealand and Canada.

Captain Bill Lawrie and Lieutenant James Sinclair had a totally altruistic means of filling their time. From August 1942 until September 1943 they worked at Kloster Haina and Obermassfeld Hospitals and thereafter at Meiningen Hospital until May 1945. They looked after the welfare and rehabilitation of seriously injured British PoWs, as well as trying to keep up their morale. Being a 5th Battalion Territorial Army officer, Captain Lawrie's civilian occupation was a physical education teacher. With his knowledge of physiology he took charge of the departments dealing with massage and physical training. They were ingenious in creating apparatus to assist in this work, using the only materials to hand, such as string from Red Cross parcels, cotton reels and odd pieces of wood. Artificial limbs were also fashioned and fitted to some of the amputees by Lieutenant Sinclair, utilizing engineering skills from his civilian occupation. One young airman, known only as 'Salt', always had a desire to be taller and when his two artificial legs were fitted by Jim Sinclair, he made them slightly longer to fulfil Salt's wish. They were well respected by their numerous patients and the reward for their dedication was that, after the war, they were honoured by each being made a Member of the Most Excellent Order of the British Empire (MBE).

At home the families could only pray that their menfolk would be safe and sending parcels and letters was one way they felt they could improve their lot. The Scottish Branch of the Red Cross produced a newsletter, entitled *Prisoners of War News*, which was the official journal of the Prisoners of War Department of the Red Cross and The Order of St John War Organization. It was issued to the next of kin of PoWs free of charge. This gave another forum for sharing news. This also sought to reassure families in Britain that their relatives were being looked after properly and that there was some oversight of the German authorities by an independent organization. This gave details of the activities of the Red Cross in providing relief to PoWs in the form of food parcels, medical supplies, clothing, musical instruments and books. The newsletter also gave praise to fundraising groups such as Ellon Secondary School, Aberdeenshire, who were specifically mentioned in the May 1943 issue as an example of the children of Scotland taking a great interest in the fate of British prisoners of war. Ellon Academy raised £310 in eighteen months by giving concerts and other activities, entirely organized by the pupils. Ellon was not alone in its efforts. In the same publication, Fintry School, near Turriff, Aberdeenshire also received praise for raising £100 for the cause. It was not all home front news which was reported as a letter was published from Gordon Highlander William Goodfellow, who wrote to the honorary secretary of the Gordon Highlanders' (Glasgow) Club enclosing a photograph of a drawing done by one of his fellow PoWs in Stalag XXID (Posen). This had won first prize in an arts and crafts exhibition and was a tangible way for him to show the prisoners' appreciation of artistic materials being sent to the camps through the auspices of the Red Cross.

Unfortunately, publications like these sometimes created the wrong impression of PoW life. This was often compounded by the PoWs themselves who sent home upbeat messages about their conditions so as not to worry their families. The drawback was that these positive messages just reinforced an erroneous impression making it look like their life behind barbed wire was fairly easy. For example they sent home photographs, in the form of postcards, of them in amateur dramatic productions or in various sports teams. In the January 1944 edition of the newsletter *Prisoner of War* page seven shows numerous groups of smiling PoWs in sports strips, or dressed casually with their hands in their pockets, including a group of officers from Oflag VIIB (Eischstätt) showing Major Tony Bruce and Captain H.M. Usher. In an article on page three of this publication, Gunner N. Gould (possibly a fictitious character), described what was purported to be a typical weekend for him in an article entitled 'Come and Spend A Week-end in My Stalag'.

In this Gould wrote:

Meet me at the factory and come back with me to the camp for the week-end. The first person you must meet is Bill, my mate. Bill finishes work an hour earlier and has already prepared our tea. His speciality is pancakes and today he has certainly lived up to his reputation. As a dutiful host I must apologize for the absence of lemon but feel thankful at any rate that there is sugar. The rest of the meal is lettuce from the garden plot (Red Cross seeds) and the oatcake biscuits are from a Scottish Red Cross parcel... . We will spare you the discomfort of an after tea conversation in competition with two accordions, a guitar and a mandolin. We're used to these budding musicians... .Sunday, of course, is a free day which means everybody can indulge by getting up later than usual... . We can obtain a fine grandstand view of the after dinner rugger match, England v Colonials, from the library window on the top floor. The other occupants of the library this afternoon are the editor of the camp magazine and a pair of script writers, busy scribbling; one of the camp artists at work on a poster for the next show; and the librarian at work on his card index system. After tea a non-denominational service is held, conducted by a Lance Corporal. Later on there is the weekly mail to be written and despatched, and to end the day the band gives the usual Sunday evening programme from the bandstand – the outdoor boxing ring.

Finally Gould asks:

What are your impressions of us? A depressed area? Certainly not! Rather we hope you left us with the picture in your mind of a small but cheerful community of Britons.

This article covered two pages and painted a very rosy picture of camp life, which was far from the grim reality of life in a PoW camp. However, it sought to express the gratitude for the gifts of food, books and musical instruments, via Red Cross parcels, and tried to convince the folks back home that their life was much better than the actuality. This had repercussions for how the PoWs themselves were perceived back in Britain, where naturally enough the PoWs' families were more than happy to believe this well-meaning deception. The newsletter did include reports from Red Cross Inspectors who visited the Stalags and work Kommandos which gave mixed appraisals, describing some unsatisfactory conditions, but often qualifying this by stating it was believed 'this was a temporary situation' *or* 'prisoners are overworked sorting private and Red Cross parcels for the whole of the Stalag', that an oversupply of gifts was their biggest problem and almost suggesting that for the men to be overworked was fine where the outcome was self-serving!

This situation was compounded further in May 1944 by the Red Cross, the Order of St John and the *Daily Telegraph* combining to produce a 'Prisoner of

War Exhibition' produced together with a catalogue comprehensively detailing the life of PoWs in German hands. The article by Gunner Gould, described above, was reprinted in full, and there was great emphasis on describing the filling and delivery of Red Cross food parcels, books and clothing. However, the stark fact that without these parcels the PoWs would have been close to starving on the rations provided by the Germans was glossed over. After describing what the Geneva Convention required the Germans to provide, it went on to quote Lord Cromwell who stated:

> This drab diet, served day after day, is not given in sufficient quantities to maintain robust health and strength. We know enough of the evils of malnutrition these days to realise that such a diet is quite inadequate and Red Cross food parcels are therefore designed to provide what is lacking.

This reality was, however, buried in a great deal of other positive stories about artistic pursuits and sporting activities, all endeavouring to indicate that morale among the PoWs was high.

Nevertheless, the Red Cross and the Order of St John were doing great work. Almost to a man the PoWs credited the food parcels and clothing as lifesavers. These did raise their spirits but many other aspects of their lives determined their morale, such as the opportunity for female liaison, or the simple act of outmanoeuvring a guard. All of these impinged on their state of mind. As the war went on and it was clear the Germans were facing setbacks, the PoWs grew more confident and assertive in their dealings with the guards. The Red Cross parcels sometimes played an important role in this. For example, if a particular guard was not liked because of his attitude, Gordon Reid (2882817) would ask the guard, 'would you like a bar of soap for your frau', which invariably got the expected reply 'oh ja ja ja'. Later, when a senior German NCO came around, Gordon would tell him the guard had 'asked' for a bar of soap, which was forbidden, and the guard was moved. The expectation was that the replacement guard would be less hostile. Gordon also bluffed the guards when he had nothing to bribe them with. If he didn't want to comply with some demand he would ask the guard if he had heard of the Geneva Convention. The guard generally replied that he had but conceded that he was not fully aware of it all in detail. This gave Gordon, a solicitor's clerk in civilian life, the chance to quote, in a convincing tone, some fictitious section and subsection of the Convention which completely forbade the action being ordered.

Despite the restrictions there were opportunities for the PoWs to have friendships or deeper relationships with some women, particularly the other foreign workers who were, like the PoWs, forced to work for the Nazi regime. In May 1943 Lance Corporal Alex Watt (2875918) was working on a building site alongside a civilian Polish carpenter. During a coffee break, the carpenter started chatting up some Polish girls who were hanging out of the windows of their accommodation opposite and asked Alex which girl he liked. Alex was already engaged to be married to Alice back in Aberdeen but expressed a liking for one of the girls who reminded him of his fiancée. The carpenter shouted this up to the girl who said something shyly and disappeared, much to the hilarity of the rest of her friends. Fairly soon notes started being passed between Alex and Hella (Helene Ossovska) with little gifts of soap or chocolate, as no fraternization was allowed. One benefit Alex derived from writing notes was that he had to start using a dictionary which helped him improve his German. Alex was, however, always a bit uneasy about his relationship with Hella but in his situation, with his future uncertain he had to live for the day. However, his platonic affair with his little Polish friend came to an abrupt end when another PoW told Hella, 'he already has a wee lassie back home and is engaged to be married'. Alex's mate George had three girlfriends at this AbKdo. He was a lorry driver's mate and so had quite a bit of freedom compared to most other PoWs. The lorry was covered in by a tarpaulin and he was prepared to take the risk to rendezvous in the back of the truck with his girlfriends after dark. The girls were also taking a considerable risk as, if caught with a PoW, they could have been sent to a concentration camp. Maurice MacLean was used by the Wehrmacht and the local police as a translator at their AbKdo at Dubensko (Dębieńsko) in southern Poland. Following a search, a guard discovered that a young British PoW, named Eddie, possessed a photo of a young Polish woman standing by a wire mesh fence. It was not stamped on the back with the Stalag censor's stamp which showed it was not legitimately held. The consequences for them both were serious, especially the girl. Since a civilian was involved the local police were contacted and Maurice knew full well that the PoW had worked near this girl in the local factory and she had given him her photo but if her identity was discovered the girl would be sent to a concentration camp. Maurice was frustrated that Eddie had been foolish enough to keep this photograph, so putting her at risk, but he wanted to help both of them avoid punishment. During the interrogation of this young PoW by the police, Maurice did his very best to concoct a story that the photo was the young man's fiancée, back home in Britain, standing next to a tennis court. He was not aware that the policeman had a limited knowledge of English until he suddenly stood up and pointed his cocked pistol at Maurice and said he wanted to hear no more lies. Luckily they were dismissed with no punishment and it was hoped that the girl's identity was not discovered.

Corporal Albert Heafield, a Regular soldier of the 1st Battalion, was a PoW at Stalag XXA (Thorn) and developed a close relationship with Eva Schultz, the widow of a German soldier who was killed on the Russian front. Albert was working on a farm in northern Silesia when he started a relationship with her which lasted to the end of the war and he requested permission to bring her and her daughter back home with him. However, this was not allowed and, after he was discharged from the army, he took a job as a stoker on a ship to return to Poland and eventually took her back to the UK and settled down in England, where the couple added to their family.

News of how the war was progressing was also vital to the state of the PoWs' morale. In this regard the Polish civilians they worked with would sometimes pass on information. However, Spud Robertson was concerned that, since his knowledge of the Polish language was limited, news would be hard to come by. However, it is clear that news was getting through fairly quickly when Spud recorded in his diary that it was rumoured that Laval and Darlan were either assassinated or had committed suicide. Admiral François Darlan was a French admiral and political figure who died in December 1942, just four days before the entry in Spud's diary. Being able to get news of how the war was progressing on clandestine radios was also a morale booster. Prior to them getting hold of radios, which was difficult and dangerous so took some time, the PoWs were dependent on German sources for information on the progress of the war.

In the first two years after their capture everything appeared to be going Germany's way and the German propaganda machine was not slow to enlighten the PoWs about their victorious advances. When they launched their offensive against the Russians in June 1941, initially making extraordinarily rapid progress, this news was jubilantly shared with the PoWs. Similarly the shock of the surprisingly quick defeat of British forces in the Far East by Germany's Axis ally, the Japanese, was trumpeted as another reason as to why Britain would soon lose the war. The 2nd Battalion Gordon Highlanders were involved in this action and it was not uncommon for family members to be serving alongside one another, particularly in the two Regular (1st and 2nd) Battalions. Consequently the news from Singapore was particularly disturbing for a large number of Gordon Highlanders who had close relatives and friends serving there. Michael Caulfield's two younger brothers, Hugh and Bryne, were among these, as was William Durward, whose two brothers, Arthur and James, had been captured at St Valéry and were now in Stalag IXC and Stalag 383 respectively. Seven other men had brothers serving with the Gordons in Singapore, including Thomas Murray whose older brother David was a sergeant, but there were not only fraternal relationships. David Greig's stepson, William Strachan, was serving with the Gordons in Singapore and he knew he could have been captured or killed by the Japanese. Many other Gordons now languishing in Stalags in Germany and Poland, such as Company Quartermaster Sergeant Joe Skinner and Private Douglas Bonnar, had many friends in the 2nd Battalion as, prior to the outbreak of the war, they themselves had been serving in Singapore with the 2nd Battalion. George Clyne, who was originally bound for Czechoslovakia with the 1st Battalion in 1938, was killed in action suffering multiple gunshot wounds trying to eliminate a Japanese machine-gun post. Bryne Caulfield was also seriously wounded in the battle for Malaya and was evacuated on the hospital ship *Talamba*; this reassuring news did reach his brother in Stalag 344. Regrettably, unlike the Germans, the Japanese did not communicate the names of their prisoners of war or the casualties to the Red Cross after the fall of Singapore. This resulted in the names of the men of almost the whole of the 2nd Battalion being listed as missing and their families had a long anxious wait for news. It was often more than a year before any news reached families in Britain and even longer before it filtered through to the PoWs in Germany. For example, David Murray was repatriated early, in October 1943, because of his medical condition after he was wounded in 1940. When he arrived home his family were still waiting for news of his brother David. Three months later, in January 1944, the family finally received a postcard from David confirming he was alive and a prisoner of the Japanese.

John Murdoch was part of a group in Lamsdorf where their radio was discovered by a German in the most unlikely circumstances. The PoWs had an almost invisibly thin aerial wire strung from the hut's brick chimney breast but the presence of the radio was betrayed by what John described as a 'Nazi blackbird spy'. A German officer was perplexed by the sight of this blackbird singing away with its wings folded and apparently perched in mid-air. Scratching his head, he deduced the bird was perched on a very thin wire. This could only mean a radio and he ordered the hut surrounded but two enterprising PoWs smuggled out the radio, right under the guards' noses. They carried it out in a breadbin which they took straight to the cookhouse and hid the radio. In another incident the Germans manacled a number of NCOs as a reprisal for the Allied raid on Dieppe in August 1942. At Lamsdorf, a British NCO who had been handcuffed as part of this action decided that he would take a bath. He soaped up his wrists and managed to squeeze off his handcuffs. However, John Murdoch recalled that the Germans appeared while he was bathing so he quickly snapped the handcuffs back on and the Germans were totally mystified as to how he had managed to take his clothes off, which was a source of great amusement among the other PoWs. All these small victories gave morale a boost. At Oflag VIIB Ran Ogilvie got his news of how the war was progressing from a secret British network which tried to maintain two or three radios at the same time as the Germans were always searching. He recounted that sometimes a radio would be hidden in a less secure place than normal so that it could be found. This satisfied the Germans that they had closed down the BBC news bulletins but they never actually succeeded in this. The radios were built with parts acquired by bribing some of the guards with soap or chocolate. It was dangerous for the guards to trade with the PoWs, especially for forbidden items such as radio parts, but once they were involved it was impossible for them to stop as they were easily blackmailed into continuing this clandestine activity. In 1944 Maurice Maclean's source of information was the camp blacksmith who secretly listened to the radio and passed on the news. Their source was almost compromised when one PoW began to taunt the German guards with news of the Allied advances. Since this information could only have come from an unauthorized source it was decided that the general dissemination had to be delayed so that it did not arouse suspicion.

Working at a granite cutting and polishing factory in the village of Freiburg, William Anderson accepted he was required to work but was always conscious that he should not aid the German war effort. In his work at this Arbeitskommando he was satisfied that he was not doing this as the main output from the factory was gravestones, which he thought could do no harm. While there he encountered another Nazi spy who emanated from the main camp at Lamsdorf but was more a wolf in sheep's clothing rather than any black-feathered villain. The PoWs had managed to loosen the bars of the toilet window and after this some sabotage occurred in the area. The hand of suspicion fell on the inmates of the camp. They were visited by the Gestapo who were very interested in a photo William had of his sister who, the Nazis thought, might be a local woman. About a week after the Gestapo's visit a solitary prisoner, named Abdul Achmet Gadel, arrived from the main camp. Abdul professed to be an Arab who had been a taxi driver in Alexandria but it was not clear how he came to be a prisoner of war and he was full of questions such as how was it possible to get out of the camp at night, which immediately made everyone suspicious of him. He did not stay long and when he left word was passed back to the main camp about him and he was never heard of again, except that it was rumoured that his body had been fished out of the fire tank.

Spud Robertson's best friend was Archie Hepburn who attempted to escape many times and was never deterred by his regular fairly swift recapture and inevitable punishment detentions. These escape attempts were seen as a blow to the Germans and acted as a morale booster for the other men who did not dare escape themselves. On several occasions Spud recorded Archie's exploits his diary, e.g. on 4 June 1942 'Archie escaped today'; 19 July 1942 'Archie contemplating another break'; 11 August 1942 'Archie prepared for another take-off'.

Chapter 5

Gambling Everything – Escape or Death

It is surprising just how many men risked their lives trying to escape. After missing the initial 'easier' escape route, immediately after their capture when they were still in France, the matter of escaping to a safe neutral country, such as Switzerland or Sweden, from eastern or central Europe was a far harder task. Malcolm (Mac) Stephen, who rose to the rank of major after the war and was second-in-command of the 1st Battalion Gordon Highlanders in Kenya in1962-3, summed up the situation very succinctly. He said that immediately after capture is the most opportune time for a successful escape. His reasoning was simple, declaring

> at this time, you are the fittest and best fed you are ever likely to be as a prisoner and your captors, who are generally front line soldiers, have very little interest in guarding prisoners.

On this basis 'Mac' did escape while in France and successfully made it back to the UK through southern France and Spain. He was subsequently commissioned in October 1941.

Escaping from a prisoner of war camp in Germany and Poland was not something to be considered lightly and some brave men died in the attempt. Among those who tried their luck and paid the ultimate price were William Collie, Robert Clarkson, John Cruickshank, John McCormack and George McKay, the latter a Reservist who had served in India with the 1st Battalion ten years earlier. Escaping PoWs who were killed in such tragic circumstances were normally awarded a posthumous Mention in Despatches but often little is known about the circumstances of their deaths. For example, John McCormack escaped from the working party in a limestone quarry near Vápenná (German Setzdorf), a village in the Olomouc region of Czechoslovakia. In a desperate attempt to avoid recapture, he attacked one member of the Nazi patrol which was hunting him down but, as he tried to get away, he was shot through the heart and died instantly. These brief details are only known through the records kept by other PoWs, even to the level of detail of the name of the German who shot John, who was Schütze (Rifleman) Paul Klumps. This only came to light after the war was over. John McCormack now lies buried in Prague, where he was re-interred after the war. In the case of Robert Clarkson, however, only a handwritten note against his name, in the Perth Infantry Records Office's register, simply records 'shot by a Warder', but fails to give any detail of the circumstances which led his death on 16 May 1943.

For some men, however, escaping was treated as a sport or a challenge. They did not think that they were engaged in a game of Russian roulette, their fate decided by the fickle nature of the guard or policeman who recaptured them, and they had to hope that the dreaded Gestapo or SS were never involved. They knew that the odds against a successful attempt were high as it was very difficult to obtain civilian clothes, they had no money, the language was difficult and, although Russia was the closest country to the PoW camps in Poland not occupied by the Nazis, they didn't know who they could trust. This was especially true following the signing in August 1939 of the Nazi-Soviet Non-Aggression Pact by Joachim von Ribbentrop and Vyacheslav Molotov, the German and Soviet Union's foreign ministers. This unlikely alliance, between the Nazis and the Bolsheviks, secretly carved up Poland and paved the way for Germany to invade Poland in September 1939 without any fear of Russian intervention. As a result of this pact the Germans and Russians were ostensibly allies and the prisoners were warned that escape to the Russian frontier was pointless as the Red Army frontier guards would shoot them on sight.

Corporal Hubert Lovegrove, was with the 4th Battalion Gordon Highlanders near Assche, Belgium, when his position was overrun on 18 May 1940. He initially avoided capture and was trying to get back to his unit but, while spending the night at a farm, he was betrayed to the Germans and captured. He was eventually taken to Stalag XXA and then sent out on a working party to Grupa, an AbKdo forty miles north of Torun. He was engaged in his civilian trade as a plasterer at a construction site for a parachutists' school. Security there was not as tight as at the main camp and he had a fair degree of freedom and managed to win the confidence of the guards and the parachute students by speaking and joking with them. His escape plan was simple. On 28 August

1940, while working, he managed to knock the solitary guard unconscious and calmly walked out of the building and into the forest. A Polish professor at the school, who was employed as a labourer, had previously given him a map and compass but he had little food. After a short distance travelling east he encountered the River Vistula and the only means of getting across was to swim. This looked impossible, but Hugh was determined to try his luck and succeeded in swimming across the river. On the eastern bank he rested while his clothes dried before striking out for Russian-occupied territory. At Ostrelenka (now Ostrołęka) in north-eastern Poland he found the frontier was heavily wired with a sentry post every kilometre although he managed to cross under the cover of darkness. His elation at escaping Nazi-occupied territory was very short-lived when he encountered what he described as a posse of Cossacks which he initially thought was splendid. In fact he could not have been more mistaken as this was the start of a dreadful period of treatment, far worse than anything he had experienced from the Germans. He was thrown into gaol, spending the next five months in a succession of filthy and overcrowded prisons, until finally being interned at Smolensk.

Private Harold Doyle, of the 5th Battalion, was also one of the earliest escapers to make a clean getaway from the Germans. He had arrived at Stalag XXA in July 1940 and two months later was sent to an Arbeitskommando at Winduga, around forty miles south of the main camp, almost the same distance away from Stalag XXA as Hugh Lovegrove but in the opposite direction. Here Harold met up with Corporal Corkery, of the Sherwood Foresters, who was captured near Lillehammer in the failed attempt to thwart the German occupation of Norway in April 1940, and Driver Louis Massey of the RASC. Louis had already made a bold escape attempt when first captured near Boulogne in May 1940. He had been wounded in the arm but, despite this, when there were too many casualties captured with him than could be accommodated by the ambulance, the German soldiers commandeered a car which Louis volunteered to drive and convey three other walking wounded to hospital. He was told to keep up with the ambulance but it was travelling quite fast and began to out-distance them. Louis took his chance and just turned off and drove south hoping to reach Allied lines. Unfortunately this was unsuccessful and they were recaptured two weeks later at le Touquet. Together Doyle, Massey and Corkery formulated a plan to escape which, by a remarkable coincidence, was very similar to Lovegrove's exploits. They noticed that the guards' mess hut had a door leading outside the main perimeter with only a simple boundary fence beyond. In preparation for their escape they stored some food, acquired a compass and stole a map. They made their attempt in the early hours of the morning of 2 December 1940 by entering the mess hut and, after waiting until the sentry passed, exited through the window, crawled under the wire fence and, with little difficulty, got clean away. They walked until daylight, putting as much distance as possible between themselves and the camp, before their absence was discovered at the morning roll call. They were careful to avoid contact with anyone, detouring around every town, and followed the course of the Vistula upstream, which they knew would take them eastwards towards the Russian-occupied part of Poland. After ten days they ran out of food and were forced to approach a Polish farmer, near Modlin, for assistance. He welcomed them and gave them food and civilian clothes; then they were guided towards Warsaw, where they were able to make contact with the Polish Resistance. Things were going well and the Polish Resistance assisted them as far as the Russian frontier near Ostrelenka where, just as Hugh Lovegrove had done before them, they crossed into Russian-occupied territory. After only five miles they were apprehended and arrested by the Russian occupying forces which they also initially thought was beneficial. To their dismay, this was the start of six months of dreadful treatment, commencing with being badly beaten when captured.

Christmas day 1940 was not a very merry one for them as they were thrown into the nearby Lomsa prison. Over the next month they were fed very little and transferred to a succession of appalling prisons, which housed mainly Polish Army officers. This was followed by a short stay in Moscow, firstly at the notorious Lubyanka prison, then the state prison, where they were interrogated continually, day and night, with the Russians insisting they were spies. They were then transferred, with a large contingent of Frenchmen, to Smolensk, where they remained for five months until it was decided to relocate them again. The entire contingent was loaded onto a train, consisting of cattle trucks, and their hearts filled with dread when they heard the rumour that their destination was Siberia as they knew the awful reputation of the Gulags (forced labour camps) there. Their spirits were very low when, suddenly, all of the British prisoners were ordered off the train and taken back to Moscow where, to their great surprise, they were put up in a hotel.

Hugh Lovegrove was also freed and at first the astonishing change in their fortunes was a mystery but it soon became clear that they had received a helping hand from a most unexpected of quarter. Hitler had torn up Ribbentrop's Nazi-Soviet Non-Aggression Pact and had launched Operation BARBAROSSA, invading Russian territory on 22 June 1941, so switching their host's allegiance to Britain against Nazi Germany. As a consequence their status had been transformed in a trice from enemies to comrades. They then enjoyed a short spell of good living with plenty of food before being released to the British Embassy in Moscow on 8 July. They returned home to Britain on 11 August 1941, sooner than many of the men who had escaped in France many months earlier. For their gallantry in escaping from their PoW camp and the hardships sustained while prisoners of the Russians, both Harold Doyle and Hubert Lovegrove were awarded the Distinguished Conduct Medal, which, for an enlisted man, is second only in significance to the Victoria Cross. They were both convinced that if it had not been for the outbreak of hostilities between Germany and Russia they would never have been released, despite all their repeated requests to be allowed to contact the British authorities in Moscow, which went unheeded.

Around the same time as Hugh Lovegrove was making his escape attempt, in August 1940, James Guy, accompanied by a friend, escaped from his work camp and were hidden by a Polish family at Leslau (now renamed Włocławek), only a few miles from Winduga, across the River Vistula. They joined forces with the Polish Resistance force A.K. (*Armia Krajowa*) loyal to the Polish government in exile in London and served with them for three years until forced to give themselves up. After one unsuccessful escape attempt they finally got away in September 1944, from a Straflager (punishment camp) at Weichselgard and re-joined the Resistance. Their luck did not hold out and only two months later they encountered two German soldiers. His friend was killed and James was wounded but, despite this, succeeded in making his way back to his Polish friends at Leslau. They hid him until the Red Army arrived in January 1945 when he was liberated. On return to Britain he was awarded the British Empire Medal for his actions.

Another Gordon Highlander who fought alongside the Polish A.K. resistance fighters was Sergeant John Duncan. He had already had a brush with the Gestapo after managing to stay at large in France after escaping shortly after the surrender at St Valéry-en-Caux. He was not keen to fall into their hands again. In August 1942, when at a work camp in Trautenau, in the Sudetenland, he made a dummy which he left in his bed to cover his absence and managed to cut the wire of the perimeter fence and get away. Unfortunately, he was recaptured in Prague only five days later. After another unsuccessful attempt, four months later, he finally made a clean getaway on 10 May 1943 from Tost, Upper Silesia, accompanied by Sergeant Hugh Brooks of the Royal Canadian Air Force. Learning from his previous experiences, he had prepared properly in advance by acquiring civilian clothes, a map, compass and food. They cut the bars on the window of their barrack room, unhooked the shutter and got away over the perimeter fence without the alarm being sounded. On reaching Czestochowa they made contact with the Polish Resistance. John Duncan served continuously until January 1945 with the A.K. in the West Besmid area of the Carpathian mountains of southern Poland, rising to second-in-command of a section. He later received a commission in the Polish Home Forces. For his gallantry he was awarded the Military Medal by Britain after his liberation.

Lovegrove and Doyle's experience of making a successful escape at the first attempt was rare. Most Gordon Highlanders incarcerated by the Germans following the fall of France were from humble backgrounds. Apart from the few Regulars who had pre-1935 service with the Regiment, few had been abroad before the war. It is therefore quite incredible that many were prepared to tackle journeys across half of eastern Europe to gain their freedom. Flexibility, quick wittedness and determination to succeed, driven by either a refusal to be beaten or a mentality that they could not endure being a prisoner any longer, were all crucial for success. William Milne (2884045), a factory worker from Peterhead, Aberdeenshire, was fairly typical, making numerous escape attempts and suffering many setbacks. In March 1942, at AbKdo 137, a salt mine near Erfurt, Germany, he made his first escape attempt, with Robert Hall of the Argyll and Sutherland Highlanders. Instead of going to work they hid in the mine buildings and waited until midnight when they came out of hiding and made off on stolen bicycles belonging to the civilian miners. They had a compass and a map and cycled by night and slept during the daytime, concealed in the forest. Their plan was to head for the Swiss border, approximately 300 miles to the south, but after only four days their hopes were dashed when they were surprised by an armed forester, apprehended and taken to the local police station. They were returned to Stalag IXC, and given twenty-one days' solitary imprisonment as a punishment. Two months later both Milne and Hall teamed up again for another unsuccessful attempt, again receiving the customary solitary confinement as their reward. Undaunted at the end of the year they made a third attempt but this time with three other 51st (Highland) Division men. They managed to reach the railway goods yard where they climbed aboard a wagon bound for Hungary. Things went well for six days, crossing through Czechoslovakia but, unluckily, when they crossed the frontier into Hungary they were discovered by police and arrested. They were initially gaoled at Komaron before transfer to the castle at Siklos, in southern Hungary, just ten miles from the Yugoslav border where they remained for over six months. Although Willie Milne considered they were reasonably well treated by the Hungarians they were still prisoners, so they planned another escape in the hope that they could join up with Yugoslav partisans operating just over the border. They considered this was the best hope of assistance in their bid for liberty. In July 1943 they made a rope using bed sheets and abseiled down the fifty-foot drop to the ground from their supposedly secure quarters. Again they were thwarted when they were apprehended by border guards. In March 1944, with the tide of the war flowing strongly against the Axis powers, Hitler became concerned that the Hungarian leadership was looking for a separate armistice with the Allies and so ordered the occupation of the country. As a consequence Allied PoWs in Hungarian hands were relocated to Austria. Willie Milne and his companions then found themselves in Rossgraben, near Ulreichsberg. Undeterred by their constant setbacks they made another escape in April 1945 and were helped by two local men. The first, Franz Wallner, took them to his house but the Germans billeted some soldiers with him so he persuaded his friend Franz Rumpler to conceal Willie and the three others. Rumpler was a local gamekeeper and knew a well-protected cave where the men stayed for five weeks and were visited by his family bringing food until the Red Army arrived in the district. Milne and his three companions were so grateful to Herr Rumpler that they wrote out and signed a statement detailing how he and his family risked their lives looking after them and protecting them during a very difficult five weeks while they were being searched for by the German police and the SS. They left this document with him so that he could show the Russians he was sympathetic to the Allies if he was accused of any crime. On 10 May 1945 they left him to travel the fifty miles to Amstetten where they knew there were American troops and safety.

Archie Hepburn was working at a mine in Hindenburg when, one day in May 1942, he just walked out of the camp through the open gate. There was a sentry on duty but his air of confidence implied he had permission to leave. This was an opportunistic attempt and, initially, it all went very well. He walked to the railway station in the town and, after reconnoitring the area, decided his best chance of getting away was to climb on board an empty coal wagon under the cover of darkness. After successfully getting onto a train Archie had no way of knowing where the train would take him but when it set off he was jubilant. His mood changed when, after fifteen hours the wagon was shunted into a siding and left, apparently after developing a fault with its brakes. He stayed silently in the truck until all was quiet outside and he thought it was all clear and safe to come out but, to his surprise, there was a sentry standing by the wagon. Fortunately this man was as surprised to see Archie as Archie was seeing him so he was able to run off. When he was trying to get back to the railway he was challenged by a German guard but was able to satisfy him that he was going about his legitimate business, only to be arrested shortly afterwards by the civil police. He was returned to the camp. Six months later he was separated from his good friend Spud Robertson when he was transferred to Sosnowiec, Poland. Archie was determined to be better prepared when he made his next escape attempt and patiently waited eighteen months while he devised his plan, although during a lot of this time he was in hospital with an injured knee and unable to walk far, so any thought of an escape was premature. In May 1944 he was fit and ready and had previously made contact with sympathetic Polish activists in the area. The first part of his plan required that he get clear of the camp and Archie included himself in a group of prisoners who were being taken to a civilian dentist in the town and managed to slip away unnoticed. He had arranged for his Polish friends to provide him with civilian clothes and they escorted him the ten miles to Myslowice, where he was able to board a train for Olkusz. Here he joined a band of Polish partisans and for the next six weeks was engaged in sabotage and raiding Nazi installations.

The next phase of his escape did not go so well. Archie was a brave man with a burning desire to be free and in June 1944 he decided to make for Switzerland, undaunted by the fact that this was over 700 miles away. He left his Polish friends and journeyed south. He had a narrow escape when he was shot at by German troops near the Czechoslovakian frontier but avoided capture and four days later made it into Slovakia. Forging on, he crossed into Hungary and after making it as far as Komaron, just over the border, almost 250 miles south of his starting point, he was arrested and, just like William Milne (2884045) before him, was sent to prison camps at Siklos, finally ending up in Esztergom. In November 1944 Archie became aware that he was likely to be transferred back to a PoW camp in Austria or Germany and so resolved to escape again, which he did with three others and they managed to make their way to Budapest where Archie was lucky enough to find someone to shelter him and laid low until the Russian army entered the city in January 1945. He reported to them and they arranged for him to be flown to Bucharest, Rumania, in March 1945 and eventually to Bari in Italy and finally back to Scotland. Archie Hepburn was awarded the Military Medal for his gallantry.

By a strange coincidence another 5th Battalion Gordon Highlander also named William (Bill) Milne (2880536), and also from Peterhead, had a fantastic escape story. He first attempted to escape from Stalag XXB in August 1941 and again in August 1943 but on both occasions was recaptured. After his arrest in 1943 he was interrogated by a Gestapo officer who, in Bill's words, 'was a master with a rubber truncheon'. On his third attempt he spent Christmas 1944 hiding in a loft in eastern Poland trying to make for the Russian lines and was astounded to find an empty herring barrel with the words 'G & P Duncan, Peterhead', a company he knew well, stencilled on the side. Bill took this as a good omen. As he neared the Russian lines he encountered another escaping PoW from Leicester and they agreed to help each other. Shortly afterwards they ran into a friendly German officer who guessed they were escaped PoWs. He advised them not to go on as, in his words, the Russians were 'shooting everything that moved'. Bill and his new-found companion chose to ignore the advice and, shortly afterwards, were ambushed by a Russian patrol who thought they were German deserters. One Russian just wanted to shoot them but it was finally agreed among them that Bill and his companion should be taken back for questioning. They were thrown into a cell with some genuine German deserters who, on hearing their story, expressed the opinion that the Russians would not spare them.

After many days and nights of questioning they still were not believed and one terrible night they were dragged from their cell with some others and put up against a wall in front of a firing squad. Bill whispered to his friend that the only possible chance was to make a bolt for freedom. At that point a Russian officer who understood some English heard this and ordered they be taken out of the line and questioned further. He asked them where Manchester United played, what was the name of the king and eventually, much to Bill's relief, they were reprieved. The Russians now accepted they were indeed escaping British PoWs. The officer explained that they would be repatriated but their euphoria did not last long, however, when he explained this would take time, so in the intervening period they would have to fight for the Red Army. He arranged that they were fully equipped with their Red Army uniforms, including a Cossack hat, and they were expected to participate fully in the Russian actions. One of their most hazardous tasks was checking out abandoned buildings. It was known the Germans often set booby traps in these situations and their Russian comrades always insisted Bill entered the building first. Despite this, Bill remembered a strong camaraderie with the Russians. They shared their vodka and Bill entertained them by playing the accordion and singing or reciting from the works of Rabbie Burns, which some of the Russians already knew well. After a few weeks advancing into Poland, almost back to his old camp at Marienburg, Bill was transported to the rear and taken by train down to Odessa, where all Allied PoWs were being assembled for repatriation.

Corporal John (Jack) Byrne, who was in France with the 1st Battalion in 1940, had an exceptional escape experience. This began when he was wounded and evacuated and so was not captured when 51st (Highland) Division surrendered at St Valéry-en-Caux. In August 1940 he volunteered to join the Commandos and the following year was hand-picked by Captain David Stirling, for L Detachment, 1 Special Service Brigade, the unit which subsequently became 1st SAS Regiment. While serving with the SAS, on a sabotage mission behind enemy lines near Benghazi, Libya, he was captured by the Germans and eventually imprisoned at several Stalag Lufts (prisoner of war camps run by the German Luftwaffe for aircrew). This was because the Germans had no idea what his unit was and did not appreciate he was a soldier, not an airman. From April to September 1942 he was held in Stalag Luft III (Sagan) later made famous by the films *The Great Escape* and *The Wooden Horse*.

He attempted his fourth escape in July 1943 when being held in a transit camp at Königsberg (Kolobrzeg), sliding down the drain which served the urinals and passed out of the camp. Exploring the town, Jack encountered a number of Frenchmen, who had considerable freedom to move around the town unguarded. He asked for their help and this was readily given, supplying him with a suit of blue overalls to cover his own uniform, a beret and a haversack of food. Jack already had a plan. While at Stalag XXIB, he had met a recently captured British airman who, before his capture, had heard a lecture given in England by Sergeant Philip Wareing. Philip Wareing had successfully escaped to neutral Sweden in December 1942 by stowing away on a ship in the harbour at Danzig (Gdansk). Wareing had been shot down near Calais in August 1940, his escape back to Britain was well celebrated at the time and he spent several months travelling around the country lecturing aircrew about his experiences.

Jack made his getaway from Königsberg on a stolen bicycle and made for Danzig which he reached in just four days, taking care to avoid some checkpoints along the way. He saw a French forced labour worker and took a great risk declaring he was British and wanted help to get to the docks and board a ship for Sweden. Fortunately the Frenchman was supportive and took him to a small station where he provided coffee and hot water so Jack could get cleaned up and have a shave. He then walked to the docks where he observed Swedish ships loading coal but there were German guards all around. Jack decided he had to try and enter the port area so he passed the first guard at a busy time and as he approached he rolled a cigarette, turned his face away and spat. Fortunately the guard assumed he was a Swedish sailor and did not challenge him. Each ship had a single guard and Jack could not at first see how to get past him. His opening came when it started to rain heavily and a number of civilian workers were passing the guard who became distracted. Jack took his chance and just walked past the German and up the companionway of the Swedish ship. He hid in the coal bunker where he remained for two days. There was a moment of panic when someone came down to the boiler room and flashed a torch around but Jack remained undiscovered and shortly afterwards the ship started to move. Jack stayed hidden for another day then surrendered to the ship's captain, who asked Jack to prove he was British, which he did with his British Army identity discs. After this reassurance he was welcomed on board, congratulated and the captain declared that Jack would be back home in a week. On arrival in Sweden Jack's story was checked by the local police and he was sent alone to Stockholm by train. There he was welcomed by the British Military Attaché who arranged accommodation for him to recuperate for almost three weeks. Jack was then flown, in a Mosquito fighter-bomber, to Leuchars in Fife, arriving back in Scotland on 15 August 1943, replicating Philip Wareing's trailblazing feat just eight months later. For his gallant actions Jack Byrne was awarded the Distinguished Conduct Medal and returned to active service.

Life as a prisoner of war for an officer was entirely different to that of an enlisted man. The absence of any requirement to work severely restricted opportunities to explore the local area surrounding the camp, such as finding the location of the nearest railway station, or the possibility of making contact with some of the local populace who might be sympathetic and assist an escape attempt. The result of this was often that, with a lot of time on their hands, officers escape attempts were more elaborately planned but they were still receptive to exploiting any serendipitous chance that presented itself.

Lieutenant Iain Price exemplified this in his second and third attempts to escape from the infamous Colditz Castle (Oflag IVC). In the summer of 1942 he knew that a party of French prisoners was due to leave the prison camp and so he changed identity with a French political prisoner named Fleury who did not wish to leave. To make his disguise more realistic Iain Price enlisted the help of one of the camp's theatrical group's make-up artists who enlarged his nose to make him more like a Frenchman. A short time after the French were marched out from the castle, Iain broke away from the column and made for Switzerland. His liberty was short-lived as he was tracked down by guards with bloodhounds and received fourteen days in the cells on a diet of bread and water. This did not dampen his enthusiasm for gaining his liberty. Another opportunity arose when, in September 1943, he and five other Allied officers were summoned, as witnesses, to attend the German court martial in Leipzig of Flight Lieutenant Tunstall, an RAF officer. Since this was a rare excursion outside the castle they viewed it as a chance to escape, although they knew they would be under close guard the whole time. The plan was to break away from the guards at a pre-arranged signal and blend into the local population, so they switched their uniforms and dressed as either Hungarian army officers, who were allied to the Germans, or as civilians. Iain Price dressed as a Hungarian count. They executed their plan after the court martial was over and all broke away at the same time but it was a complete failure as they were rounded up within half an hour. Possibly the Germans were aware that these men were all determined escapers, which is why they were in Colditz, and were suspicious of their unusual mode of dress. In another incident where the escape plan hinged on a disguise, Captain Hector Christie was one of a group of five would-be escapers who, in June 1943, tried to walk out of Oflag VIIB (Eischstätt) dressed as German dignitaries. They were dressed as a German general, a hauptmann (captain), an unteroffiziere (NCO) together with two civilians, posing as an architect and a surveyor, all purporting to be making plans for an extension to the camp. Everything went to plan and they were free. Unfortunately, their escape was discovered by the innocent act of the sentry on the gate telephoning the camp commandant to inform him the 'General' had just left the camp, which raised the alarm and they were caught only a mile away from the camp. Iain Price never escaped from Colditz but he still proved a nuisance to the Germans. In conjunction with an RAF officer he devised a scheme to steal potatoes from a cellar in the castle. This was an audacious plan as it involved making duplicate keys to unlock doors, but the fruits of their thieving activities were very welcome as it took place over the period of six months from October 1944 until March 1945 when food was in very short supply. When they were finally caught they were charged and set to be court-martialled by the Germans but this never took place as Colditz was liberated by the American Third Army on 16 April 1945.

One of the low points for British officers during their time as PoWs occurred in March 1941 when the Germans alleged ill-treatment of German prisoners in Canada and their response was to send 500 young officers to a punishment camp, namely Fort VIII at Stalag XXID (Posen), Poland. This building dated from the nineteenth century and was one of a number which ringed the city. The officers arrived there on 6 March 1941 and Lieutenants Ran Ogilvie, Peter de Winton and Iain Price were among them. Their time there was a sort of subterranean existence and conditions were deplorable. Fortunately their stretch was relatively short and, after some negotiations between Britain and Germany, through a third party, they were moved back to other camps in Germany in June. On hearing the camp was to be evacuated and seeking to capitalize on the inevitable chaos of evacuating such a large number of unco-operative individuals, Peter de Winton organized the construction of a false wall in a dungeon, effectively creating a hidden room. He and three others walled themselves in, with a supply of food and water, and hid. When the evacuation of the camp took place and the roll call was conducted it was assumed they had escaped. They remained hidden for three days, and then, unseen, made good their escape. Lieutenant de Winton managed to get to Warsaw where he spent sixteen months working with the Polish Resistance, becoming fairly fluent in Polish and Russian, all the while hoping he would be assisted to reach a neutral country. This episode ended badly, however, when, in October 1942, he was arrested while couriering another British escaped prisoner of war to a new address. He spent the next four months in the hands of the Gestapo before being sent to join Iain Price in Colditz Castle (Oflag VIC). Lieutenant de Winton never gave up trying to escape and was involved in four other unsuccessful attempts which involved sawing through the bars of his cell, digging two separate tunnels and exchanging identity with an orderly who was being sent to another, less secure, camp. He was awarded the Military Cross in recognition of his brave endeavours.

Like Peter de Winton, Iain Price made several other unsuccessful escape attempts, involving tunnelling and other forms of subterfuge but his first foray was almost successful as he jumped off a moving train near Munich and was only re-captured trying to board another train, at Lansberg, within striking distance of Switzerland. Captain Hector Christie came even closer to entering Swiss territory in June 1941 after being carried out of Oflag VB (Biberach) by hiding in the cart which came into the camp to take away the rubbish. Freedom was within sight when he was re-captured by a German patrol just a short distance east of Schafhausen, Switzerland. Frustratingly the patrol was actually hunting for escaped French PoWs and this bad luck was a feature of a number of his escape attempts but his escaping activities were highly praised by no less a person than Major General Victor Fortune. Hector Christie eventually joined his fellow Gordon Highlander officer brethren in Colditz where all three were finally liberated by the American Army with both Captain Christie and Lieutenant Price being honoured by each being made a Member of the Most Excellent Order of the British Empire (MBE).

Escape was not the only way to escape from incarceration in the PoW camps in Germany and Poland. There was provision under the Articles of the

Geneva Convention that required the warring parties to return to their own country prisoners of war who were seriously ill or wounded. For the purposes of determining which PoWs would be eligible for repatriation there was a requirement to form Mixed Medical Commissions to examine affected prisoners and make decisions with regard to their future status. The commissions were to be chaired by a medical officer from a neutral country. One aspect of this was that there was not to be any quota system and those repatriated were to be solely on the merits of their case, not their rank or the numbers involved. One other provision of the Convention, which was relevant in respect of repatriations, was that non-combatants, such as medical staff and chaplains, should be repatriated as soon as possible. There was one difficulty with regard to medical staff. It was common practice for regimental musicians to be trained as first-aiders and act as stretcher-bearers in the combat zone but if this was not documented properly, e.g. recorded in their pay-books, or their documents were lost or destroyed for some reason, then their status remained uncertain.

Negotiations between Britain and Germany to repatriate eligible personnel began as early as 1940 but the Germans did not adhere strictly to the Convention and argued that the numbers of persons exchanged should be similar. At that time, however, the number of British servicemen in German hands far outnumbered the number of captive Germans in Allied hands, partly because of the numbers of British captured at Dunkirk and St Valéry but also because, at the fall of France, all Germans held by the French were released immediately. The balance of numbers only began to swing the other way when the British were making substantial gains in North Africa.

Men who were deemed to qualify for repatriation on health grounds were examined by the Mixed Medical Commissions. These commissions comprised of three members, two of whom came from a neutral country, one of them chairing proceedings, while a third member was appointed by the Germans. These commission members decided the fate of the sick or wounded prisoner on a majority basis, with no party having a veto. The first exchange of British and German PoWs was made in October 1943. A list of men had been compiled and as the date of their exchange drew near they were assembled to make ready for their journey to Sweden. It was over three years since the surrender of 51st (Highland) Division at St Valéry and over that period many men had been examined and deemed appropriate for repatriation due to their physical condition. As part of this process they were given a certificate of approval which they kept. Tom Murray, who had been wounded during the fighting in France in 1940, was examined by the Medical Commission at Reserve Lazaret Obermassfeld, a military hospital serving Stalag IXC, on 13 November 1941. His condition was judged as qualifying him for medical repatriation. In the intervening two years his health had improved, so he was concerned that he would not be allowed to leave his camp and travel to Sweden but was pleased when his fears were not realized. The Germans were very correct in their behaviour, complying with the articles of the Geneva Convention to the letter. This required the men's private property to be safeguarded, so they gave each man a receipt for wages owing to them. Tom was given a receipt which stated ten Reichsmarks were being 'safely held in custody for him' but no doubt he wondered how he would ever be able to access this money. He considered its loss was a small price to pay for his freedom. In any event, nobody trusted the Germans and they were still nervous that their repatriation was just another false hope.

The PoWs being repatriated travelled by train to the Baltic coast at Rugen then by ferry to Trelleborg, the southernmost tip of Sweden, where they knew they were truly free. Boarding trains, they continued their journey almost 200 miles northwards to the Swedish port of Gothenburg. Prisoner exchanges were always made through a neutral country and the Swedish ships *Gripsholm* and *Drottningholm* played a major role in transferring British and American PoWs home. These ships were painted white with the words 'Diplomat', the name of the vessel and 'Sverige' prominently emblazoned on their sides. During the hours of darkness they sailed fully lit up so that they could be easily identified and there could be no mistaking them for anything other than a mercy ship. On this first PoW exchange there were over 4,000 mainly British PoWs exchanged, although the party also had a small number of Canadians and Americans. Before they could begin their voyage to Britain they had to await the arrival of a party of around 800 Germans for whom they were being exchanged, most of whom had been held in camps in Canada. To balance the numbers of German PoWs being exchanged for the 4,000 British PoWs there was a similar exercise being undertaken through Barcelona in neutral Spain. The German PoWs arrived in Gothenburg aboard the *Empress of Russia* and the *Atlantis* which, in turn, together with the *Drottningholm* were to accommodate the large numbers of British PoWs for their voyage back to Britain. As the Germans disembarked it was reported that they complained about the quality of the food they had received in Britain and during their passage to Sweden. Chief among their grouses was that they did not like the white bread, apparently preferring the black rye bread British PoWs disliked, but there were no reports of complaints from the British about this as their euphoria at release put all other considerations in perspective.

Between 6.15 and 8.00 am on the morning of 21 October 1943 the hospital ship *Drottningholm* together with the liners *Atlantis* and the *Empress of Russia* sailed out of Gothenburg bound for Britain. The *Drottningholm* and the *Empress of Russia* arrived in the Firth of Forth at Leith in the early hours of Monday 22 October 1943, carrying 2,400 passengers. The *Atlantis* sailed round the north of Scotland and into the Mersey to dock at Liverpool. At Leith General Sir Ronald Adam, the Adjutant General, went aboard to deliver a greetings message from the King. It read:

> The Queen and I bid you a very warm welcome. We hope with all our hearts that your release from captivity may bring you restored health and a full measure of happiness.

Before the ships docked, each man was given a telegram form and a letter card to notify his family of his impending arrival home and these were to be despatched as soon as the ship arrived in port and even before the men had disembarked. The ships had anchored in the estuary so disembarkation of the PoWs was by a flotilla of tenders. As the men arrived at the quayside, their first sight was the word 'WELCOME' spelled out in enormous letters. A military band struck up a spirited tune followed by the Pipe Band of the King's Own Scottish Borderers as thunderous cheers came from a crowd of well-wishers at the dock gates. A warehouse had been transformed into a reception/banqueting hall with the importation of thousands of chairs and tables, where some 8,000 sandwiches, copious draughts of beer and tea were served, and gifts of cigarettes and sweets handed out. There were some short speeches and the men boarded a fleet of buses and were taken to the railway station to take them on to hospitals for a medical assessment and treatment if required. As a consequence, family reunions were delayed in the short term.

Dougie Thow, a bandsman (stretcher bearer), was among this first batch to arrive. Other men who believed they also qualified under this category, such as Pipers George McLennan, Gordon Reid, Bill Maitland, Drummer Spud Robertson, and Bandsman Bill Lawrie, were not so lucky and although their hopes had been raised, they were dismayed when their likely repatriations fell through. None of them was ever repatriated early. To them the process appeared to be something of a lottery. Piper Curly Allan was, however, fortunate in that he was successful in qualifying for repatriation, but this was not because he was a piper acting in a medical role. He had been seriously wounded, losing part of his heel, in the mortar shell incident at Manneville-ès-Plains. John Jarvis has been examined by a Mixed Medical Commission on 1 September 1943 and declared medically unfit for further combat operations and sufficiently injured to be repatriated. His injuries were received while he was working on a building site and a brick fell from a great height and struck him on the head. On his return to the UK he was immediately transferred to Bangour Hospital, Broxburn, where he remained until January 1944. Shortly afterwards he was discharged from the Army.

Among the other repatriated PoWs there were some sad family stories awaiting their return. Private Tom Tilney's mother had died while he was being held as a PoW and Lance Corporal George Watson, a 5th Battalion man from Methlick, and a farm servant pre-war, was also keen to get back to look after his family of four children as his wife had died while he was a prisoner. Perhaps the most heartrending case was that of Regimental Quartermaster Sergeant James Mackie, repatriated to Liverpool on the *Atlantis*. His 14-year-old daughter Gladys died in Aberdeen City Hospital the day before he arrived back in the UK. She had been ill for four weeks before she died and, although his wife had written to him to tell him Gladys had been admitted to hospital, he had not received the news as he had been in transit as part of the repatriation exercise.

The MS *Gripsholm*, which sailed from Barcelona to Southampton, also played its part in repatriating British PoWs, including some Gordon Highlanders. James Moir was transferred from Stalag IXC to Barcelona and with Alex Brockie they came home on her. Some men were wrongly sent to Barcelona for repatriation and this port was used as many of the German PoWs being repatriated had been taken in North Africa, so it was logistically simpler and safer to use nearby Spain for them, rather than taking them north to Sweden. On his return home William Gordon was asked to speak to some of the local groups in the Huntly area who had supported PoWs and he rightly praised their efforts. People with relatives still in PoW camps in Germany and Poland were also anxious to know if he had any news of their loved ones and he was able to give some families reassurances. Incredibly he also revealed that the British doctor in charge of the medical block at Lamsdorf, where he was a patient for two years before his repatriation, was Captain George I. Davidson of the Royal Army Medical Corps. Doctor Davidson, a local GP from the Huntly area, was the Medical Officer attached to the 5th Battalion. There were later repatriations. Henry Hudson had spent three months in hospital, due to a fractured skull he received as a result of an accident at work. He went before a Medical Commission on 26 October 1944 when his case for repatriation, on medical grounds, was approved. This was good news for a return home by Christmas. Allan Walker, who had to have a serious operation and was in hospital for two years, was also repatriated together with Quartermaster Major Bill Craig. Allan Walker was an old soldier with twenty-three years continuous service, for which he had a Long Service and Good Conduct Medal, but he had not served the Regiment as long as Bill Craig, who had been unlucky enough to have also been a PoW in the Great War.

On return to the UK the men were given a warm welcome and sent to reception centres where they were processed as quickly as possible, with their medical needs being quickly assessed and the necessary actions taken. They were given an advance payment of £6 to a private and £8 to a sergeant and issued with their ration books. It was recognized that these returning PoWs were malnourished and so their ration books were stamped to allow them double rations for the period of their leave. In general these were not well men and Henry Hudson, for example, was given detailed instructions to cover the eventuality that he might fall ill during his leave. In the pre-National Health Service era this could be an expensive business if he had to see a doctor and the Army made provision that only immediate medical care should be given until he could be treated by a doctor at the nearest military facility. In addition, they each received a gift from the Queensland Country Women's Association of Australia and were urged to write and thank them for their kindness and generosity. When James Moir returned home he and his family were treated to a formal reception, hosted by the Lord Provost and held in the splendour of the Town House. This was not unusual and many other civic receptions were held in towns and cities all over Scotland.

Chapter 6

A Bitter Winter

As the 1945 New Year dawned the Gordons captured in the early summer of 1940, at St Valéry and elsewhere in France and Belgium, had already endured four and a half years of captivity. This incarceration without knowing how long it would continue was dispiriting and began to tell on morale. At the beginning of 1945 Albert King posed himself a question, which he wrote in his diary, 'will this year see the end of this heart-breaking monotonous life?' In the autumn of 1944 Albert had become seriously disheartened and decided that, until he was a free man again, he would put away his trumpet, which had given him and so many others much pleasure during those long years behind barbed wire. He had also stopped writing home to his mother and his wife-to-be Ena Bruce, although they still wrote to him. This New Year, however, things looked a little different with almost everyone, except the most fanatical Nazis, believing that the war in Europe would end soon with a victory for the Allies. For the PoWs, however, the concern was not just when it would end but how would it end? Would the Germans accept that defeat was inevitable and surrender soon to avoid the total destruction of their country? This could mean the PoWs would be released to the Allies in an orderly disciplined manner. Alternatively, would the Nazis put up a fanatical last stand, in some Bavarian alpine fortress redoubt, with the PoWs as hostages? The actuality was what was the least expected, which made making preparations to mitigate the consequences of the last few months of the futile Nazi resistance impossible. For the PoWs held in eastern and southern Poland the next few months would be very testing as they faced another severe Polish winter.

The PoWs were aware that the Red Army was making large gains and had pushed back the German Army into Poland. At the beginning of 1945 the Russians were at the gates of Warsaw, callously failing to come to the aid of the Polish partisans in the Warsaw uprising. At the end of 1944 they had been massing their forces for a major offensive which began on 12 January 1945.

The Western Allies were still some way off, having not yet crossed the River Rhine. The PoWs had come to hope that their liberation by the Russians would only be a matter of weeks away and some could hear the rumble of guns in the distance. It was, therefore, a considerable shock and disappointment for many when, around 20 January 1945, they were roused from their beds in the middle of the night and, given virtually no notice, told they were to leave their camps and march towards Germany and away from the advancing Red Army. In other instances, the day started normally and they went to work in the morning but part way through the day, they were ordered back to the camp and given an hour or less to prepare to go on the road and march off into the unknown. Maurice MacLean was working at a farm near Dubensko (Dębieńsko) in southern Poland and could hear the sound of Russian artillery in the distance. He anticipated the Germans would evacuate them so decided this was going to be his best chance of freedom. His plan was to escape and hide in the nearby forest for a short time until the Russians arrived. He prepared for his breakout by hoarding some food and loosening the bars on his window and waited for the right time. He thought there would be some notice of the evacuation and so believed he could wait until then before making his move. Maurice's plans were completely thwarted when, without any warning, the Germans rounded up all the PoWs one afternoon and told them they were leaving within the hour. He could not put his plan into action in broad daylight and so was forced to march out into the snow with the others.

The various Arbeitskommandos were given orders to rendezvous at various specific locations from where they set off westwards, normally in columns of 500 or 600 men. The PoWs had few belongings, so packing up did not take long but some had the foresight to pack food from Red Cross parcels. They wore all the clothes they could as protection against the bitterly cold Siberian wind and driving snow and took any prized possessions if they could carry them. Alex Watt (2875918) took his guitar but after only two days on the road it proved such a burden that he reluctantly left it in a barn where he had spent the night. At a rendezvous point in the railway station at Freystadt, David Thom and his friend Jock Harper were anticipating that they would be travelling by train and, remembering their train journey to Poland, in 1940, were somewhat apprehensive about this. In considering the weather conditions at the time, with deep snow on the ground and the temperature around minus twenty degrees

Centigrade, they were glad to have a roof over their heads while they waited for their train to arrive. They were, however, dismayed when told they were travelling on foot and were forced to set off in the teeth of a blizzard. David noticed that next to him was a fire-fighting point with a ladder and an axe so, without hesitation, Jock used the axe to chop off a length of the ladder, which they used as a sledge, and loaded it with their kit. Being so low and having two readymade runners on either side it proved very stable and ideal for the journey. The only thing which was unorthodox was that in order to pull it they needed a rope but none was available. The problem was solved by using a pair of David Thom's long johns. As they marched out into the freezing weather their breath froze on their coat fronts and they had to cover up as much as they could so that very little bare flesh was exposed to the elements. Where possible only their eyes were exposed. They were not alone on the roads and many other parties had gone before them. These included Wehrmacht units moving up to the front, all mixed up with hordes of civilian refugees fleeing the terrible reputation of the Red Army, hell-bent on avenging the atrocities meted out to their countrymen when the Germans invaded Russia in 1942. Into this mix was thrown the groups of PoWs and political prisoners. Walking around eighteen to twenty-five miles most days, in the intense cold, was not the only problem to contend with. They slipped and slid along for mile after mile and Charlie Morrison observed that walking on the polished hard-packed snow and ice was like walking on a surface resembling the icing on a wedding cake. This severely strained the leg muscles which rebelled at the unaccustomed actions as they tried to maintain balance. They spent the nights in various barns, factories, or other abandoned buildings along the way but it was clear the guards were just opportunistic about the buildings they used. Sometimes another group commandeered the shelter first so they had to carry on farther in the hope of finding shelter for the night not too far away.

The cold was so intense that their boots froze and frostbite in their fingers and toes was a constant danger. It was imperative to get their boots off at night and vigorously rub their feet to get the circulation going. As the blood began to pump into their frozen toes some men cried with the excruciating pain but this was a critically important practice if the loss of a finger or toe from frostbite was to be avoided. Some men got together in groups of seven or eight, pooling their blankets and huddling together to keep warm as they slept. The buildings were often as cold inside as it was outside, but at least there was shelter from the biting wind. There was no possibility of washing and the most a man could do was to rub his hands and face with snow. Clothes were never taken off and so they became infested with lice which mainly came to life at night, reacting to the man gaining some warmth. One of David Thom's friends had a peculiar result when he never took off his balaclava. He had to be cut out of it when his beard grew through it and became firmly entwined with the material. The physical exertions of the march, the lack of food and sometimes the onset of dysentery were just too much for a lot of men. David Thom had a severe attack of dysentery and felt so miserable that he despaired of ever seeing his home again, describing his situation as spending two full days in the latrines with his trousers around his ankles. Fortunately for David his group were on a rest stop for three days but he felt like throwing in the towel. Others were not so lucky and, after two months, George Murray and Harold King died, on 11 March 1945.

The cold was not the only danger the PoWs faced. The Wehrmacht guards were often nervous, having to control large bodies of men who were numerically superior and although unarmed were no longer confined. The only thing keeping most of them together was the uncertainty of their location and the belief that it was better sticking with the crowd. David Thom witnessed a near mutiny among the PoWs when he saw a Nazi guard shooting a defenceless woman, who was part of a column of Jews also being moved westwards. Exhausted, she had stopped and was bent double when she was brutally kicked in the face and shot as she lay in the snow. The PoWs were well used to abuse and unjust punishments but this was much more brutal than even they were familiar with. They gave a roar of angry protest but were forced to back away when faced with a line of grim-faced SS guards levelling their sub-machine guns at them. On 16 March 1945 Maurice MacLean was asked to conduct the funeral service of Jock (John) Kerr, a fellow Scot who served with the Royal Army Service Corps. Jock's friends knew of Maurice's ecumenical training and asked for his help, explaining that Jock had been shot by a 'trigger happy guard' at the small village of Kornhaus. In another incident, during an overnight stop, around Hanover, John Taylor was with his companions Robert Dolier and John Duthie who had already managed to secure a comfortable place to sleep in the hay loft of a barn. John had not been so fortunate and remained on the ground floor. As the night wore on John became aware of a bad-tempered Nazi guard becoming increasingly agitated by the behaviour of a few of the many men in the loft who were trying to wrestle a bit more room for themselves in the crowded space. In a fit of temper the guard fired his rifle indiscriminately into the floorboards of the loft. This was presumably meant as a warning but it had tragic consequences. The bullet hit the sleeping Robert Dolier in the hip and was deflected into his stomach, a fatal wound from which he died on 14 April 1945. The event was doubly sad in that he had survived five years of imprisonment and hardship to be killed on the eve of his deliverance by Allied forces. The whole group were liberated the next day but, before he died, John promised he would visit Robert's wife, Jane, in Glasgow and tell her what had happened to him.

The provision of food was not very organized and the PoWs had to scrounge as best they could. They were generally given some bread and watery soup each evening, but this was hardly enough to keep them going with the strain of the cold and physical demands of the march. At some farms the PoWs would steal potatoes or sugar beets and boil them up on small fires. If any small animals were kept at the farm they were promptly killed and eaten. Alex Watt (2875918) managed to kill and pluck a duck at one farm, while Maurice MacLean's group slaughtered and butchered a horse. There were occasional issues of Red Cross parcels, each being shared by four or more men. In addition to living off the land the PoWs would loot anything edible if the guards were amenable. Often the German guards were no better off than the men they were guarding, so it was often in their interest to find extra food. Alex Watt (2875918) and some others passed a cheese factory where a free for all was taking place but when they arrived there was little left. At a nearby schnapps distillery there was an abundance of spirit still available but Alex considered it undrinkable. This view was not, however, universally shared. Some German soldiers were filling their water bottles with the liquor while one German was flat on his back drinking directly from the tap of the vat. His attitude was a mixture of drowning his sorrows and a determination not to leave anything for the advancing Russians, who were close on his heels.

The march away from the advancing Western Allies began much later for the camps in Germany. Albert King was working at Erfurt, in central Germany, when the order to evacuate the camp was given. This was not entirely unexpected as there were rumours that British tanks were only sixty miles away. Machine-gun fire could be heard during the performance of the camp's Easter Sunday show, which Albert watched rather than playing his trumpet in. Next morning, 2 April 1945, the German guards woke the PoWs at 6:00 am, telling them to make ready to immediately evacuate the camp. In a positive frame of mind now, Albert reflected 'this time we are marching out of bondage, not into it. They can march us where they like but it will do them no good'. Albert's group initially fared reasonably well for food, being issued with Red Cross parcels every two or three days, each parcel being shared between four men. Albert found this new phase of his time in captivity quite uplifting. Although his feet were hurting from the long daily marches and he was frustrated to hear that the Allies had liberated Erfurt, where they had just left, he met up with John Kemp and, a couple of days later, with John Donaldson, both of whom he had trained with but hadn't seen during his five years of captivity. One low point was when they were caught in a town which was being bombed by the RAF and he was hit in the face by a flying roof tile. After this the Germans decided it was only safe to travel at night.

The threat from the air was ever present, with the Allies having complete control of the skies. The danger was that the Allied pilots were not aware of the drama unfolding to the PoWs on the ground and to them a column of marching men was a target of opportunity. Bill Reaper was working on the construction of a huge new chemical plant at BAB 20 (Bau und Arbeits Battalion 20, Hydebreck) for I.G. Farben, a large German chemical industry conglomerate, which was a prime target for American B-17 Flying Fortress bombers. They carpet-bombed the site and the PoWs were in constant danger. During one raid in 1944 Bill was buried alive but fortunately rescued. Early in 1945 another raid destroyed a large part of the plant, including the accommodation, and there were no lights or water. After some negotiations between the Senior British Officer and his German counterpart, it was decided to evacuate the camp. The Russians were very close to the camp at this time and the crump of their artillery could be heard. Nobly, the German camp commandant agreed PoWs could remain and wait for the Russians to arrive if they wished. Most, however, including Bill, decided not to risk waiting for the unpredictable Russians and stayed with the rest for safety reasons although, disappointingly, this meant four months on the road braving the worst of winter weather. At Oflag VIIB,

Germany, the close proximity of the Americans forced the Germans to evacuate the camp and the officers were marched out on 14 April 1945. They were marching, in a column which extended for almost three quarters of a mile, along a wide valley with parallel roads on either side. After travelling only a short distance disaster struck. Ran Ogilvie noticed a motorized column of German troops travelling up the opposite side of the steep-sided alpine valley when an American reconnaissance plane appeared and circled over the scene several times before departing. Shortly afterwards a flight of P-51 Mustang fighter-bombers arrived and attacked the Germans. The PoWs had a ringside seat as this spectacle unfolded and stopped to watch the action as the German column was completely destroyed and left as a line of blazing wrecks. They were cheering for all they were worth when suddenly their mood changed from jubilation to blind terror as the Mustangs formed up in a line again and tore down their side of the valley, machine guns blazing, strafing the entire length of their column. The steep sides of valley meant it was difficult for PoWs and German guards alike to scatter off the road for cover. After the planes had gone they left fifteen dead and around fifty men wounded. Since they had not travelled far they retraced their steps and returned to their camp. The German camp commandant was determined to set off again next morning but the Senior British Officer flatly refused. Common sense finally prevailed and it was agreed that they would only travel at night and lie up during the day. As an added precaution, the PoWs commandeered every scrap of red, white and blue material in the camp and made a huge Union Jack. They carried this with them as they travelled and the Germans also appeared happy to receive the protection of the Union flag. These incidents were not common, but by no means exceptional, as Maurice MacLean and his fellow travellers had to dive for cover on 24 April 1945 when Mustangs arrived overhead as his column was travelling through Bavaria.

Maurice and his companions knew the Americans were close but they knew this was a dangerous time if they were caught in the middle of a firefight between the Americans and their guards. Maurice befriended a young German guard who was worried about his family at nearby Lake Constance. Together they developed a plan to help each other. This required that one PoW would feign an attack of dysentery and Maurice would assist his PoW friend while their friendly guard would volunteer to stay and guard them. Once the main column was out of sight they would slip away into the wood. If they met Germans they thought it would be alright as the friendly German guard was with them, but if they met Americans they would speak up for him and see if he would be allowed to visit his family. Their plan never came to fruition as a drama soon developed. They had spent the night at a farm and in the morning were awakened by the sound of a fierce battle raging for the small town in the valley below. Some of the PoWs mutinied and told the German officer they refused to go on as many were too sick and exhausted to carry on and demanded that they be allowed to go directly to the American lines. For a short time there was a stand-off, with the guards cocking their weapons, but eventually the German hauptmann marched off with his men, leaving them. Shortly afterwards two armed guards returned to the farm and surrendered to Maurice. This was the young German with whom Maurice had conspired earlier together with a companion. It was agreed these Germans would patrol the perimeter of the farm to give the appearance the PoWs were still in German hands. While Maurice and the others watched the battle go on between the Americans and SS in the valley below, a group of Hitler Youth came into the farm. These disillusioned young boys, whose officers had deserted them, surrendered when they saw the British uniforms of the PoWs but this set up a very tense time as they also knew that in their area there was a band of fanatical Nazi military police shooting and hanging German deserters in an effort to keep them fighting. Surmising that the Americans would probably not all be below them, one of the PoWs worked his way up the valley and made contact with another group of Americans, of General Patton's Third Army, who were holding a bridgehead about five miles upriver. The Americans sent a tank and an armoured car to the farm and, after mopping up the resistance in the town below, the PoWs were free. Maurice spoke to an American officer to stress how helpful the young German guard had been, hoping it would do him some good, but with so many Germans falling into Allied hands it was not certain any special allowance would be made on his behalf. Next day the PoWs and their German prisoners were escorted by a tank to the Stalag at Moosburg, which had already been liberated.

The chaos of the general evacuation of the camps created an opportunity for some PoWs to slip away. The guards were not fully in control as the columns stretched out over long distances. The fittest moved ahead quickly, trying to get to the next rest point, secure a good place to spend the night and have the first chance of scrounging any food that might be available. Meanwhile, the less fit and injured men struggled on as best they could and often fell behind. With the poor diet and lack of hygiene at the overnight stops, where men were answering the call of nature all around their temporary billet, dysentery was not uncommon. This resulted in men having to drop out of the column to attend to their urgent needs and sometimes when they re-emerged from the trees the column had moved on and they found that they were alone. This could be a dangerous situation as being alone in a strange area, weakened by disease and physical exertion, with no food and the possibility of being found by the dreaded SS meant a man could easily die. After their foray to the cheese and schnapps factories, Alex Watt (2875918) and his two companions returned to where they had left the column. They had gone with the consent of the guard but when they returned the column had gone. They saw a nearby farm where the woman who answered their knock on her door told them Germans were billeted with her and so asked them to keep out of sight and go away. It was now getting dark and they were alone on the road and were becoming increasingly anxious about where they were going to find shelter for the night. As they pressed on, trying to catch up to their column, a Polish farmer with a pony and trap caught up with them. He stopped and enquired where they were going and offered them a lift. After it was clear they had lost contact with the others he suggested they go home with him and, with few options, they agreed. They stayed with the Polish farmer and his family for almost two weeks until the farmer decided that it was too dangerous for his family to remain at the farm, the front line was becoming too close. Alex and his companions were left alone in a sort of no man's land as the battle ebbed and flowed around them. One day a German tank rolled into the farmyard and they hid to avoid discovery. A few days later Russian mortar shells landed in the yard but fortunately did little damage, apart from setting some small haystacks alight. After a few days of this they decided it was probably best to go out and see if it was possible to make contact with the Russians. They set off down a country road and after a short distance Alex heard the distinctive sound of a rifle bolt and a shout. They raised their hands and, as taught by the Polish farmer, shouted 'Angleachan, Angleachan!' (more correctly Anglichanin) which they had been told was Russian for Englishmen. With rifles pointed at them they were taken to a Russian officer who questioned them. They were then taken to the Russian battalion HQ, fed and questioned again by an Intelligence officer, who spoke excellent English. He eventually accepted their story and surprised them by saying they would have to make their own way to Moscow. At first their spirits fell as they had absolutely any idea how they could accomplish this.

In January 1945 John McCulloch was in a work camp near Grudziadz, Poland, where he was planning to escape with Harry Steel, of the Queen's Own Cameron Highlanders. Harry's brothers, Bill and Allan, were Gordon Highlanders who had also been captured at St Valéry. They decided that instead of waiting for their camp to be evacuated it would be better to take matters into their own hands and they got through the wire on 19 January. Their original plan was to get to Thorn, where they believed the Russian lines were, but once they were free they changed their minds and crossed the River Vistula and headed west. They were not well prepared for their escape and had no stock of food or a compass but did have civilian clothes. After ten days they were short of food and struggling to go on. They reached Stalag IIB (Hammerstein), Pomerania, where preparations were underway to evacuate this large PoW camp holding mainly Americans. Fortuitously, there was a large group of French forced labourers going through the gates so John and Harry mingled with them and once inside identified themselves to an American sergeant. They were able to collect Red Cross parcels and cigarettes and left the camp with the Americans the next day. Once clear of the camp they absconded again. A week later, while walking down the street in Polzin, they were approached by a German officer, an approach which was entirely unexpected. He addressed them in English and instead of arresting them gave them a meal and asked them to work with the wounded in a group of hospitals in the area, being given a pass so they could travel freely between them. Then, at the beginning of March, they were told they had to leave and were taken to a collection centre, where they joined a large number of other Allied PoWs from around Danzig. Seeing they were again in captivity John and Harry absconded yet again and made their own way to Neubrandenburg where Stalag IIA was a stopping-off point for the columns of Allied prisoners from PoW camps farther east. They approached the gate, gave their particulars and, because the once super-efficient Nazi administration system had broken down, they were assumed to be stragglers from one of the groups passing through. At Neubrandenburg, John McCulloch met up with his friend Private Norman Alexander of the 1st Battalion. They learned that next day some 200 American PoWs were being evacuated from the camp and so they exchanged identities with some of them and left with the American contingent. After two days, while billeted overnight in a barn, they absconded for a fourth time. They eventually made it to Stendal which, shortly after their arrival, the Germans declared an open town and the American forces arrived to liberate them on 3 April 1945.

Some men's experience was less stressful than Alex Watt's (2875918) or John McCulloch's. Charles Leighton was marched out of his working camp, at Kosel, a Kommando attached to Stalag 344, on 22 January 1945. With four others, Charles planned to escape at the first opportunity. They didn't have to wait long as, just two hours after leaving the camp, they were able to get into some woods near the River Oder and deserted the column. For the next six days they hid near an oil factory in the area and obtained food from the canteen and plundered farm produce. They were assisted by local Poles who introduced them to other British PoWs who were also evading the Germans. Shortly afterwards the group set off and encountered some Russians, who advised them to go east and head for Odessa. This they did, initially travelling south through Czestochowa and Krakow and on to Odessa, on the Black Sea, 600 miles away. Odessa was used by the Russians to assemble all the Allied PoWs they liberated. The Geneva Convention required that prisoners should be removed from the front line as soon as possible, but the Russians, who were not signatories to the treaty, had an agenda of their own. Stalin was determined to ensure that Russian PoWs and refugees who had been liberated by the Allies would be returned to Russia, regardless of their own wishes. This was agreed at the conference held at Yalta, the Black Sea resort in the Crimea, where the terms of the administration of post-war Europe were agreed by the three Allied leaders, Prime Minister Winston Churchill, President Franklin D. Roosevelt and Premier Joseph Stalin. Stalin made certain Britain and America would co-operate with his goal by channelling all of the Allied PoWs liberated by his Red Army back east to Odessa, almost as far as possible from the advancing British and American armies. Allied PoWs, therefore, unwittingly became pawns in a larger game.

At this time, when the Nazi grip on their country had loosened, the local population in Poland were sympathetic and where possible helpful to escaping PoWs. John Hutchison received food and blankets from a woman in Danzig and Duncan McEwan was hidden for a month by a Polish family. James Gordon received assistance from an unlikely quarter when he dropped out of his column in Upper Silesia in late January 1945. He was accompanied by a deserting German guard and together they reached the Russian lines at Vogsdorf. James was directed to travel east to Odesa but the fate of the German is not known; it is unlikely he was treated very well.

After dodging out of his column in southern Poland, Bill Stuart eventually made his way to Krakow where he hoped he could board a train to freedom. While at the railway station he encountered a Polish woman stealing coal. Bill spoke to her and offered to help her collect some coal then helped her take it home. Despite appreciating the danger, the family decided to help Bill so hid him for six weeks until the Russians entered the city. Although Krakow was a regional capital, the Germans had no interest in defending it against the Red Army's advance. Fortunately therefore, Krakow did not suffer from the heavy fighting and destruction of many other Polish cities. The Germans evacuated their troops from the city and did little other than blow up bridges to slow down the Russians' advance, so buying time to establish their positions in Upper Silesia on the line of the River Oder. Once the situation in the city was calm, Bill surrendered to the Russian authorities. During his time in captivity, Bill had learned to speak German fluently so the Russians used him for a time as a translator before he too was directed to Odessa.

Not every city was as fortunate as Krakow. The war was almost over but in Prague a unit of fanatical SS troops refused to surrender. The local partisans, aided by many of the population, tried to liberate their city. The partisans were only lightly armed but on 5 May they gained control of the radio station. It didn't take long for German forces outside Prague to rally to the aid of their Nazi comrades in the city. At this point an unlikely actor took centre stage in the form of Gordon Highlander Private Bill Greig. Bill had previously escaped when his PoW camp, Stalag VIIIB (Teschen), near the Czech border, was evacuated. While on the run he was assisted by a Czech family who gave him civilian clothes, food and shelter then guided him to the railway station where he got on a train to Prague. It had been arranged that he would be met in Prague by a friend of the family and on reaching Prague this all went to plan. When the uprising against the German garrison began Bill joined forces with the local Resistance fighters. He was aware the beautiful city was in danger and, being a native English speaker, agreed to broadcast an appeal to the Allies for assistance. Bill was certainly not accustomed to public speaking so was extremely nervous when the microphone was placed in front of him, his mouth suddenly dry. He stiffened himself, cleared the frog in his throat and spoke, fully mindful his broadcast could save one of Europe's most iconic cities and thousands of its citizens. He began:

> Prague is in great danger. The Germans are attacking us with tanks and planes. We are calling urgently our allies to help. Send immediately tanks and aircraft. Help us defend Prague. At present, we are broadcasting from the broadcasting station and outside there is a battle raging.

The Czech capital, Prague, was seriously damaged when the Germans bombed the city on 7 May 1945, setting fire to the 600-year-old Town Hall, which was completely destroyed, although the tower was saved, but not without damage to the famous Astronomical Clock. Fortunately Bill's appeal had been heard by the American military, which sent planes to destroy a column of German reinforcements. On 9 May the Red Army entered Prague and the city was saved. Bill was awarded the Czechoslovakian Military Cross for his efforts.

William Anderson, of the 5th Battalion, also escaped to Prague, arriving there at the time of the uprising. He had escaped from a working party in a limestone quarry near Setsdorf and merged into a large stream of refugees escaping from the eastern front. He made his way south into Czechoslovakia via Brünn (now Brno) and then after some weeks on the road reached Prague. On the outskirts of the city he came to a small railway station where there was a group of Germans who were stripped to the waist with red swastikas painted on their chests and backs. They were being guarded by Czech partisans armed with rifles and wearing armbands and bandoliers. They watched over them while these captured Nazis loaded railway sleepers 'as if their life depended on it', which William thought meant it probably did. Inside the station a trainload of wounded German soldiers was being guarded by another group of partisans. At this time the Russians had not yet reached the outskirts of the city, while the Americans had halted their advance at Pilsen. Arrangements were made for William and some other Allied soldiers to be taken by train, through the Russian lines, to the Americans. After a thorough interrogation, they were released through Regensburg, flown to Brussels and on to England. These men were lucky and some of a few who didn't have to travel eastwards to Odessa.

Around twenty-five Gordon Highlanders are known to have been liberated by the Russians in 1945 and sent back east to Odessa. (This is a small number considering the several thousands of Allied PoWs who were liberated through Odessa and the actual number of Gordons may be significantly higher but it is almost impossible to quantify accurately.) This journey was far from easy as few had a map or compass and although individual Russians were generally happy to help there did not appear to be any system in place to convey the PoWs to Odessa. After Alex Watt (2875918) and his party were told by a Russian major just to make their own way east, they initially came to a Russian temporary depot where they were given some food. They explained their predicament to a Russian officer who scribbled out a note for them. This was incomprehensible to Alex but he assured him it would secure assistance and food as they travelled east. During their journey they mixed with other PoWs and French, Belgian, Dutch, Czech and Hungarian forced labour workers, all pursuing the same objective as them. After some six weeks of walking eastwards, finding food and shelter any way they could, they arrived in Warsaw on 9 March 1945. Here they caught a train to Lublin and made contact with British Consul staff. After a few days delay, the Consul staff made arrangements for them to join a train to Odessa which was specifically for PoWs and refugees. It was a slow journey taking about nine days to cover the 600-mile journey, stopping in sidings and taking on other passengers, such as Auschwitz survivors en route to Palestine. Arriving in Odessa on 23 March 1945 they were deloused and accommodated in an old school.

Not everyone was keen to go back east through the Russian lines. Corporal Jimmy Nicol's Arbeitskommando farm in Upper Silesia was evacuated and their route westwards meant they trekked over 250 miles passing Peenemünde, the V-2 weapon research site, in northern Germany. They were eventually liberated by the Red Army. With their rapid advances the Russians were in celebratory mood and treated Jimmy and his companions well and their time together was marked by singing and accordion playing. Following their normal procedures, the Russians were sending the PoWs back east to Odessa and most complied, just happy they were no longer prisoners in German hands. Jimmy knew the British lines were not far away, so he refused to go east and was allowed to walk away and got to the British lines where he had to prove who he said he was. He had kept his pay-book so he could do this easily.

When the gap between the Western and Eastern Allied armies was closing, squeezing the German army and the PoWs, it was a very dangerous time. David Thom summed up his experiences during the early part of 1945 as having been 'chased by the Russians, bombed by the RAF, bombed and machine gunned by the Yanks and scandalously and criminally treated by the Germans'. Albert King's group were lucky to have just left the town of Hernsdorf when it was heavily damaged. A few days later the farmer whose barn they were using for shelter wanted them moved on as there were American tanks in the area and shells were already landing all around them as they were in no man's land. He told the guards he did not want to get involved with anything to do with the PoWs. This was now the middle of April and Albert wrote in his diary that the German guards had begun to 'bail out' and he didn't blame them. They had obviously decided it was pointless for them to go on with the Americans so close but Albert had another five nerve-racking days before he could write in his diary, in large letters, 'Monday 16th April – FREE at last. Today at 09:45, standing with a white flag in my hand, I shook hands with a Yank officer. The Yanks are here'. The Americans enlisted Albert's help and used him as an interpreter, a role he enjoyed now the tables were turned.

At the time of his liberation Corporal Jimmy Nicol found himself at an assembly point near Lüneburg Heath, just south of Hamburg. There were many hundreds more liberated PoWs around him who had being force-marched hundreds of miles across Europe. The German surrender to Field Marshal Bernard Montgomery was taking place but there was a little bit of trouble getting the German soldiers to disperse so that the surrender could get under way. Some British officers suggested to the PoWs that they should get involved so, without much further encouragement needed, they soon got the Germans, who were now the PoWs, moving in the same manner as the British had been treated in 1940. They shouted 'raus raus' at them and the Germans soon got the idea that they had to move. Shortly after this Jimmy saw a large German red-and-black Nazi swastika flag on a flagpole so he took it for a souvenir, which he has kept to this day, lending it on one occasion to his grandson, for a school project.

Chapter 7

Homeward Bound

With the war in Europe over, the PoWs' five long years of captivity was at an end. Europe was in a hugely disorganized state with many cities in Germany and Eastern Europe reduced to rubble. In addition to the hundreds of thousands of Allied PoWs who required repatriation, there were also millions of displaced people from many nations. Not unexpectedly, thoughts of getting home as soon as possible after liberation were uppermost in most PoWs' minds. This proved to be a frustrating time as the logistics of repatriating so many men proved challenging. Albert King was transferred back to Erfurt where he was registered for repatriation but he found the administration system slow and bureaucratic. He was frustrated that he was now killing time until it was his turn to fly out. On 23 April, a week after his liberation, he wrote 'hope to be on the road tomorrow', but subsequent entries for the next ten days are variations of, 'still in barracks', or, 'spent the day loafing around in barracks,' until, on 3 May 1945, he was able to jubilantly record, '4pm - sitting in a plane, engine roaring'; then later that day, '11:05pm - Landed in England (Surrey)'. Maurice MacLean's wait for repatriation was less frustrating as he was sent to Landshut aerodrome where there was a steady procession of C-47 Dakotas landing and taking off, carrying around twenty-five PoWs on each flight. Maurice slept on the grass on the airfield and his turn came on his second day there. He was airlifted to Brussels where he was deloused and given a clean battledress. A canteen was being run by a group of Scots women and the sound of female Scottish accents was a great lift, giving him the feeling that home was, at last, very close now. The next stage of his journey was by Lancaster bomber, as part of the RAF's Operation EXODUS and he was lucky enough to be allowed into the mid-upper gun turret just as they crossed the English coast, the unmistakable iconic panorama marking his first sight of Britain. This was a bit of a routine 'bus run' for one of these Lancaster pilots. This was Royan Yule, himself an Aberdonian, who against all the odds had just been awarded the Distinguished Flying Cross for completing thirty hazardous bombing missions over Germany and occupied Europe.

After a short debrief by an Intelligence Officer, Maurice was given a telegram form to send home and next day he got on a train to Dundee where nobody was there to meet him as his telegram had failed to arrive. A helpful policeman contacted his family home for him and he was finally met by his sister. For months his family had not known if he was dead or alive and there was great delight in having him home. This was tinged with some sadness, however, when another returning PoW told the family that Maurice's brother, Robin, had been killed in Germany during an American air raid. Robin had been captured, like Maurice, by forces under the command of General Erwin Rommel, but in North Africa. Fortunately, it was not long before good news was received, in the form of a telegram, announcing Robin was in fact safe and back in England.

For the men liberated by the Red Army and now in Odessa the outlook was still uncertain, many having been there for some time, arriving all through February and March. Red Cross food and medical attention was provided and the British Military Mission was also available to assist the PoWs but to the ordinary soldier there was no obvious plan as to when, or how, they would get home. British and American ships were, however, repatriating Russian PoWs who had been liberated by the Allies. These were being delivered to Odessa so the ships were turned around as quickly as possible to get the Allied soldiers home. On 27 March word came to the waiting PoWs that they were to march to the quayside. This had only been a delay of two days for Alex Watt (2875918) but for many others it was a day long overdue. The sight that greeted them was a huge ship with the Union flag hanging over the side, which brought tears to many an eye. This was the *Duchess of Richmond* and they were greeted by the sailors throwing oranges to them. On board they were given good food, cigarettes and chocolate but were gently reminded they were now back in the Army so military discipline was restored. Each PoW was issued with a booklet, entitled *Happy Returns* which was both informative and entertaining. There was a welcome from the ship's master, Captain E.A. Shergold, together with other articles. One explained seafaring terms in a light-hearted manner, for the benefit of the Army personnel. There was also a tongue in cheek article, composed in rhyme, which even gave advice to men returning to long estranged wives and sweethearts as to how they should rekindle the flames of their romance but the sting in the tail was the final line. This warned, 'But don't let her think she is having her way'. The more serious articles explained the work of the Red Cross, for which every PoW had reason to be grateful, and some information on the ship's history and its wartime service. This concluded:

> The ship's company want you to know that, of the various jobs we have done, none has seemed more important than bringing you home, nor given us greater pleasure. We know you are eager to get home and hope you will not find the trip too irksome. We wish you GOOD LUCK.

Their route home was through the Black Sea, anchoring for a short time at Constantinople (Istanbul) then through the Dardanelles, the Aegean Sea and into the Mediterranean, anchoring again in the Bay of Naples for five days, then on to Malta and a transfer onto HMS *Orion*. On 7 April 1945 they sailed for Gibraltar and the voyage through the Mediterranean was a nervous one. There were several submarine alerts and there was some alarm when there was the unmistakeable sound of depth charges being dropped. Despite these scares, they completed their passage safely and sailed into the Firth of Clyde, back to where the *Duchess* was built in 1928, and arrived safely at Greenock on 17 April. It was very frustrating for the Scots contingent to learn that they were next to be transported all the way south to Beaconsfield, Buckinghamshire, to have a medical check-up and be debriefed by an Intelligence Officer before being released to go home for three months' leave. Compassion was shown to the returning PoWs with the necessary formalities being completed as quickly as possible.

For the returning PoWs there was much catching up to do. The world had moved on in the five years they had been incarcerated. It was difficult for them to adjust to the new situation of 1945 Britain. Women had a newfound self-confidence, having become used to having their own money, running their own affairs and enjoying regular employment in skilled jobs, often previously reserved for men. Many women had also learned to cope with supporting a family without a man around. In addition, everything was much more modern and mechanized. In the realm of the military, new weapons were in service which they had never imagined before their capture. David Thom encountered

Americans for the first time when he was liberated and was bemused by their Jeep, which he had never seen before and thought it 'an unusual looking car', not being aware that it was a ubiquitous piece of equipment which had played a vital war role in the years after his capture. Nevertheless, the most pressing matter to resolve on their return home was their personal lives and picking up cherished relationships which had been on hold for over five long years.

For those returning PoWs a telegram had normally preceded their arrival. After travelling by the overnight train, Alex Watt (2875918) arrived back to Aberdeen early in the morning of 22 April 1945, five days after his original arrival at Greenock. He was met by his fiancée Alice Ross and they took a taxi home where his mother had breakfast ready for them. Their wedding had been set for his first leave home from France in 1940 but, as Alex remarked, he had forgotten to ask 'the Führer's' permission. There was now a frenzy of activity to arrange the big day and both families were busy getting the dresses sewn for the bride and bridesmaids and organizing the food for the reception which, under the rationing restrictions, was a challenge. Alex's allotted task was to get in the celebratory drinks. He went to a licensed grocer and after he mentioned he was a newly-liberated PoW getting married he did manage to obtain some spirits. The big day was 5 May 1945, less than two weeks after arriving home and their story was carried that evening in the local *Evening Express* and the next day in the national newspaper, the *Sunday Post*. This was also a day to remember for another PoW's family. Albert King's parents received a message early in the morning of 5 May informing them that Albert would be travelling home by train and arriving in Aberdeen at 11:30 pm that night. They telephoned Albert's long-term girlfriend Ena Bruce at her work to tell her the good news. Following the call Ena was really excited, especially since Albert had been out of communication for so long and, understandably, she found it hard to concentrate on her work that day. Five years apart was a long time, especially since the restrictions applied to PoW correspondence and the work of the censors meant that it was not easy for them to express themselves properly. In the circumstances news was meagre and often delayed. Ena went with Albert's family to the railway station to meet him off the train. Once the family reunion was over and Albert and Ena were alone together they knew immediately they still felt the same way as before their enforced separation. They walked home and, despite the late hour, all the neighbours were out in the street to welcome Albert. Albert and Ena became engaged to be married but it could not be made official until the jewellers were open for business on Thursday 10 May as they had been closed since Albert's return due to the weekend and the Victory in Europe (VE) Day holidays. The couple were married just three weeks later, less than a month after Albert's return to Britain.

The welcome Albert had received from his friends and neighbours was not uncommon. As Private James Norrie arrived home he was met by a group of pipers. In addition, friends had hung up a large flag at his garden gate and bunting across the street. Similarly, when Robert Smith arrived back home in Aberdeen he was greeted by a crowd of almost 200 well-wishers. One of his neighbours played the bagpipes as he walked up the road, hand in hand with his two daughters whom he had not seen for over five years. When Herbert Petrie arrived at Aberdeen railway station he was introduced to his 5-year-old daughter for the first time. After her initial shyness they became inseparable and she would not let him out of her sight. Similarly, Captain David Morren met his daughter Collette, conceived on his last leave before capture at St Valéry. Brothers Harry and William Tocher, who had spent the war together in Stalag 344, were re-united with their brother who had lost a leg at Dunkirk. Although they had suffered five years of hardship and a loss of freedom, it was sobering to note that their ordeal was over while he had to live with the disability for the rest of his life.

After virtually all the PoWs had been repatriated the Gordon Highlanders still had unfinished business in Germany. The drums of the 5th Battalion, which had been stored at Metz in May 1940, were considered lost. That entire area had been occupied by the Germans for the remainder of the war, so the experience of the loss of 2nd Battalion's drums in the Great War had been repeated. In early February 1945, the 10th Armored Division of the Seventh US Army re-assembled at Metz and was able to rest briefly. Shortly after this period they attacked and broke through the German lines and reached the River Saar, going on to capture the important bridge over the River Moselle and the heavily defended strategic city of Trier. This success prompted the visits of the Supreme Allied Commander, Dwight Eisenhower, and General George Patton to congratulate them. Lionized by these eminent figures, they drove forwards towards Bavaria where, on 23 March, Captain Thomas

O'Rorke found a drum in the officers' quarters of the Kasserine Artillery near Baumholden. This was one of the 5th Battalion's drums and was recognized as such. When he was told of the find, Lieutenant General Alexander M. Patch, Commander of Seventh Army, decided it was only appropriate that the drum be returned to the Gordon Highlanders and invited a representative party from the 5th/7th Battalion to take part in a historic ceremony in Munich on 7 June 1945. The 51st (Highland) Division had been resurrected from 9th (Highland) Division and continued to play a vital role in the war, taking part in many important actions in North Africa, Italy and going back to France on D Day. They fought all through North West Europe, finishing the war in northern Germany, around Bremerhaven. The 'phoenix' 51st (Highland) Division included 153 Brigade. This brigade mirrored the former formation lost at St Valéry and included the Gordon Highlanders. A new 1st Battalion Gordon Highlanders had been reconstituted at Aberdeen before the end of June 1940 and the 5th/7th Battalion Gordon Highlanders was restored by simply renaming the 7th Battalion. Probably the Division's most satisfying action was avenging the surrender of the old 51st (Highland) Division when they liberated St Valéry-en-Caux, on 11 September 1944. This was a mission allocated to them as a direct order from the newly-promoted Field Marshal Bernard Montgomery.

In Munich Brigadier J.R. Sinclair DSO, a Gordon Highlander commanding 153 Brigade, represented the Regiment at the ceremony to return the 5th Battalion's drum. The Battalion party was represented by the Commanding Officer, Lieutenant Colonel C.F. Irvine MC, together with two other officers, fourteen pipers, nine drummers and twenty-four other ranks. The party arrived at Seventh US Army's Headquarters at Augsburg on Tuesday 5 June where they met General Sandy Patch. He expressed his deep regret at being unable to take part in the ceremony but explained that he had been recalled to Washington to take over another command as the war in the Pacific was far from over. (Tragically he died of pneumonia only five months later.) The handover ceremony took place on Munich's Königsplatz, a stunning setting with neoclassical Greek architecture, where the Nazis had staged mass rallies and Hitler once welcomed the Italian dictator, Mussolini. On 7 June 1945, a brilliant sunny day, there was a breath-taking pageant with huge numbers of spectators lined up on every side of the square and perched on every vantage point all around. On parade were several American Army units, including a troop of tanks and tank destroyers together with a carrying party of the flags of the forty-eight American states (Alaska and Hawaii had not joined the Union in 1945). A guard of honour of the 10th Armored ('Tiger') Division carried the drum onto the parade ground which, after the general salute and a short speech by the American Lieutenant General Wade Haislip, was handed over by Captain O'Rorke. In receiving the drum, Lieutenant Colonel Irvine expressed the gratitude of the Regiment for the honour done to them by the American Army. He expressed the opinion that there would be none more delighted than the men of the old 5th Battalion, who had recently returned home after their five years as prisoners of war. Lieutenant Colonel Irvine gave a short history of the 5th Battalion and of the drum, which had originally been presented to the Battalion before 1914 by Captain W. Stephen of Peterhead. To conclude, the Gordon Highlanders' guard of honour, headed by the Drums and Pipes, led the march past, and took up a position on one side of the square while the United States forces marched past, headed by the Band of the 45th Division. Corporal Willie Sim was given the honour of beating the drum at the ceremony. The whole ceremony was broadcast by the BBC and all American radio networks. That evening the officers of the Gordon Highlanders were guests of honour at a party given by officers of the Seventh US Army Headquarters and, to reciprocate, the Americans were entertained the following evening by the Drums and Pipes of the Gordons beating 'Retreat' and an exhibition of highland dancing.

It appears that the experience of the 2nd Battalion in the Great War was well and truly lost on the other Battalions of the Regiment as the 4th Battalion also went on to lose both pipes and drums in France in 1940. These instruments were in prominence, in October 1939, when the 4th Battalion Pipe Band led the Battalion through the streets of Aberdeen to the railway station, bound for Aldershot and France. The Battalion was billeted in the French town of Roubaix, just outside Lille, from early December 1939 until the start of the German offensive in May 1940 when they moved into Belgium with the majority of the British Expeditionary Force. They decided to leave a number of their drums and pipes with a French Army officer who promised to keep them in his cellar. Despite the area being occupied by the Germans, the 4th Battalion's drums and pipes did not fall into enemy hands. They were kept safe but, with the passage of time, during the turbulent period France experienced until 1945, knowledge of their whereabouts had been lost. It was, therefore, a happy accident when an RASC officer discovered some of them, purely by chance, when he was searching Roubaix for billets for his men. Others were handed over by the French Resistance (the FFI) who, knowing the symbolic importance of these instruments to the Regiment went far beyond their intrinsic worth, had kept them safe throughout the war, fully expecting the return of British forces to Roubaix. The thrilling news of their discovery was widely welcomed by the Battalion and in their home city.

Once their leave was over, those men who were considered physically fit were required to report back to their units or placed in Reserve or holding units. There was a range of experiences for these men. After his leave Harry Tobin was sent to a camp in the south of England where he was given heavy duty training to build him back up to full strength and then transferred to Bonhill Barracks, Dunbartonshire (a former print works), for jungle warfare training. This was a three-month course and he was on a list to be posted to Burma to fight the Japanese. Fortunately for Harry, the atomic bombs dropped on Hiroshima and Nagasaki forced the unconditional surrender of the Japanese on 15 August 1945 and so he did not have to go overseas again. The two Gammack brothers, Sandy and Douglas, who were both 5th Battalion Territorial Army soldiers before the war, were placed in holding camps in different parts of the UK, Douglas in Langholm, Dumfries-shire, while Sandy was in Perth, having previously been in Lambton, County Durham, Otley, Yorkshire and Barhill, Dumbarton, since his liberation. In a letter Douglas wrote to his brother Sandy in October 1945 he complained about the boredom and the uncertainty of a date for his release from the army and a return to civilian life. A passage from his letter is very illuminating:

You'll see we are aye in this God forsaken dump, but for how long I can't say, there are rumours, we might have to go any moment. All the recruits have gone (mostly overseas). Our training has finished, we've only being doing fatigues this week, sweeping up leaves, washing dishes, loading coal etc. Twice I've been in the NAAFI from 9am until 9.30pm. Nothing to do, but got to be there, I just patter away with the women staff all day. All the other jobs are cushy, stop about 2 hours in the morning and 2 in the afternoon; it's just like being in Germany, dodging all the time.

This is my half day but I didn't go out, I spent the afternoon in bed and the evening writing letters. Have you started any classes to make you ready for Civvy Street? Most of the places have started a school of some sort. What are you going in for?

You should be out by Xmas. I expect Rob to be out about the 8th of November. No word of Willie yet is there? He should be on his way home now you should think. (Reproduced by courtesy of Stan Robertson)

This final reference to 'Willie' is to their half-brother, William Angus, who was a Regular soldier with the 2nd Battalion Gordon Highlanders, captured by the Japanese at Singapore and was a prisoner of war forced to work on the Thai-Burma railway, where hundreds of Gordon Highlanders died, suffering brutal treatment from a cruel enemy and barely surviving on starvation rations. Like all the prisoners of the Japanese there had been very little news heard of Willie Angus during his captivity, a very different situation from the treatment both Sandy and Douglas had experienced at the hands of the Germans.

After his liberation leave, Maurice MacLean spent time in various camps around Britain. In the autumn of 1945 he was called to see his commanding officer who informed him that the Church of Scotland had managed to arrange for his early release from the Army to allow him to return to St Andrews University to resume his theological studies that October. Maurice confessed to his superior that he had decided to depart from his original plan and hoped to qualify as a teacher, so was unable to accept the early release. The CO told Maurice that he was far too honest as in his opinion most people would have accepted the opportunity of an early release and then changed their mind about the studies. Shortly afterwards, the CO urged him to accept his recommendation for a commission but Maurice had seen enough of soldiering and returned to university the following year.

Chapter 8

Epilogue

There is no doubt that the events of the summer of 1940 and the aftermath for almost 2,000 Gordon Highlanders who ended up as prisoners of war in Germany and Poland for five long years had a considerable effect on their character and outlook for the rest of their lives. Every man was proud of their collective courage. Even their enemy had complimented them on the stout resistance they had put up but with only light weapons at their disposal they could not hold out for long against the Germans' heavy armour and superior numbers. Charles Irvine, Harry Steel and Bill Jamieson are just a few of the men who named their daughters Valerie, after the town in Normandy where they had lost their liberty, giving them a constant reminder of that day. Bob Stewart, who died aged 81, on 10 June 2000, just two days before the sixtieth anniversary of the St Valéry surrender, literally took the memory to his grave. He had a figure of soldier engraved at the top of his headstone with the words 'Ex St Valéry' proudly inscribed in gold letters below.

The ex-PoWs tried to make sense of it all, reading the many books about the fall of France, becoming frustrated in seeing what became to be known as 'the miracle of Dunkirk' passing into the nation's folk memory but with St Valéry forgotten, or just rolled into the Dunkirk story. A few wrote their story for posterity, but of the Gordon Highlanders only Charles Morrison's was published. It was entitled *We've Been A Long Time Coming Boys* which were the first words he heard uttered, in a deep southern drawl, by a tall American soldier who liberated him on 5 May 1945. Maurice MacLean summed up his war experience, which would probably be echoed by a lot of the former PoWs. He had lost seven years of his normal growing up. From starting his service, after a sheltered upbringing, he gained self-confidence and found that he could face physical hardship as well as most. He had learned German and got to know the Germans far better than if he had just fought them, but his religious beliefs were tested to a point where he found there were parts of the doctrine that made him uneasy and he would have found it difficult to preach them to others. In effect he had to re-evaluate his values but he was more confident in his own abilities.

Winston Churchill has often been blamed for the loss of 51st (Highland) Division by his insistence that General Fortune stay with the French under whose command his Division was operating. This was, perhaps, underlined by the title, but not the conclusion, of a book written by the celebrated author and historian Saul David, which is entitled *Churchill's Sacrifice of The Highland Division*. Churchill's actions can partly be explained by his realization that the French were wavering and defeatism was taking hold. His enthusiasm for supporting the French is beyond question and in mid–May he had to be dissuaded, by Air Chief Marshal Hugh Dowding, from sending more Royal Air Force planes to France as they were unlikely to achieve a decisive result there but would leave Fighter Command too weak to defend Britain. Churchill believed that the longer he could keep the French Army in the fight against Germany the better the chances of victory would be when Hitler turned his full attention to Britain. In his own book *Memoirs of the Second World War*, Churchill stated:

> I was vexed that the French had not allowed our Division to retire on Rouen in good time, but had kept it waiting till it could neither reach le Havre or retreat southward, and thus forced it to surrender with their own troops. The fate of the Highland Division was hard … .

Churchill knew full well what the fate of the captured men would be as he had been a prisoner of war himself during the Boer War, when he was captured in the company of Gordon Highlander Captain James Haldane (later General Sir James Aylmer Lowthorpe Haldane GCMG KCB DSO). While imprisoned in Pretoria, Haldane planned the escape which made Winston Churchill famous. Haldane failed to escape at the same time and later complained of Churchill's lack of regard for those who should have escaped with him. However, Haldane later managed his own escape. Churchill said of his PoW experience:

> You are in the power of the enemy. You owe your life to his humanity, your daily bread to his compassion. You must obey his orders, await his

pleasure, possess your soul in patience. The days are long; hours crawl by like paralytic centipedes. Moreover, the whole atmosphere of prison is odious. You feel a constant humiliation at being fenced in by wire, watched by armed men and webbed about by a tangle of regulations and restrictions.

This was to be the experience of the men captured in France and Belgium some forty years later. In addition, through his wife, Clementine, he was acutely aware of the plight of her nephew, Giles Romilly. He was a war correspondent working for the *Daily Express* when captured in Narvik, Norway, in May 1940. Through his connection to the British prime minister, he became the first German prisoner to be classified as a 'Prominente', who the Nazis considered valuable political hostages. Because of his importance to Hitler, Romilly was imprisoned in Oflag IVC (Colditz) but unlike the PoWs at Colditz, the 'Prominente' lived in relative luxury. Romilly did escape in 1945 by abseiling down the castle walls, whilst at Oflag VIID (Tittmoning), then reaching Allied lines and freedom.

After the war Aberdonians did not hold any grudges and recognized the huge debt the nation owed to Churchill's leadership throughout the war. Winston Churchill was given the Freedom of the City of Aberdeen on 27 April 1946. He visited the city with Clementine and their daughter Mary for the presentation of the honour, made by Lord Provost Sir Thomas Mitchell. He was a wily orator and knew how to win over any audience. The opening words of his speech were:

The qualities and firmness of character for which the Scottish race is renowned are thought to reach their fullest and most profound manifestation in the granite city of Aberdeen. But Aberdeen is also famed for warm hearts, keen affection and bright eyes. I am deeply moved by your welcome.

During his speech there was a massive cheer when he mentioned the 51st (Highland) Division. He also received an honorary degree from Aberdeen University later that day.

Another man who bore no grudge against his old enemy and gaolers was Charlie Aitchison. He had only been at home for a few days when he took his 11-year-old daughter out for a walk to get to know her better, after his five year absence from her life while she was growing up. As they walked along the street, they came across some German PoWs working on the roads. Charlie stopped and spoke to them in fluent German. Then, after speaking to them for a few minutes, he went into a shop and returned with four pies and twenty cigarettes which he gave to the Germans. When his daughter asked him why he gave the men the gifts he said, 'they're just Jerries, working men like me who had been captured fighting for their country'.

In 1945 nobody thought to offer counselling or any other form of psychological support to the returning soldiers. Both PoWs and the men who had spent years in mortal danger in combat situations were just expected to get on with life. Perhaps the most common reason given by families to explain why they know very little of what their fathers or grandfathers did during the war years is 'he never talked about it'. There are probably many reasons for this. All men of combat age were in the forces so everyone had a story but didn't really think they were any different from anyone else. Some just wanted to forget the war and get on with their lives but in this silence some men suffered depression, anger and anxiety. Most got back to normal very quickly and led successful lives. When David Morren came home he was very thin and his face showed signs of malnutrition. He also suffered from depression and loved to walk in the open countryside while playing the piano was also a great solace. His family's granite business declined after the war and when this was sold he took up full time farming in the Huntly area. He also became an Aberdeenshire councillor, becoming convenor of the Planning Committee. He was immensely proud when, in 1963, his daughter, Alison, a doctor, married Captain Peter Graham of the Gordon Highlanders. Peter Graham went on to have a successful military career, going on to command the 1st Battalion Gordon Highlanders in 1976, became General Officer Commanding Scotland and Governor of Edinburgh Castle in 1991 and retired in 1993 with the rank of lieutenant general. He was also the last Colonel of the Regiment. PoWs who had been Regular soldiers of the 1st Battalion before the war had seen their careers put on hold while their contemporaries and juniors rose up the ranks quickly, serving in North Africa and continental Europe. After his liberation, Ran Ogilvie stayed in the Army finishing his career with the rank of major and took up farming in the Scottish Borders, inspired by the lectures and discussions with his PoW friend David Morren. Drummer Les Burlton continued to serve with the Regiment and was posted with the 1st Battalion to Malaya in the 1950s where they were involved in dealing with the Communist insurgency. He was promoted to drum major and in the 1954 New Year's Honours list was awarded the British Empire Medal. He continued to serve with the 1st Battalion until 1965. Service in Malaya with the Gordons was to prove less positive for Major Charles Watt, who was killed there on 23 July 1953.

Some men were able to pick up their lives where they left off before the war. Harry Milne went back to milk retail and when he retired in 1983 estimated he had delivered at least 160 million gallons of the white stuff. Bill Reaper went back to farming and towards the end of his life liked to reminisce on how the world had changed in his lifetime but he still enjoyed traditional verse, particularly in the Doric but despite the changes, he was not complaining about the 'new-fangled' creature comforts. Sergeant Bill Inglis was proud when his son John joined the Gordon Highlanders and served with the Regiment in Germany, Singapore, Cyprus, Belize and Northern Ireland. After being demobbed in May 1946 Harry Tobin trained as a jeweller and watchmaker and spent his working life in Aberdeen and lived to the marvellous age of ninety-five. On the other hand some men hankered after an entirely new life. Thomas Murray, who had been a full-time Regular soldier before the war, trained as a bricklayer, going on one of the government's retraining schemes for men discharged from the Army at the end of the war. He met his future wife at a New Year's dance in Peterhead in 1949 and, after a whirlwind romance, they were married in March 1950. They had two daughters and emigrated to Australia in the summer of 1958 on the £10 scheme where their family was increased by the addition of four more daughters, all immensely proud of their father's war record.

In later life a few men were able to return to Poland to lay to rest the ghosts of the past. Brothers Gordon and Albert (Romeo) Holmes, who had both been PoWs, went to Poland in 1985 and were surprised that all that was left of Stalag XXB were the gates. They found the farm at Jenkau, where George had worked as a PoW but the farm buildings were in ruins, although his old billet and the latrines were still standing. They were pleasantly surprised to find the daughter of one of the Polish cowmen still living nearby. She was a young girl when they were PoWs and in her early fifties when they met her again. Mary Hutcheon had a less nostalgic reason to visit Poland as she travelled to visit the grave of her husband Jack, who died in Stalag XXA in March 1941 and was later reinterred at Marienburg. Mary and her son Cecil travelled to Poland four times to visit his grave and were pleasantly surprised to meet a Polish family who had tended his and other PoWs' graves. They struck up a lasting friendship with these local people. Mary joined the Royal Household in the 1940s, working at Buckingham Place at the time Princess Elizabeth (later Queen Elizabeth II) was married to Prince Philip. She also worked at Windsor Castle, Sandringham, Holyrood Palace and Balmoral Castle. Their son Cecil was a Volunteer Guide at the Gordon Highlanders' Museum for over twenty years.

The 5th/7th Battalion Gordon Highlanders held their first annual reunion dinner in Aberdeen on 11 December 1948. Their chairman was Brigadier Alick Buchanan-Smith, who had been their CO before the war and took the 5th Battalion to France in 1940. The menu card had a very inclusive design with all of the Battalion's roles over the previous twenty-five years in a variety of theatres of war encapsulated in a simple single drawing. It showed a Great War soldier emerging from the trenches shaking hands with a 'skinny' kilted PoW standing by a high barbed-wire fence, who in turn is shaking hands with a soldier, standing by a palm tree in desert uniform. Jack Caldwell was an enthusiastic member of the Association and enjoyed the company of what he termed 'the Methlick Loons', a group of men who like him had been PoWs and originally hailed from the Aberdeenshire village of Methlick. Alex Watt's (2875918) copy of his menu card has a large number of signatures of other attendees at the reunion, many of them, like him, having been 5th Battalion PoWs and Jack Caldwell's signature features prominently on the front cover. The Lamsdorf Loons continued their association long after the war, even though their members became widely dispersed. On one occasion Henry Simpson returned to Scotland from his adopted home in Northern Rhodesia (now Zambia) to attend one of the re-unions. The members had a club tie and their honorary secretary would send the members a birthday greeting. One such card read, 'The Lamsdorf loons now free from brutal Nazi treatings, send you, their pal and comrade, their heartiest birthday greetings'.

The events at St Valéry in 1940 were especially significant for the east and north of Scotland, from where the Highland regiments traditionally drew their recruits. Almost every family had a relative or a friend who was affected and it was inevitable that the momentous events of 1940 would be commemorated. In 1946 a committee, presided over by Gordon Highlander Brigadier James Roderick Sinclair, 19th Earl of Caithness CBE DSO, recommended honouring the sacrifices of both the old and new 51st (Highland) Division between 1939 and 1945, by the erection of a memorial at St Valéry-en-Caux. A public appeal was launched through the press and by the lord provosts of all the main towns in the Divisional area. The French became aware of the plans for an unveiling ceremony at St Valéry and in 1948 the town of St Valéry-en-Caux was awarded the Croix de Guerre with Silver Star for the part the population played in the momentous events in 1940. The order conferring the honour contained the words 'St Valéry . . . made illustrious by the heroic resistance of the 51st Scottish Division'. The French Army also decided to erect a memorial to their forces in the hope that there would be a joint ceremony. Separately, but in parallel to these arrangements, the north-eastern counties of Scotland made an appeal, sponsored by the *Press and Journal*, a daily newspaper which circulates in the area concerned, which raised a considerable amount of money to be used to provide memorial gates for the cemetery at St Valéry. The plan was that these were to be unveiled with the main memorial. The design of the 51st (Highland) Division Memorial is a fifteen-ton, seventeen-feet high, monolith of roughly-hewn grey Aberdeenshire granite, quarried from Inver Quarry, just three miles from the sovereign's summer residence at Balmoral Castle. This is also just ten miles from the town of Ballater, which has a long association with the Gordon Highlanders. The cobbled paving at the base of the Memorial is laid in such a way as to depict the St Andrew's cross.

The logistics of creating and transporting the memorial to Normandy involved moving the massive block of granite from the Inver quarry the fifty miles to John Fyfe's granite works in Aberdeen, where the stone was sculpted and engraved to create the memorial and the pillars for the cemetery gates. These were then loaded onto two lorries, which left Aberdeen for Gosport on 15 April 1950. The Royal Navy provided a tank landing craft (LCT) to carry them to Dieppe, where they were carefully lifted off onto French Army trucks and taken to the site and erected by French contractors. The memorial is set high on the cliff above the town with an inscription on the face overlooking the harbour which reads:

In proud and grateful memory of all ranks of the 51st Highland Division who gave their lives during the War, 1939-45.

Immediately below this is the Gaelic inscription, 'Là a'bhlair 's math na càirdean' which translates into English as 'Friends are good on the day of battle'. A further inscription, in French, is on the reverse side of the memorial. The literal translation from the French is 'To the memory of its glorious children, Officers, Sub-Officers and Soldiers of 51st Scotland Division. This monument was raised in the ground of their Auld Allies 1939–1945'. The French memorial sits on the opposing clifftop on the other side of the town.

The unveiling and dedication ceremonies took place over the week-end of 10 and 11 June 1950 (the tenth anniversary of the surrender). Representatives of all the regiments of the 51st (Highland) Division were present together with many relatives of the fallen, to whom some financial assistance had been offered to allow them to attend. The Guard of Honour, comprising men from all the Division's Highland Regiments, saw Gordon Highlander RSM David Shore, a PoW for five years in Stalag 383, leading the march of the other ranks. The entrance to the War Cemetery at St Valéry-en-Caux lies up a wooded lane named 'Avenue D' Ecosse' and the two simple grey granite pillars, supporting low wooden gates, were the gift of the people of north and north-east Scotland. A granite St Andrew's shield given by the Marchioness of Huntly is set into the base of the Cross of Sacrifice, which forms a central feature, standing between the French and British sections of the War Cemetery. Among the 165 British servicemen buried here are twenty-two Gordon Highlanders. There are, however, other graves in some of the local village cemeteries in the vicinity of St Valéry-en-Caux. At Manneville-ès-Plains are the graves of William Neilson and the four pipers, Patrick (known as Peter) Stewart, Duncan Reid, John McLennan and George Rennie, killed in the orchard just a short distance from the church. After the war the authorities were planning to disinter the bodies of these British soldiers and take them to the main military cemetery at St Valéry-en-Caux only a few miles away. The villagers raised a hue and cry, pointing out that it was for their village the men died and pleaded with the authorities that 'the Jocks' be allowed to remain among them, where they could continue to care for their graves. The villagers have been true to their word and these men's graves are appropriately planted with heather.

When Mrs Nancy Wilson, the daughter of Piper Peter Stewart, attended the seventy-fifth anniversary commemoration ceremony at St Valéry in June 2015 she naturally went to Manneville-ès-Plains. She was just sitting alone in the churchyard, thinking about her father and admiring the beauty and peacefulness of this place when she was approached by a Frenchman who had just come out of the church. He enquired if she had someone buried in the cemetery and she replied that her father was. He took her to the graveside where he, and some others, conducted a short impromptu ceremony of remembrance and she was very touched and greatly appreciated their thoughtfulness and kindness. There were originally also nine French soldiers buried here, including a father and his son, but the villagers met the expenses for them to be moved to their own towns and villages, a gesture which was much appreciated by the families of the men involved. Nancy had visited her father's grave with her mother many years before but she has not been alone in making a pilgrimage to this spot. Piper Bill Maitland, who was wounded in the same incident as those buried at Manneville, visited the village and played his pipes by the graves of his comrades, contemplating the fact that, although he had to suffer five hard years of captivity, he was at least still alive and able to venerate his fallen friends. George McLennan visited his brother Johnny's grave there in 1947 and Alex Watt (2875918) returned to the village with his wife and family in 1986. After paying their respects at the gravesides of his friends, whose deaths he witnessed at close hand, they took a walk into the nearby orchard and stumbled across the barn where the men were killed forty-six years before and the painful memories came flooding back. The barn was still in everyday use and exactly as Alex remembered it. The only difference was that the roof and floor, which had been damaged by the mortar shell, had been repaired.

Over the years the little town of St Valéry-en-Caux has seen many commemoration ceremonies. The people of Normandy have a strong affinity with the 51st (Highland) Division and appreciated their friendship and support during both world wars. The Highland Division has erected another significant memorial at Beaumont-Hamel, a little less than 100 miles north-west of St Valéry. Here a number of battalions of Gordon Highlanders fought, suffering a high number of casualties, during the battles of the Somme in 1916. In 1990, at the fiftieth anniversary commemoration of the surrender, a commemorative window was unveiled and dedicated in the church in St Valéry. After the civic functions and a march past, commemorative medals were presented by local children to all the veterans present, a gesture which was greatly appreciated. Although no longer worked, it was thought fitting that the quarry at Inver, near Balmoral, Aberdeenshire, should be the source of a rock for another notable occasion. A suitable piece of granite was donated by Invercauld Estate which was then dressed and engraved to mark Queen Elizabeth's Diamond Jubilee in 2012 and it tops off a memorial cairn in the centre of Ballater. A small plaque proudly advises the many thousands of tourists who visit Banchory every year that the Jubilee commemoration stone is from the same source as the 51st (Highland) Division Memorial at St Valéry-en-Caux.

A casual visitor to St Valéry-en-Caux today could be forgiven for being oblivious of the momentous events which occurred there in the summer of 1940. St Valéry is a neat, pretty, fairly typical, small Normandy town. The harbour, where the soldiers of the 51st (Highland) Division waited in vain for the ships which were to rescue them, is now a smart marina packed with pleasure yachts. There is a funfair at the end of the promenade. Families with young children play happily on the beach in the lee of the high chalk cliffs where there once was utter carnage with many men being gunned down mercilessly as they tried desperately to escape. Perhaps this is only fitting. The men who are the subject of this book gave their lives and their freedom so that these children, and all of us, can have the freedom and peace we all enjoy today. It is without any exaggeration that they gave their lives and freedom for ours.

Appendix

Gordon Highlanders Captured or Killed In France in 1940

Name / Army Number	Photo	PoW Camp
Aberdein, Andrew / 2881739	No Photo	XXA (Thorn)
Aberdein, John / 2870035		383 (Hohenfels)
Aberdein, William / 2879001	No Photo	383 (Hohenfels)
Adam, A.C.G. / 75276		O.VIIB (Eischstätt)
Adam, Robert Ritchie / 2882841	No Photo	XXA (Thorn)
Adams, Alexander / 2880801	No Photo	XXID (Poznan)
Adams, John / 2877028	No Photo	XXB (Marienburg)
Adams, John / 2882003		IXC (Muhlhausen)
Addison, Charles / 2880021		344 (Lamsdorf)
Addison, William / 2879042		344 (Lamsdorf)

Name / Army Number	Photo	PoW Camp
Adie, Colin / 2834033	No Photo	XXID (Poznan)
Aitchison, Charles / 2871743	No Photo	344 (Lamsdorf)
Aitchison, James / 2878868		344 (Lamsdorf)
Aitken, Charles / 2877133	No Photo	XXB (Marienburg)
ALEXANDER, DONALD / 67199		KIA
Alexander, Norman / 2873860		XXA (Thorn)
Alexander, William / 2872319	No Photo	344 (Lamsdorf)
Allan, Charles / 2881867	No Photo	XXID (Poznan)
Allan, Edwin / 2074458	No Photo	IXC (Muhlhausen)
Allan, Gilbert / 2873473	No Photo	XXID (Poznan)

Name	Photo	PoW Camp
Army Number		
Allan, James A. (Curly)		Repatriated in 1943
2873473		
Allan, Leslie	No Photo	IXC (Muhlhausen)
2873173		
Allen, Joseph	No Photo	XXA (Thorn)
2875548		
Allward, D.R. Stewart	No Photo	O.VIIB (Eischstätt)
99776		
ALTHAM, NORMAN	No Photo	344 (Lamsdorf)
78907		
Anderson, Andrew	No Photo	XXB (Marienburg)
2878348		
ANDERSON, FORBES	No Photo	XXB (Marienburg)
2881890		
Anderson, George		XXB (Marienburg)
2868544		
Anderson, G.	No Photo	344 (Lamsdorf)
3048641		
Anderson, Tom	No Photo	317 (Markt Pongau)
2883937		
Anderson, William	No Photo	344 (Lamsdorf)
2883125		
Andrew, James	No Photo	XXA (Thorn)
2871648		
Andrews, Leonard	No Photo	Escaped
2879532		
Angus, Alexander		XXB (Marienburg)
2876859		

Name	Photo	PoW Camp
Army Number		
Angus, Alexander W.		XXB (Marienburg)
2875189		
Angus, Archibald		344 (Lamsdorf)
2879200		
Angus, David		IXC (Muhlhausen)
2880001		
Archibald, George	No Photo	344 (Lamsdorf)
2881847		
Armour, R.	No Photo	N/a – Evacuated
2869969		
Armstrong, William	No Photo	XXA (Thorn)
2880006		
ARMSTRONG, IRWIN	No Photo	KIA
2873323		
Astlew, W.	No Photo	344 (Lamsdorf)
5567143		
Auld, Archibald		Unknown
2874183		
Aylmer, Stuart		0.9A/Z (Rotenburg Fulda)
40649		
Baillie, John	No Photo	344 (Lamsdorf)
2882911		
BAIN, ALEXANDER		KIA
2882005		

Name / Army Number	Photo	PoW Camp
Bain, William / 2875829	No Photo	344 (Lamsdorf)
Baker, John / 2872523		383 (Hohenfels)
Ballantyne, A. / 3059547	No Photo	XXA (Thorn)
Barclay, George / 2878341	No Photo	344 (Lamsdorf)
Barclay, John / 2879152		IXC (Muhlhausen)
Barclay, John / 2880715		344 (Lamsdorf)
Barclay, William / 2876434		357 (Kopernikus)
Barclay, William / 2880708	No Photo	344 (Lamsdorf)
Barnes, William / 2879201	No Photo	IXC (Muhlhausen)
Barnes, Thomas / 2880746	No Photo	XXB (Marienburg)
Barnett, J.G. / 93984		O.VIIB (Eischstätt)
Barr, John / 2879435	No Photo	XXID (Poznan)
Barrack, John / 2881017	No Photo	XXA (Thorn)

Name / Army Number	Photo	PoW Camp
Barrack, Stuart / 2881184		344 (Lamsdorf)
Barrett, I / 6139231	No Photo	N/a – Evacuated
Barrett, Thomas / 2882912	No Photo	IXC (Muhlhausen)
Barron, William / 2881526	No Photo	XXA (Thorn)
Bass, Thomas A. / 2874350	No Photo	344 (Lamsdorf)
BASSETT, SAMUEL / 2872423	No Photo	KIA
Bates, S. / 4854923	No Photo	344 (Lamsdorf)
Baxter, Anthony / 2882913	No Photo	344 (Lamsdorf)
Beagrie, Andrew / 2878790		IXC (Muhlhausen)
Beaton, Frank / 2883786	No Photo	344 (Lamsdorf)
Beaton, George / Unknown		Unknown
Beaton, Lewis / 2874504	No Photo	XXB (Marienburg)
Beattie, Alan / 2886105		344 (Lamsdorf)

Name	Photo	PoW Camp
Army Number		
Beattie, David	No Photo	XXA (Thorn)
2877206		
Beattie, James		Escaped
2880258		
BEEDHAM, HERBERT	No Photo	KIA
2876311		
Bell, J.	No Photo	344 (Lamsdorf)
3055306		
Bell, J.	No Photo	XXA (Thorn)
4267942		
Bennett, Charles	No Photo	XXB (Marienburg)
2883862		
Bennett, Henry		344 (Lamsdorf)
2881451		
Benzies, Percy		Repatriated October 1943
Unknown		
Bettley, Charles	No Photo	IXC (Muhlhausen)
2883923		
Bews, John	No Photo	IXC (Muhlhausen)
2879350		
Birnie, Charles		IXC (Muhlhausen)
2878807		
Birnie, Ivor Herron		344 (Lamsdorf)
2884009		

Name	Photo	PoW Camp
Army Number		
Birnie, Robert		344 (Lamsdorf)
2882902		
Birnie, Ronald	No Photo	XXA (Thorn)
2880749		
Birse, Ernest		XXB (Marienburg)
2876869		
Birse, Robert		XXB (Marienburg)
2878489		
Bisset, James A.	No Photo	XXB (Marienburg)
2872099		
Blackie, Thomas	No Photo	344 (Lamsdorf)
2883225		
Blades, E.	No Photo	XXB (Marienburg)
4853645		
Blair, John		344 (Lamsdorf)
2876918		
Blanche, Robert Gunn		344 (Lamsdorf)
2876656		
Blood, L.A.	No Photo	XXA (Thorn)
4852963		
Bonnar, Douglas	No Photo	383 (Hohenfels)
2875580		
Bonner, Frank	No Photo	IXC (Muhlhausen)
2882268		
Booth, Douglas	No Photo	IXC (Muhlhausen)
2882781		

Name	Photo	PoW Camp
Army Number		
Booth, Guthrie	No Photo	XXA (Thorn)
2883968		
Booth, Jack		344 (Lamsdorf)
2876772		
Born, Thomas H.		XXA (Thorn)
2867963		
Borthwick, Thomas	No Photo	XXA (Thorn)
2878773		
Borthwick, William	No Photo	XXA (Thorn)
2884025		
Boulby, Frank	No Photo	BAB 20 (Hydebreck)
4742974		
Bowman, Thomas	No Photo	XXB (Marienburg)
2877825		
Boyd, James W.	No Photo	XXID (Poznan)
2883920		
Boyes, Jack		IXC (Muhlhausen)
2875396		
Bradshaw, R.		344 (Lamsdorf)
6137071		
Brandon, John	No Photo	344 (Lamsdorf)
2883249		
Brankin, Alexander	No Photo	XXB (Marienburg)
2751974		
Brannen, Alexander	No Photo	XXB (Marienburg)
2879236		

Name	Photo	PoW Camp
Army Number		
Brebner, John	No Photo	344 (Lamsdorf)
2881848		
BRECHIN, ROBERT	No Photo	KIA
3051463		
BREMNER, JAMES		Died of wounds
2876021		
BREMNER, WILLIAM		KIA
2873444		
Bridger, Charles	No Photo	XXA (Thorn)
2881527		
Brockie, Alexander		Repatriated October 1943
2878219		
Brodie, Matthew	No Photo	XXB (Marienburg)
2878478		
Brooke, Basil Arthur		O.VIIB (Eischstätt)
75449		
Brown, James	No Photo	XXB (Marienburg)
2878963		
Brown, Alexander	No Photo	XXID (Poznan)
2881426		
Brown, Alexander	No Photo	344 (Lamsdorf)
2882916		
Brown, E.J.	No Photo	383 (Hohenfels)
3188900		
Brown, George		Repatriated October 1943
2871151		

Name	Photo	PoW Camp
Army Number		
Brown, L.J.	No Photo	XXA (Thorn)
2882025		
Brown, Richard	No Photo	XXB (Marienburg)
2883864		
Brown, Thomas		344 (Lamsdorf)
2879066		
BROWN, WALTER	No Photo	KIA
2881465		
Brown, William		344 (Lamsdorf)
2875472		
Brown, W.L.	No Photo	XXB (Marienburg)
2224023		
Brownlie, J.	No Photo	XXB (Marienburg)
3308370		
Bruce, George W. (Tony)		O.IXA/H (Spangenburg)
36961		
Bruce, Henry	No Photo	IXC (Muhlhausen)
2880062		
Bruce, Hugh	No Photo	344 (Lamsdorf)
2879268		
Bruce, James	No Photo	XXA (Thorn)
2875046		
Bruce, John	No Photo	XXB (Marienburg)
2883326		
Bruce, Robert	No Photo	XXA (Thorn)
2880082		
Bruce, William	No Photo	IXC (Muhlhausen)
2878366		
BRYDON, JAMES	No Photo	KIA
2874395		

Name	Photo	PoW Camp
Army Number		
Bryson, Andrew	No Photo	XXB (Marienburg)
2875200		
Buchan, Alexander	No Photo	XXA (Thorn)
2879371		
Buchan, George	No Photo	IXC (Muhlhausen)
2878627		
Buchan, James	No Photo	344 (Lamsdorf)
2874153		
Buchan, William	No Photo	344 (Lamsdorf)
2871278		
Buchan, William	No Photo	344 (Lamsdorf)
2880709		
Buchanan, James		XXID (Poznan)
2876922		
BUCHANAN, MATTHEW	No Photo	KIA
2873346		
Buchanan-Smith, Alick		Evacuated
Unknown		
Buist, Neil	No Photo	344 (Lamsdorf)
2191482		
Burgen, John	No Photo	344 (Lamsdorf)
2879270		
Burgess, James		344 (Lamsdorf)
1662909		
Burgess, James A.	No Photo	XXB (Marienburg)
2881602		
Burgess, John	No Photo	XXID (Poznan)
2882102		

Name	Photo	PoW Camp
Army Number		
Burke, John	No Photo	XXB (Marienburg)
891020		
Burlton, Lesley G.		344 (Lamsdorf)
2876482		
Burnett, Ernest		IXC (Muhlhausen)
2878952		
Burnett, Norman		XXB (Marienburg)
2879132		
Burnett, William		XXB (Marienburg)
2879045		
BURNEY, GEORGE		Died in Captviy
Uknown		
Burns, Duncan		XXB (Marienburg)
2876901		
Burr, William		L3 (Sagan & Belaria)
2882356		
Burrell, A.R.	No Photo	383 (Hohenfels)
5988450		
Burt, Robert William		XXA (Thorn)
2876999		

Name	Photo	PoW Camp
Army Number		
Bush, John	No Photo	BAB 21 (Blechammer)
2882770		
Butler, John	No Photo	344 (Lamsdorf)
2033760		
Byrne, John (Jack) Vincent		Luft III (Sagan)
2060658		
Cairns, James	No Photo	IXC (Muhlhausen)
2882918		
Calder, James	No Photo	XXB (Marienburg)
2874541		
Calderwood, Gavin	No Photo	344 (Lamsdorf)
2874406		
Caldwell, John		XXA (Thorn)
2880474		
Cameron, Colin	No Photo	IXC (Muhlhausen)
2879346		
Cameron, George	No Photo	XXIA (Schildberg)
2879484		
Cameron, James		XXB (Marienburg)
2873453		
Campbell, Alex	No Photo	XXB (Marienburg)
2878809		
Campbell, Alex	No Photo	344 (Lamsdorf)
2880741		
Campbell, Alexander M.		XXB (Marienburg)
2876797		

Name	Photo	PoW Camp
Army Number		
CAMPBELL, ARCHIBALD		KIA
2876919		
Campbell, Duncan Cameron		O.9A/Z (Rotenburg Fulda)
66602		
CAMPBELL, JAMES	No Photo	KIA
2879358		
Campbell, John Kirkwood	No Photo	XXB (Marienburg)
2882920		
CAMPBELL, JOSEPH	No Photo	KIA
2879506		
Campbell, Robert	No Photo	N/a – Evacuated
2873877		
Campbell, Thomas	No Photo	344 (Lamsdorf)
2883866		
Canty, Walter	No Photo	XXA (Thorn)
3853362		
Cardno, A.	No Photo	344 (Lamsdorf)
1664202		
Cargill, James	No Photo	XXB (Marienburg)
919979		
Carle, Charles		XXB (Marienburg)
2876764		
CARLE, GEORGE		KIA
2879146		

Name	Photo	PoW Camp
Army Number		
Carle, James Gordon	No Photo	344 (Lamsdorf)
2879237		
Carle, Robert		XXB (Marienburg)
2879143		
Carle, William		Evacuated
2875567		
Carnochan, J.		344 (Lamsdorf)
3241188		
Carr, John Doig	No Photo	XXA (Thorn)
2882826		
Carroll, J.	No Photo	XXID (Poznan)
3050852		
Carroll, John	No Photo	N/a
2883238		
Cassie, Alexander	No Photo	XXB (Marienburg)
2878778		
Cassie, Alexander	No Photo	XXB (Marienburg)
2878923		
Cassie, James	No Photo	383 (Hohenfels)
2875455		
CATTO, DAVID	No Photo	KIA
2879217		
Caulfield, Michael		344 (Lamsdorf)
2871569		
CHALMERS, DOUGLAS	No Photo	KIA
2872603		

Name	Photo	PoW Camp
Army Number		
Chalmers, George	No Photo	XXB (Marienburg)
2876563		
Chalmers, Hugh		344 (Lamsdorf)
2876722		
Chalmers, James		344 (Lamsdorf)
2881697		
CHAPMAN, DONALD	No Photo	KIA
2872816		
Cheyne, A.	No Photo	344 (Lamsdorf)
2679253		
Cheyne, George		XXA (Thorn)
2879096		
CHEYNE, ROBERT		Died in Captivity
2882365		
Chisholm, Stanley	No Photo	XXA (Thorn)
2874830		
Christie, Charles John		XXB (Marienburg)
2882892		
Christie, Donald		383 (Hohenfels)
2872205		
Christie, George	No Photo	XXB (Marienburg)
2881479		
CHRISTIE, GEORGE	No Photo	KIA
2879428		

Name	Photo	PoW Camp
Army Number		
Christie, George	No Photo	XXA (Thorn)
2882062		
Christie, Hector	No Photo	O.IVC (Colditz)
38881		
Christie, Meston Charles		XXID (Poznan)
2883101		
Christie, Rupert N.		O.XIIB (Mainz)
20230		
Christie, Sidney	No Photo	XXB (Marienburg)
2881015		
Christie, William		XXB (Marienburg)
2879202		
CHRYSTALL, JAMES	No Photo	KIA
2878810		
Clark, Albert	No Photo	XXB (Marienburg)
2882777		
Clark, Forbes	No Photo	344 (Lamsdorf)
2881466		
Clark, George		XXA (Thorn)
2876923		
Clark, J.		O.IXA/H (Spangenburg)
19867		
Clark, James Shearer		XXA (Thorn)
2882793		

Name	Photo	PoW Camp
Army Number		
Clark, Thomas	No Photo	IXC (Muhlhausen)
2883868		
Clark, Thomas	No Photo	344 (Lamsdorf)
2883870		
Clark, William J.	No Photo	N/a – Escaped
793956		
Clark, William	No Photo	344 (Lamsdorf)
2879463		
Clarke, Richard	No Photo	344 (Lamsdorf)
2882923		
Clarke, William	No Photo	IXC (Muhlhausen)
2877696		
Clarkson, John	No Photo	344 (Lamsdorf)
2883271		
CLARKSON, ROBERT DAVID		Killed while a POW
2876983		
Clauson, Emil George		383 (Hohenfels)
2876461		
Cleland, A.W.	No Photo	XXB (Marienburg)
6007247		
Clifford, James	No Photo	XXA (Thorn)
2883872		
Close, G.R.	No Photo	344 (Lamsdorf)
2882924		
Clubbs, Robert		N/a – Escaped
2875390		
Cobb, F.I.	No Photo	O.VIIB (Eischstätt
67971		
Cockburn, J.	No Photo	IVA (Hohenstein)
98591		
Cocker, A.	No Photo	XXB (Marienburg)
8122763		

Name	Photo	PoW Camp
Army Number		
Colleran, James	No Photo	383 (Hohenfels)
2869181		
Collie, Andrew	No Photo	344 (Lamsdorf)
2872514		
COLLIE, WILLIAM		IXC (Muhlhausen) Shot escaping
2876639		
Collie, William	No Photo	XXB (Marienburg)
2882784		
Collin, William Maltman		344 (Lamsdorf)
2879007		
Collins, James	No Photo	XXA (Thorn)
2881742		
COLVILLE, FREDERICK		KIA
50797		
Conn, Robert	No Photo	XXB (Marienburg)
2883873		
Conn, William		XXB (Marienburg)
2875134		
Connan, Adam	No Photo	XIIIC (Hammelburg am Main)
2883235		
Cook, George		344 (Lamsdorf)
2876519		
Cooper, Alex		344 (Lamsdorf)
2877828		
Cooper, Charles	No Photo	IXC (Muhlhausen)
2883839		

Name	Photo	PoW Camp
Army Number		
Cooper, Walter	No Photo	XXB (Marienburg)
2878991		
Cooper, Walter	No Photo	383 (Hohenfels)
2877138		
Cooper, William		XXB (Marienburg)
2873168		
Copland, Robert	No Photo	N/a – Escaped
2874837		
Copland, Thomas Aitken		XXB (Marienburg)
2876498		
Copland, William	No Photo	XXB (Marienburg)
2883899		
Corbett, George Duncan		XXIA (Schildberg)
2882785		
Cormack, Douglas	No Photo	XXA (Thorn)
2878189		
Cormack, George	No Photo	344 (Lamsdorf)
2873914		
Coull, James	No Photo	XXA (Thorn)
2880472		
Coull, Peter		O.VIIB (Eichstatt)
2879100		
COURAGE, JAMES		KIA
2869551		
Coutts, David	No Photo	XXB (Marienburg)
2879340		

Name	Photo	PoW Camp
Army Number		
Cowie, Alexander	No Photo	344 (Lamsdorf)
2882929		
Cowie, George	No Photo	344 (Lamsdorf)
2878827		
Cowie, George M.	No Photo	XXA (Thorn)
2883226		
Cowie, George S.	No Photo	IXC (Muhlhausen)
2883991		
Cowie, Hugh Wilson		BAB 20 (Hydebreck)
2876924		
Cowie, James	No Photo	344 (Lamsdorf)
2878844		
Cowie, William		IXC (Muhlhausen)
2882312		
Coyle, Henry	No Photo	BAB 20 (Hydebreck)
2883929		
Craib, Leslie	No Photo	344 (Lamsdorf)
2877831		
Craib, William	No Photo	XXID (Poznan)
2878362		
Craig, James	No Photo	XXB (Marienburg)
2882827		
Craig, James G		XXA (Thorn)
2879113		
Craig, W.H.		O.IXA/H (Spangenburg)
37492		
Craig, William H	No Photo	XXB (Marienburg)
2882861		
Craigen, Alex	No Photo	IXC (Muhlhausen)
2884004		

Name	Photo	PoW Camp
Army Number		
Craigen, William	No Photo	XXB (Marienburg)
2882930		
CRAIGIE, DAVID		KIA
2875645		
Cran, James		Unknown
Unknown		
Crawford, C.G.	No Photo	344 (Lamsdorf)
782922		
Crawford, James		344 (Lamsdorf)
2878891		
Crawford, Stanley	No Photo	XXB (Marienburg)
2879316		
Crawford, William	No Photo	IXC (Muhlhausen)
2883900		
CRICHTON, DAVID STURGE	No Photo	Died while a PoW
70723		
Croker, John	No Photo	XXB (Marienburg)
2882894		
Cromar, James		Escaped
2879013		
Cruden, James	No Photo	IXC (Muhlhausen)
2882007		
Cruden, Walter Fowlie		344 (Lamsdorf)
2879105		

Name	Photo	PoW Camp
Army Number		
Cruickshank, A.	No Photo	XXA (Thorn)
2885852		
Cruickshank, Arthur	No Photo	344 (Lamsdorf)
2879326		
Cruickshank, Edward Inglis		IXC (Muhlhausen)
2882782		
Cruickshank, G.C.		O.VIIB (Eischstätt)
95380		
Cruickshank, George		Unknown
2868001		
Cruickshank, George McG.		XXID (Poznan)
2884012		
Cruickshank, James	No Photo	IXC (Muhlhausen)
2875292		
Cruickshank, John		IXC (Muhlhausen)
2876794		
Cruickshank, Joseph		IXC (Muhlhausen)
2878221		
Cryle, Robert	No Photo	IXC (Muhlhausen)
2878628		
Cumming, Charles	No Photo	XXB (Marienburg)
2881369		

Name	Photo	PoW Camp
Army Number		
Cumming, David		XXA (Thorn)
2210580		
CURRIE, ANDREW		KIA
2876847		
Cushnie, James Hay	No Photo	XXB (Marienburg)
2882868		
Cuthbertson, Charles	No Photo	XXB (Marienburg)
2873880		
Dalgarno, Edward	No Photo	XXB (Marienburg)
2881682		
Dalrymple, David	No Photo	XXA (Thorn)
2883186		
DANN, EDWARD	No Photo	Died while a PoW
1020138		
Davidson, Andrew	No Photo	XXB (Marienburg)
2874486		
Davidson, Alexander	No Photo	XXID (Poznan)
2884042		
Davidson, Charles	No Photo	344 (Lamsdorf)
2880022		
Davidson, Douglas Fraser		XXB (Marienburg)
2882794		
Davidson, Duncan	No Photo	344 (Lamsdorf)
2883816		
Davidson, Forbes		383 (Hohenfels)
2870334		

Name	Photo	PoW Camp
Army Number		
Davidson, George I.		344 (Lamsdorf)
97960		
Davidson, Gilbert (George)	No Photo	344 (Lamsdorf)
753368		
Davidson, James	No Photo	VIIIB (Teschen)
4268006		
Davidson, James Alexander		344 (Lamsdorf)
2881743		
Davidson, James Algie	No Photo	344 (Lamsdorf)
2883258		
Davidson, James Rettie Mutch		8A (Gorlitz)
2882072		
Davidson, John Adair		XXB (Marienburg)
2880381		
Davidson, John Falconer		8A (Gorlitz)
2880487		
Davidson, Joseph	No Photo	344 (Lamsdorf)
2880159		
Davidson, Peter	No Photo	344 (Lamsdorf)
2883091		
Davidson, W.		XXB (Marienburg)
2879157		

Name	Photo	PoW Camp
Army Number		
DAVIDSON, WILLIAM	No Photo	KIA
2873443		
Davidson, William J.R.	No Photo	VIIIB (Teschen)
2877458		
Davie, John (Jack)		XXB (Marienburg)
2880753		
Dawson, William	No Photo	XXID (Poznan)
2878412		
Dawson, William George		IXC (Muhlhausen)
2882873		
De Jersey, N.	No Photo	344 (Lamsdorf)
5494448		
Deacon, Andrew	No Photo	XXB (Marienburg)
2883939		
Deakins, William	No Photo	XXB (Marienburg)
2879465		
Dempster, David		344 (Lamsdorf)
2876538		
Dempster, Robert	No Photo	344 (Lamsdorf)
2883902		
Denholm, Thomas		344 (Lamsdorf)
3055571		
Derry, Joseph		XXB (Marienburg)
2876973		

Name	Photo	PoW Camp
Army Number		
Devine, Matthew	No Photo	IXC (Muhlhausen)
2883938		
Dewar, J	No Photo	344 (Lamsdorf)
3247843		
Dey, Frank		XXB (Marienburg)
2876850		
Dey, Frederick		XXB (Marienburg)
2877329		
Dey, William	No Photo	344 (Lamsdorf)
2877444		
Diack, Gordon	No Photo	O.VIIB (Eischstätt)
113407		
DIACK, WILLIAM		KIA
63002		
DICK, EDWARD		KIA
2876992		
Dick, John	No Photo	N/a – Escaped
2883903		
Dickie, Alexander		344 (Lamsdorf)
2880158		
Dickie, Frederick	No Photo	344 (Lamsdorf)
2881461		
DICKIE, JOHN	No Photo	Died of wounds
2868848		
Dickinson, Mark	No Photo	IXC (Muhlhausen)
2879321		

Name	Photo	PoW Camp
Dickson, David	No Photo	344 (Lamsdorf)
2883228		
Dickson, Robert	No Photo	IXC (Muhlhausen)
2883189		
Dickson, Ronald	No Photo	XXA (Thorn)
2883204		
Digan, William	No Photo	XXID (Poznan)
2883904		
Dingwall, W.		344 (Lamsdorf)
771415		
Docherty, Dominick	No Photo	344 (Lamsdorf)
2882936		
Dodds, James T.	No Photo	IXC (Muhlhausen)
2879271		
Donald, Albert	No Photo	344 (Lamsdorf)
2881870		
Donald, Alexander	No Photo	IXC (Muhlhausen)
2878479		
Donald, Alexander	No Photo	XXB (Marienburg)
2880734		
Donald, Frederick	No Photo	XXB (Marienburg)
2874403		
Donald, James	No Photo	IXC (Muhlhausen)
2882351		
Donald, Peter	No Photo	344 (Lamsdorf)
2872017		
Donald, William	No Photo	N/a – Escaped
2880305		
Donaldson, Allan		VIIIB (Teschen)
2881429		

Name	Photo	PoW Camp
Donaldson, John		IXC (Muhlhausen)
2882796		
Donaldson, William	No Photo	344 (Lamsdorf)
2883160		
Done, George	No Photo	XXA (Thorn)
2879238		
Donnelly, Frank	No Photo	XXB (Marienburg)
2883906		
Donnelly, John	No Photo	344 (Lamsdorf)
2883907		
Donnelly, Michael	No Photo	N/a – Escaped
2883908		
Doolan, John		IXC (Muhlhausen)
2883909		
Dorris, James	No Photo	344 (Lamsdorf)
2878765		
Douglas, George	No Photo	XXB (Marienburg)
2883992		
DOUGLAS, WILLIAM		KIA
923200		
Dowell, Robert	No Photo	XXA (Thorn)
2879231		
Downie, Thomas	No Photo	XXA (Thorn)
2882812		
Downs, John	No Photo	XXB (Marienburg)
2883912		
Doyce, Edward	No Photo	XXB (Marienburg)
2883954		
Doyle, Harold R.	No Photo	XXA (Thorn)
3301080		

Name	Photo	PoW Camp
Army Number		
Duff, Alexander	No Photo	XXB (Marienburg)
2873457		
Duguid, Evander	No Photo	Evacuated wounded
Unknown		
Duguid, James	No Photo	IXC (Muhlhausen)
2883810		
Duke, Robert W.	No Photo	VIIA (Mooseburg)
4744980		
Dunbar, Cosmo	No Photo	VIIIB (Teschen)
2881418		
Dunbar, Douglas	No Photo	Repatriated in 1944
Unknown		
Dunbar, James Kelman Fraser		XXA (Thorn)
2878267		
Dunbar, Robert	No Photo	383 (Hohenfels)
2874442		
Dunbar, Robert		Escaped
2879107		
Duncan, Alexander		XXB (Marienburg)
2877668		
Duncan, Alexander	No Photo	IXC (Muhlhausen)
2879332		
Duncan, Allan G.	No Photo	344 (Lamsdorf)
2873445		
Duncan, Andrew	No Photo	VIIIB (Teschen)
2883079		
Duncan, Charles	No Photo	XXB (Marienburg)
2880694		
Duncan, Charles	No Photo	344 (Lamsdorf)
2882301		

Name	Photo	PoW Camp
Army Number		
Duncan, Charles A.	No Photo	IXC (Muhlhausen)
2882334		
Duncan, Douglas	No Photo	IXC (Muhlhausen)
2868644		
Duncan, Douglas	No Photo	344 (Lamsdorf)
2873795		
Duncan, George		8A (Gorlitz)
2873795		
Duncan, George F.	No Photo	XXB (Marienburg)
2884010		
Duncan, James	No Photo	XXB (Marienburg)
2874381		
Duncan, James		344 (Lamsdorf)
2875492		
Duncan, James P.		XXB (Marienburg)
2878257		
Duncan, John	No Photo	VIIIB (Teschen)
2873963		
Duncan, Lewis	No Photo	XXB (Marienburg)
2884015		
DUNCAN, NORMAN		KIA
75278		
DUNCAN, PETER		XXID (Poznan)
2879274		
Duncan, Robert	No Photo	IXC (Muhlhausen)
2883096		

Name	Photo	PoW Camp
Army Number		
Duncan, Robert B.	No Photo	8A (Gorlitz)
2883155		
Duncan, Thomas	No Photo	IXC (Muhlhausen)
2880520		
Duncan, Walter	No Photo	344 (Lamsdorf)
2883097		
Duncan, Wm K.	No Photo	IXC (Muhlhausen)
2875570		
Duncan, Wm M.	No Photo	XXB (Marienburg)
2869494		
Duncan, Wilson	No Photo	XXA (Thorn)
2881500		
Dunlop, James	No Photo	Evacuated wounded
Unknown		
Dunn, George		IXC (Muhlhausen)
2874105		
Dunn, Robert	No Photo	BAB 20 (Hydebreck
2879493		
Dunne, Michael	No Photo	IXC (Muhlhausen)
2883263		
Durward, Arthur		IXC (Muhlhausen)
2870435		
Durward, James		383 (Hohenfels)
2786438		
Duthie, Andrew	No Photo	344 (Lamsdorf)
2876486		
Duthie, Archibald	No Photo	344 (Lamsdorf)
2881854		
Duthie, John	No Photo	XXA (Thorn)
2881189		
DUTHIE, JOHN	No Photo	Died of wounds
3314110		

Name	Photo	PoW Camp
Army Number		
Easton, John	No Photo	344 (Lamsdorf)
2883163		
Eddie, Alexander	No Photo	XXB (Marienburg)
2881531		
EDDIE, GEORGE		KIA
2881668		
Eddie, Roger		344 (Lamsdorf)
2881481		
Edgar, John	No Photo	N/a – Escaped
6630518		
Edwards, C.W.	No Photo	XXB (Marienburg)
6137956		
Edwards, William	No Photo	344 (Lamsdorf)
2876036		
Elder, Robert		344 (Lamsdorf)
2876579		
Elliott, William	No Photo	XXB (Marienburg)
2874710		
Ellis, Anthony	No Photo	344 (Lamsdorf)
2076740		
Ellis, James	No Photo	XXB (Marienburg)
2878397		
Elphinstone, Alex	No Photo	XXID (Poznan)
2882906		
Elrick, Alexander	No Photo	XXA (Thorn)
2880806		
Elrick, William		IXC (Muhlhausen)
2881977		
EMSLIE, ARTHUR	No Photo	KIA
2877212		

Name	Photo	PoW Camp
Emslie, James	No Photo	XXB (Marienburg)
2880475		
Endersby, Jack		383 (Hohenfels)
2876842		
England, Ralph		IXC (Muhlhausen)
2881430		
Espie, Alexander	No Photo	XXA (Thorn)
2880756		
Esson, William	No Photo	383 (Hohenfels)
2881467		
Ettles, William J.		XXB (Marienburg)
2876049		
Evans, William	No Photo	XXA (Thorn)
2874359		
Evans, W.O.	No Photo	XXB (Marienburg)
3852682		
Ewen, Harry		VIIA (Mooseburg)
2875146		
Ewen, Harry		383 (Hohenfels)
2876497		
Ewen, James		344 (Lamsdorf)
2876775		
Ewen, John		XXB (Marienburg)
2877166		

Name	Photo	PoW Camp
Ewen, Robert	No Photo	344 (Lamsdorf)
2877613		
Ewen, William		N/a – Escaped
2875565		
Fairbairn, William	No Photo	XXB (Marienburg)
2883268		
FAIREY, THOMAS		KIA
2879185		
Falconer, Harry	No Photo	XXA (Thorn)
2873604		
Falconer, James		XXA (Thorn)
2877838		
Farquhar, Alex	No Photo	XXB (Marienburg)
2881922		
Farquhar, Charles	No Photo	XXB (Marienburg)
2881836		
Farquhar, G.L.		Unknown
Unknown		
Farquhar, James	No Photo	XXB (Marienburg)
2882938		
Farquhar, James C.	No Photo	XXA (Thorn)
2877957		
Farquhar, Robert		XXB (Marienburg)
2878977		
Farquhar, Thomas		11B (Fallingbostel)
2879074		

Name / Army Number	Photo	PoW Camp
Farrell, Jack / 2879393	No Photo	383 (Hohenfels)
Farrington, James / 2883311	No Photo	XXB (Marienburg)
Fawns, Edward / 2873780	No Photo	383 (Hohenfels)
Ferguson, James / 2882485	No Photo	383 (Hohenfels)
Ferguson, Robert / 2883243	No Photo	XXA (Thorn)
Ferguson, Thomas / 2883877	No Photo	IXC (Muhlhausen)
Ferguson, William / 2876066	No Photo	XXA (Thorn)
Ferries, Nathaniel / 2881699		XXB (Marienburg)
Ferry, Charles / 2883878	No Photo	IXC (Muhlhausen)
Fettes, Andrew / 2883797		IXC (Muhlhausen)
Fettes, James / 2880539	No Photo	IXC (Muhlhausen)
Fincham, J. / 6139756	No Photo	383 (Hohenfels)
Findell, H. / 4855011	No Photo	IXC (Muhlhausen)
Findlay, Alexander / 859420	No Photo	XXB (Marienburg)
Findlay, Robert / 2873931	No Photo	XXB (Marienburg)
Findlay, Alexander / 2880755	No Photo	IXC (Muhlhausen)

Name / Army Number	Photo	PoW Camp
Findlay, Thomas / 2883822	No Photo	XXID (Poznan)
Finnie, Alexander / 2880710	No Photo	344 (Lamsdorf)
Finnie, John / 2876586		383 (Hohenfels)
Fitzgerald, J.J. / 6221035	No Photo	XXA (Thorn)
Flinn, George / 2880094	No Photo	344 (Lamsdorf)
Flockhart, Thomas / 2876815		VIIIB (Teschen)
Forbes, Alexander / 2882828	No Photo	344 (Lamsdorf)
Forbes, Alexander Christie / 2879116		XXB (Marienburg)
FORBES, DOUGLAS / 3318438	No Photo	KIA
Forbes, Edwin / 2865879	No Photo	XXA (Thorn)
Forbes, George / 2880023		344 (Lamsdorf)
Forbes, George / 2881190	No Photo	XXID (Poznan)
Forbes, Robert / 2874781	No Photo	XXB (Marienburg)
Forbes, William / 2877408	No Photo	XXB (Marienburg)

Name	Photo	PoW Camp
Army Number		
Ford, Phillip	No Photo	XXA (Thorn)
2883184		
Forrest, Charles	No Photo	344 (Lamsdorf)
2881746		
Forrest, Eric	No Photo	XXB (Marienburg)
2882874		
Forrester, Hugh	No Photo	344 (Lamsdorf)
2879447		
Forsyth, George		344 (Lamsdorf)
2881871		
Forsyth, Herbert	No Photo	XXA (Thorn)
2873758		
Forsyth, Roderick	No Photo	344 (Lamsdorf)
2874492		
FORSYTH, WALTER	No Photo	KIA
2882942		
Forsyth, William		XXA (Thorn)
2881191		
Foster, C.	No Photo	XXB (Marienburg)
4854739		
Foster, Henry	No Photo	Evacuated
Unknown		
FRAME, ROBERT	No Photo	Died Calvarienberg Hospital
3247891		
Fraser, Alexander	No Photo	344 (Lamsdorf)
2875014		
Fraser, Archibald	No Photo	XXB (Marienburg)
2872543		
Fraser, Charles	No Photo	344 (Lamsdorf)
2882880		
Fraser, Cuthbert	No Photo	IXC (Muhlhausen)
2873950		

Name	Photo	PoW Camp
Army Number		
Fraser, David	No Photo	XXB (Marienburg)
2873579		
Fraser, Douglas		344 (Lamsdorf)
2880587		
Fraser, Frank	No Photo	IXC (Muhlhausen)
2881370		
Fraser, George M	No Photo	344 (Lamsdorf)
2874187		
Fraser, George	No Photo	344 (Lamsdorf)
2880156		
Fraser, J.	No Photo	383 (Hohenfels)
2866658		
Fraser, James	No Photo	XXID (Poznan)
2874963		
Fraser, John	No Photo	IXC (Muhlhausen)
2883275		
Fraser, John A.	No Photo	XXB (Marienburg)
2882844		
Fraser, John McD.	No Photo	XXB (Marienburg)
2873527		
FRASER, RICHARD DANIEL		KIA
2868354		
Fraser, Thomas	No Photo	IXC (Muhlhausen)
2883137		
Freel, Lawrence	No Photo	344 (Lamsdorf)
2874571		
Fullerton Charles	No Photo	N/a – Escaped
2871816		
Fullerton David	No Photo	XXA (Thorn)
2874593		

Name	Photo	PoW Camp
Army Number		
Fullerton, Charles		N/a
2871816		
Fulton, William	No Photo	XXB (Marienburg)
2883284		
FYFE, ALEXANDER	No Photo	Died of wounds
2883094		
Fyfe, John	No Photo	344 (Lamsdorf)
2874444		
Fyfe, William	No Photo	344 (Lamsdorf)
2880408		
Gair, Henry	No Photo	XXA (Thorn)
2874831		
Glashan, Robert	No Photo	XXB (Marienburg)
2877864		
Galbraith, Joseph	No Photo	XXA (Thorn)
2883206		
Gall, George		IXC (Muhlhausen)
2928930		
Gall, Herbert		O.VIIB (Eischstätt)
78973		
Gammack, Alexander		IXC (Muhlhausen)
2878808		
Gammack, Douglas		IXC (Muhlhausen)
2878630		
Ganson, James		IXC (Muhlhausen)
2881669		

Name	Photo	PoW Camp
Army Number		
GARDEN, EDWARD	No Photo	Died at XXB (Marienburg)
2877210		
GARDEN, GEORGE	No Photo	KIA
2878398		
Garden, William		IXC (Muhlhausen)
2876029		
Garden, W.M.R.	No Photo	344 (Lamsdorf)
2822304		
Gardener, James	No Photo	IXC (Muhlhausen)
2878968		
Gardener, Robert	No Photo	XXB (Marienburg)
2879474		
Garner, Alfred	No Photo	344 (Lamsdorf)
2871162		
Garrick, John	No Photo	344 (Lamsdorf)
2871720		
Gaull, James		IXC (Muhlhausen)
2878780		
Gavin, John		344 (Lamsdorf)
2001192		
Geater, Richard	No Photo	XXB (Marienburg)
2883940		
Geddes, Andrew		XXB (Marienburg)
2881521		
Geddes, G.A.M.		O.VIIB (Eischstätt)
69906		

Name / Army Number	Photo	PoW Camp
Geddes, George / 2878986		344 (Lamsdorf)
Geddes, James / 2882010	No Photo	XXB (Marienburg)
Geddes, John / 2875606		383 (Hohenfels)
Geddes, William / 2875159	No Photo	XXB (Marienburg)
GEORGE, HERBERT / 2873791	No Photo	Died of wounds
Gerrard, George / 2881501	No Photo	IXC (Muhlhausen)
Gerrard, George / 2881792	No Photo	IXC (Muhlhausen)
Gerrard, John / 2881502	No Photo	IXC (Muhlhausen)
GERRIE, ANDREW / 2874081		KIA
Gibb, Douglas / 2880436	No Photo	XXB (Marienburg)
Gibb, George / 2875964		XXB (Marienburg)
Gibb, William / 2880711		344 (Lamsdorf)
Gibbon, George / 2876045		383 (Hohenfels)

Name / Army Number	Photo	PoW Camp
Gibson, Harold / 2873710	No Photo	11A (Altengrabow)
Gibson, H. / 3247873	No Photo	XXA (Thorn)
Gibson, John / 2879437	No Photo	344 (Lamsdorf)
Gilbert, E. / 4854675	No Photo	344 (Lamsdorf)
Gilhooley, John / 2883178	No Photo	344 (Lamsdorf)
Gillies, James / 2882837	No Photo	344 (Lamsdorf)
Gilmour, W.C. / 3307693	No Photo	383 (Hohenfels)
Gilsenan, Thomas / 2882948	No Photo	344 (Lamsdorf)
GIRVAN, WILLIAM / 2691991	No Photo	KIA
Glancy, Mark / 2883192	No Photo	XXB (Marienburg)
Glass, Stanley / 2872812	No Photo	344 (Lamsdorf)
Glennie, James / 2874586		BAB 20 (Hydebreck
Goodall, Charles / 2874351	No Photo	344 (Lamsdorf)
Goodbrand, James / 2880613		IXC (Muhlhausen)
Goodfellow, William / 2872927	No Photo	XXID (Poznan)

Name	Photo	PoW Camp
Army Number		
Goodwin, F.	No Photo	Evacuated
6086574		
Goonan, Martin	No Photo	XXA (Thorn)
2883987		
Gordon, Alexander		IXC (Muhlhausen)
2875845		
Gordon, Alexander		XXB (Marienburg)
2876133		
Gordon, Alexander		XXA (Thorn)
2876428		
Gordon, Alfred	No Photo	VIIIB (Teschen)
2877810		
Gordon, D.G.I.A.		Unknown
Unknown		
GORDON, DOUGLAS W	No Photo	KIA
11557		
Gordon, James	No Photo	VIIIB (Teschen)
2875370		
Gordon, James	No Photo	344 (Lamsdorf)
2877605		
Gordon, John	No Photo	XXB (Marienburg)
2874933		
Gordon, Lewis	No Photo	O.VIIB (Eischstätt)
85691		
Gordon, Robert	No Photo	XXB (Marienburg)
3051578		
Gordon, Thomas	No Photo	344 (Lamsdorf)
2880201		

Name	Photo	PoW Camp
Army Number		
Gordon, William	No Photo	344 (Lamsdorf)
2876058		
GORDON, WILLIAM	No Photo	KIA
2881747		
Gordon, William C.	No Photo	XXB (Marienburg)
2878652		
Gordon, William J.	No Photo	VIIIB (Teschen)
2878413		
Gourlay, John Anderson	No Photo	XXB (Marienburg)
2883272		
Gourley, George	No Photo	XXB (Marienburg)
2883880		
Gow, James	No Photo	383 (Hohenfels)
2883050		
GRAHAM, DAVID	No Photo	KIA
7010626		
Graham, Donald	No Photo	344 (Lamsdorf)
2879481		
Graham, James	No Photo	344 (Lamsdorf)
2877893		
Graham, T.	No Photo	XXA (Thorn)
4275486		
Graham, William		VIIIA (Gorlitz)
2870772		
GRANT, ALEXANDER	No Photo	KIA
2873960		
Grant, Alexander Reid		XXB (Marienburg)
2883988		
Grant, Charles	No Photo	357 (Kopernikus)
2875005		

Name / Army Number	Photo	PoW Camp
Grant, Charles / 2876445		XXA (Thorn)
Grant, David / 2026877	No Photo	XXA (Thorn)
Grant, George / 2879065		XXB (Marienburg)
Grant, James Ian / 2876475	No Photo	344 (Lamsdorf)
Grant, James M. / 2882863	No Photo	XXA (Thorn)
Grant, William / 2882904	No Photo	383 (Hohenfels)
Grassick, John / 2880800	No Photo	344 (Lamsdorf)
Gray, Albert / 2876878		XXA (Thorn)
Gray, Alexander / 2873036	No Photo	344 (Lamsdorf)
GRAY, ALEXANDER / 2880589		Died of wounds
Gray, Alexander / 2882011	No Photo	XXB (Marienburg)
Gray, Alexander K. / 2878399	No Photo	IXC (Muhlhausen)
Gray, Allen / 2879515	No Photo	XXA (Thorn)

Name / Army Number	Photo	PoW Camp
Gray, Arthur / 2882366		344 (Lamsdorf)
Gray, George / 2879154		XXA (Thorn)
Gray, George B. / 2882352	No Photo	XXB (Marienburg)
Gray, James / 2881894	No Photo	8A (Gorlitz)
Gray, James D. / 2881700		XXB (Marienburg)
Gray, Leslie / 2875069		344 (Lamsdorf)
Gray, Norman / 2877778		O.IXA (Spangenburg)
Gray, Robert / 2882951	No Photo	XXA (Thorn)
Gray, Thomas A. / 2875068		344 (Lamsdorf)
Gray, Thomas C. / 2873676		IXC (Muhlhausen)
Gray, Walter / 2883882	No Photo	XXA (Thorn)

Name	Photo	PoW Camp
Army Number		
Gray, William	No Photo	344 (Lamsdorf)
2881978		
Gray, William Park	No Photo	XXA (Thorn)
2882033		
Green, Peter		344 (Lamsdorf)
2875510		
Greig, David		XXB (Marienburg)
2882461		
Greig, Hugh	No Photo	Repatriated October 1943
2874595		
Greig, Lawrie	No Photo	IXC (Muhlhausen)
807543		
Greig, Peter	No Photo	IXC (Muhlhausen)
2883823		
Greig, William		VIIIB (Teschen)
2879373		
Grieve, W.F.		Early repatriation
Unknown		
Griffin, John	No Photo	XXB (Marienburg)
2883884		
Gunn, Alexander	No Photo	XXB (Marienburg)
2875388		
Guthrie, Hugh		344 (Lamsdorf)
2874150		

Name	Photo	PoW Camp
Army Number		
Guthrie, James		IXC (Muhlhausen)
2883791		
Guthrie, William		344 (Lamsdorf)
2876817		
Guy, James	No Photo	XXA (Thorn)
2883886		
Hadden, George		XXB (Marienburg)
2882323		
Hadden, John		383 (Hohenfels)
2879197		
Hadden, Stephen		IXC (Muhlhausen)
2883068		
Haig, Robert	No Photo	344 (Lamsdorf)
1669797		
Haines, John		IXC (Muhlhausen)
2876759		
Hall, James	No Photo	344 (Lamsdorf)
2874964		
Halliday, Gavin		344 (Lamsdorf)
2873562		
Hamilton, Alexander		IXC (Muhlhausen)
2883917		
Hamilton, Gavin	No Photo	XXA (Thorn)
2883887		

Name / Army Number	Photo	PoW Camp
Hamilton, James / 2883911	No Photo	XXB (Marienburg)
Hamilton, John / 2883889	No Photo	IXC (Muhlhausen)
Hamilton, W. / 3313773	No Photo	XXA (Thorn)
Hamilton, William E. / 2883890	No Photo	XXB (Marienburg)
Hanlon, W. / 4265907	No Photo	XXB (Marienburg)
Hanna, David / 2876621		XXA (Thorn)
Hannah, John / 2883891	No Photo	344 (Lamsdorf)
Hardie, Alexander / 2875493		344 (Lamsdorf)
Hardie, Nathaniel / 2875498	No Photo	11B (Fallingbostel)
Hardie, William / 2875498		O.VIIB (Eichstatt)
Hare, Andrew / 2883892	No Photo	344 (Lamsdorf)
Harkness, Robert / 2876900		XXB (Marienburg)
Harper, Alexander / 2879108		Escaped

Name / Army Number	Photo	PoW Camp
Harper, James / 2872764		XXB (Marienburg)
Harper, William / 2875484		XXB (Marienburg)
Harris, Harry / 909873		XXA (Thorn)
HARRISON, DAVID / 2874463	No Photo	KIA
HARRISON, LEONARD / 2873529	No Photo	KIA
Harrop, J. / 6910752	No Photo	344 (Lamsdorf)
Harrower, Douglas / 2878132	No Photo	KIA
Hartie, J. / 410134	No Photo	IXC (Muhlhausen)
Harvey, David / 2882879	No Photo	XXB (Marienburg)
Hastie, Robert / 2882830		XXB (Marienburg)
Hastings, R.J. / 2876986	No Photo	XXID (Poznan)
Hatt, John / 2881533	No Photo	XXA (Thorn)
Hattemore, Arthur / 2873724		344 (Lamsdorf)

Name / Army Number	Photo	PoW Camp
Hay, Albert / 2879213	No Photo	XXB (Marienburg)
Hay, Alexander / 2876658	No Photo	XXB (Marienburg)
HAY, CHARLES / 2875401		KIA
Hay, Douglas / 2881701	No Photo	XXB (Marienburg)
Hay, G / 3051633	No Photo	XXB (Marienburg)
HAY, GEORGE / 2875503		KIA
Hay, George R. / 2875949		XXB (Marienburg)
Hay, James / 2882897	No Photo	XXB (Marienburg)
Hay, Joseph / 2871889	No Photo	344 (Lamsdorf)
Hay, P. Brian / 77689		O.VIIB (Eischstätt)
Hay, William / 2875105	No Photo	344 (Lamsdorf)
Hayes, C. / 5824287	No Photo	XXB (Marienburg)
Hayton, Cyril / 2876936	No Photo	344 (Lamsdorf)
Heafield, Albert / 2876539		XXA (Thorn)

Name / Army Number	Photo	PoW Camp
Heatherwick, George / 2878311		IXC (Muhlhausen)
Henderson, Charles / 2880092	No Photo	XXA (Thorn)
Henderson, Dawson / 2880477	No Photo	344 (Lamsdorf)
HENDERSON, GEORGE / 2875481		KIA
Henderson, John / 2883149	No Photo	XXB (Marienburg)
Henderson, John / 2883894	No Photo	N/a – Escaped
Henderson, Peter / 2884026	No Photo	344 (Lamsdorf)
Henderson, William / 2881332	No Photo	XXA (Thorn)
Hendry, James / 2871433	No Photo	XXB (Marienburg)
Hendry, Lewis / 2881703		IXC (Muhlhausen)
Henry, Archibald / 2881886		XXA (Thorn)
Henshall, Philip / 2873845	No Photo	344 (Lamsdorf)
Hepburn, Archibald / 2873454		344 (Lamsdorf)

Name	Photo	PoW Camp
Army Number		
Hibbs, John	No Photo	Escaped
Unknown		
Highet, Hugh	No Photo	344 (Lamsdorf)
2876078		
Hignett, George	No Photo	Escaped
2874699		
Hill, Alex	No Photo	XXB (Marienburg)
2873208		
Hill, Cecil		XXB (Marienburg)
2881324		
Hill, T.	No Photo	344 (Lamsdorf)
3241738		
Hilton, A.	No Photo	XXB (Marienburg)
6780644		
Hilton, William		383 (Hohenfels)
2869924		
Hinds, Robert J.	No Photo	XXB (Marienburg)
2872428		
Hird, Duncan	No Photo	IXC (Muhlhausen)
2877913		
Hird, George	No Photo	XXB (Marienburg)
2877914		
Holmes, Albert		344 (Lamsdorf)
2829312		
Holmes, Gordon		XXB (Marienburg)
2879263		
Home, William	No Photo	344 (Lamsdorf)
2878087		

Name	Photo	PoW Camp
Army Number		
Hood, David	No Photo	IXC (Muhlhausen)
2883265		
Horn, James		XXB (Marienburg)
2876012		
Horne, J.		XXA (Thorn)
3054343		
Hosie, Jack	No Photo	XXA (Thorn)
2881368		
Houston, Robert	No Photo	XXA (Thorn)
2881704		
Houston, Samuel		N/a
2877854		
HOWELLS, WILLIAM	No Photo	Died at 344 (Lamsdorf)
2876782		
Howie, William		IXC (Muhlhausen)
2878631		
HOWISON, ROBERT	No Photo	Died of wounds
2872385		
Hudson, Henry		XXA (Thorn)
3307891		
Hudson, R.F.	No Photo	XXB (Marienburg)
4272364		
Hughes, Arthur	No Photo	XXID (Poznan)
2883300		
Hughes, C.B.		O.VIIB (Eischstätt)
195384		

Name	Photo	PoW Camp
Army Number		
Hughes, D.	No Photo	XXB (Marienburg)
3052928		
Hughes, Francis	No Photo	XXB (Marienburg)
2879518		
Hulls, Leslie	No Photo	Escaped
Unknown		
HUME, LAWRENCE	No Photo	Died of wounds
2882958		
Hunt, William	No Photo	XXB (Marienburg)
2044521		
Hunter, George		344 (Lamsdorf)
2873927		
Hunter, James		XXB (Marienburg)
2876689		
Hunter, John		XXB (Marienburg)
2874961		
Hunter, Robert	No Photo	IXC (Muhlhausen)
2882014		
Hutcheon, Archibald		XXB (Marienburg)
2880059		
HUTCHEON, JOHN		Died at XXA (Thorn)
2881534		
Hutcheon, Richard		IXC (Muhlhausen)
2878474		

Name	Photo	PoW Camp
Army Number		
Hutcheon, William		XXB (Marienburg)
2881535		
Hutchins, C.D.McD.		O.IXA/H (Spangenburg)
5205		
Hutchinson, John	No Photo	XXB (Marienburg)
2874114		
Hutchison, Robert	No Photo	XXID (Poznan)
2879468		
Hutton, Robert		XXB (Marienburg)
2881536		
Imlach, Douglas		344 (Lamsdorf)
2882836		
Imlach, William		XXB (Marienburg)
2876631		
Ingle, J.R.	No Photo	383 (Hohenfels)
5044830		
INGLIS, ALEXANDER		KIA
2876451		
Inglis, William		383 (Hohenfels)
2873017		
Ingram, David		IXC (Muhlhausen)
2876531		

Name	Photo	PoW Camp
Army Number		
Ingram, Forbes	No Photo	344 (Lamsdorf)
2878705		
Ingram, Peter		383 (Hohenfels)
2876516		
INGRAM, ROBERT		Killed escaping
2882961		
Innes, Alexander	No Photo	XXID (Poznan)
2878688		
INNES, ALEXANDER K.	No Photo	KIA
2879251		
INNES, DOUGLAS	No Photo	KIA
105768		
Innes, George		IXC (Muhlhausen)
2878632		
Innes, James		Evacuated
Unknown		
Innes, John		383 (Hohenfels)
2876556		
Innes, Robert	No Photo	344 (Lamsdorf)
2876556		
Ironside, Leslie		IXC (Muhlhausen)
2879070		
Irvine, Charles		XXB (Marienburg)
2880718		

Name	Photo	PoW Camp
Army Number		
Irvine, Edward		XXB (Marienburg)
2880719		
Irvine, Joseph	No Photo	XXID (Poznan)
2882962		
Isaac, James	No Photo	344 (Lamsdorf)
2873941		
Jack, John		XXB (Marienburg)
2881572		
Jackson, John		XXID (Poznan)
2875393		
Jaffrey, George	No Photo	344 (Lamsdorf)
2875689		
Jaffrey, James		XXB (Marienburg)
2879254		
James Packman	No Photo	XXB (Marienburg)
2873772		
Jamieson, George	No Photo	344 (Lamsdorf)
2874446		
Jamieson, James		344 (Lamsdorf)
2876014		
Jamieson, Wilfred		N/a – Escaped
2876440		
Jamieson, William	No Photo	XXB (Marienburg)
2881483		

Name / Army Number	Photo	PoW Camp
Jamieson, William / 2871802		IXC (Muhlhausen)
Jamieson, William / 2883828		IXC (Muhlhausen)
Jappy, Alex / 2872548		344 (Lamsdorf)
Jarvis, John / 2881705		IXC (Muhlhausen)
Jeal, Archibald / 2746436	No Photo	IXC (Muhlhausen)
Jeffray, Robert S / 2875621	No Photo	344 (Lamsdorf)
Jenson, Harry / 2873069	No Photo	XXID (Poznan)
Jessiman, Albert / 2880757		344 (Lamsdorf)
Johnson, James / 2879375	No Photo	344 (Lamsdorf)
Johnston, Alex / 2879075		XXA (Thorn)
Johnston, James / 2873815		BAB 20 (Hydebreck)
Johnston, James Lyon (Alias Lyon, J.) / 2874282	No Photo	XXA (Thorn)

Name / Army Number	Photo	PoW Camp
Johnston, James / 2882701	No Photo	XXA (Thorn)
JOHNSTON, JOSEPH / 2882353	No Photo	KIA
Johnston, Thomas / 2875472		XXA (Thorn)
Johnstone, Frederick / 2881330		IXC (Muhlhausen)
JOHNSTONE, JAMES / 2883931	No Photo	KIA
Johnstone, Robert / 2879259	No Photo	XXB (Marienburg)
Johnstone, Thomas / 2876369	No Photo	XXA (Thorn)
Jolly, Robert / 2879461	No Photo	XXB (Marienburg)
Jones, Andrew / 2883321	No Photo	344 (Lamsdorf)
Keating, Alexander / 2871778	No Photo	XXA (Thorn)
Keenan, Tomas / 2876529		4A (Hohenstein)
Keiller, A. / 2879168	No Photo	344 (Lamsdorf)
Keith, Alexander / 2882511	No Photo	IXC (Muhlhausen)
Keith, Angus Nelson / 2883078		344 (Lamsdorf)

Name / Army Number	Photo	PoW Camp
Keith, Nelson 75281		O.VIIB (Eischstätt)
Keith, Robert 2883808	No Photo	XXA (Thorn)
Keith, William 2883939	No Photo	344 (Lamsdorf)
Kelly, Thomas 3051206	No Photo	11A (Altengrabow)
Kelman, John 2869703	No Photo	XXB (Marienburg)
Kemp, Alexander 2882867		IXC (Muhlhausen)
Kemp, James (Peter) 2871872		344 (Lamsdorf)
Kennedy, Robert 2879071		XXID (Poznan)
Kerr, Allan 2876904		344 (Lamsdorf)
Kerr, James 2876600		344 (Lamsdorf)
KERR, WILLIAM 2873692	No Photo	KIA
Kilgour, Ronald 2880375	No Photo	IXC (Muhlhausen)
Killem, J. 3308598	No Photo	344 (Lamsdorf)

Name / Army Number	Photo	PoW Camp
Kimmett, Andrew 2879320	No Photo	XXID (Poznan)
Kindness, Alex. 2879267	No Photo	IXC (Muhlhausen)
Kindness, Robert 2874966	No Photo	XXB (Marienburg)
King, Albert 2882818		IXC (Muhlhausen)
King, Arthur Unknown	No Photo	Repatriated in October 1943
KING, HAROLD 2881749	No Photo	XXID (Poznan)
King, John 2879530	No Photo	XXB (Marienburg)
Kinnear, J.W. 2882966	No Photo	XXA (Thorn)
Kinning, Samuel 2879488	No Photo	XXA (Thorn)
Kirk, George 2883897	No Photo	IXC (Muhlhausen)
Kirkwood, Samuel 2883898	No Photo	Wounded; possibly evacuated
Knight, Alan 2880410	No Photo	344 (Lamsdorf)
Knight, R.J. 4685538	No Photo	XXB (Marienburg)
Knowles, Rodney 2880682	No Photo	344 (Lamsdorf)
Knox, Harry 2882965		IXC (Muhlhausen)
Kydd, Alexander Unknown	No Photo	Escaped

Name	Photo	PoW Camp
Army Number		
Kynoch, Hector	No Photo	344 (Lamsdorf)
2877015		
Kynoch, Thomas	No Photo	XXB (Marienburg)
2874386		
Laing, Peter	No Photo	XXA (Thorn)
2882064		
LAING, WILLIAM		Died - XXB (Marienburg)
2881421		
Laird, William	No Photo	XXID (Poznan)
2883855		
LAMBERT, JOHN		KIA
2876835		
Lamont, William	No Photo	XXID (Poznan)
2883856		
Lang, DB	No Photo	XXA (Thorn)
3247783		
Langham, G.A.	No Photo	0.9A/Z (Rotenburg Fulda)
75930		
Langham, Mike		0.9A/Z (Rotenburg Fulda)
78866		
Law, John	No Photo	XXA (Thorn)
2874895		
Lawrence, Andrew	No Photo	XXID (Poznan)
2873513		
Lawrence, T.W.E.	No Photo	IXC (Muhlhausen)
3319000		
LAWRIE, ALEXANDER		KIA
2869057		

Name	Photo	PoW Camp
Army Number		
Lawrie, Alexander		XXB (Marienburg)
2881334		
Lawrie, George		XXA (Thorn)
2882815		
Lawrie, William H.		IXC (Muhlhausen)
65061		
Lawrie, William R.		344 (Lamsdorf)
2874360		
Lawson, William	No Photo	344 (Lamsdorf)
2875015		
Laybourn, Ernest	No Photo	XXID (Poznan)
2875123		
Leal, Edward	No Photo	344 (Lamsdorf)
2874960		
Leal, John	No Photo	XXB (Marienburg)
2875169		
Learmouth, John		XXB (Marienburg)
2879030		
LEASK, EDWARD		KIA
2875271		
Lee, J.H.	No Photo	IXC (Muhlhausen)
3319001		
Lee, Joseph H.		IXC (Muhlhausen)
4267734		

Name	Photo	PoW Camp
Army Number		
Lee, R	No Photo	344 (Lamsdorf)
4798846		
LEEL, JAMES	No Photo	KIA
2968660		
Leighton, Alexander		IXC (Muhlhausen)
2875447		
Leighton, Charles	No Photo	344 (Lamsdorf)
2881432		
Leighton, Ronald		344 (Lamsdorf)
2876522		
Leiper, John		XXA (Thorn)
2884002		
Leiper, William	No Photo	XXB (Marienburg)
918781		
Leitch, George	No Photo	XXB (Marienburg)
2565576		
Leitch, James	No Photo	XXB (Marienburg)
2877705		
Leslie, Alexander	No Photo	XXA (Thorn)
2878296		
Leslie, Andrew	No Photo	XXB (Marienburg)
2883104		
Leslie, John		383 (Hohenfels)
2875559		
Linden, Thomas	No Photo	344 (Lamsdorf)
2882824		
Lindsay, J.	No Photo	383 (Hohenfels)
3300304		

Name	Photo	PoW Camp
Army Number		
Lindsay, John	No Photo	XXB (Marienburg)
3319082		
Linklater, Andrew	No Photo	XXB (Marienburg)
2873778		
Linton, William		344 (Lamsdorf)
2875435		
Lippe, James	No Photo	IXC (Muhlhausen)
2878878		
Little, C.	No Photo	XXB (Marienburg)
3318589		
Little, Robert	No Photo	XXB (Marienburg)
2882895		
Littlejohn, Albert		XXA (Thorn)
2882870		
Littlejohn, Colin	No Photo	XXB (Marienburg)
2882970		
Littlejohn, George	No Photo	383 (Hohenfels)
2874433		
Livingstone, Robert		Unknown
2878475		
Livingstone, Samuel	No Photo	344 (Lamsdorf)
2883927		
LOGAN, ANDREW	No Photo	KIA
2873516		
Logan, George	No Photo	XXB (Marienburg)
2883193		
Logan, John	No Photo	XXB (Marienburg)
2884016		
Logan, Robert	No Photo	Unknown
2875442		

Name	Photo	PoW Camp
Army Number		
LOMAS, SAMUEL		KIA
3529319		
Longmuir, Alfred	No Photo	XXID (Poznan)
2877836		
Lonsdale, J.H.	No Photo	XXB (Marienburg)
5049231		
Looker, R.J.	No Photo	XXB (Marienburg)
3319114		
Loughren, John R.	No Photo	XXA (Thorn)
2866269		
Love, William		XXB (Marienburg)
2879064		
Lovegrove, Hubert	No Photo	XXA (Thorn)
6137165		
Lovie, Henry R.	No Photo	XXB (Marienburg)
2877604		
Low, Alexander	No Photo	XXB (Marienburg)
2883200		
Low, Robert	No Photo	XXB (Marienburg)
2873122		
LOWE, ALEXANDER		KIA
2878526		
Lowe, George	No Photo	IXC (Muhlhausen)
2880024		
Lowery, T.	No Photo	IXC (Muhlhausen)
3319002		
Lowes, L.B.	No Photo	XXB (Marienburg)
3319003		
Lyddiatt, George	No Photo	XXA (Thorn)
2871551		

Name	Photo	PoW Camp
Army Number		
Lydon, J.	No Photo	IXC (Muhlhausen)
3319005		
Lyon, Alexander	No Photo	Repatriated October 1943
2870623		
Lyon, John C.	No Photo	344 (Lamsdorf)
2882331		
Macara, W.J.B.	No Photo	383 (Hohenfels)
3054340		
Macaulay, John	No Photo	Escaped
3245405		
Macaulay, Robert	No Photo	XXB (Marienburg)
2883986		
MacDonald, Edward	No Photo	VIIIA (Gorlitz)
2873475		
MacDonald, George	No Photo	BAB 20 (Hydebreck
3319037		
Macdonald, Ian	No Photo	383 (Hohenfels)
2883210		
Macdonald, James		XXA (Thorn)
2873448		
Macdonald, James	No Photo	XXA (Thorn)
2873677		
Macdonald, John	No Photo	XXID (Poznan)
2884054		
Macdonald, John G.	No Photo	XXA (Thorn)
2883942		
MacDonald, Percy	No Photo	XXB (Marienburg)
2874995		
MacDonald, Robert		XXIB (Schubin)
2876479		

Name	Photo	PoW Camp
Army Number		
MacDuff, R.J.A.	No Photo	344 (Lamsdorf)
2882243		
MacEwan, Duncan	No Photo	XXB (Marienburg)
6210423		
MacFarquhar, Harold	No Photo	XXB (Marienburg)
2874679		
MacGuinness, P.	No Photo	XXA (Thorn)
3319062		
Mack, Edward	No Photo	383 (Hohenfels)
2871421		
Mackay, A	No Photo	XXA (Thorn)
2820312		
Mackay, Colin	No Photo	IXC (Muhlhausen)
2881195		
Mackay, James		344 (Lamsdorf)
2876007		
MacKenzie, Daniel	No Photo	XXB (Marienburg)
2874142		
MACKENZIE, KENNETH	No Photo	Died at 344 (Lamsdorf)
2879808		
Mackie, Albert	No Photo	344 (Lamsdorf)
2867920		
Mackie, Alan	No Photo	IXC (Muhlhausen)
2873261		
Mackie, Alexander		XXB (Marienburg)
2876523		
Mackie, James		Repatriated October 1943
2869208		

Name	Photo	PoW Camp
Army Number		
Mackie, John	No Photo	IXC (Muhlhausen)
2883107		
Mackie, John		4G (Oschatz)
2881196		
MACKINTOSH, MALCOLM	No Photo	Died trying to escape
2882858		
Maclean, Maurice		344 (Lamsdorf)
2756514		
MacLennan, J.	No Photo	344 (Lamsdorf)
2820886		
Macleod, W.	No Photo	383 (Hohenfels)
2816110		
MacMillan, J.	No Photo	IXC (Muhlhausen)
2877677		
MacQueen, Alexander	No Photo	Escaped
2877677		
Maitland, John		344 (Lamsdorf)
2881504		
Maitland, William		XXB (Marienburg)
2877427		
Malcolm, A.	No Photo	XXA (Thorn)
2814940		
Marr, Edward	No Photo	XXA (Thorn)
2875641		
Marr, George		11B (Fallingbostel)
2875564		

Name	Photo	PoW Camp
Army Number		
Marr, James		XXA (Thorn)
2875212		
Marshall, Richard	No Photo	Repatriated October 1943
Unknown		
Marshall, T.	No Photo	Unknown
2867523		
Marshall, Victor		383 (Hohenfels)
2878708		
Martell, Albert		XXB (Marienburg)
2876686		
MARTIN, ROBERT		KIA
2032977		
Martin, W.D.	No Photo	XXB (Marienburg)
3318867		
Massie, James	No Photo	XXID (Poznan)
2877317		
MASSIE, WILLIAM	No Photo	KIA
2869613		
Masson, J.		XXA (Thorn)
2882761		
Masson, William	No Photo	N/a – Escaped
2874921		
Mathers, Edward	No Photo	XXB (Marienburg)
2882776		
Mathers, Robert	No Photo	IXC (Muhlhausen)
2881683		

Name	Photo	PoW Camp
Army Number		
Matthew, David	No Photo	N/a – Escaped
2879344		
Matthews, D.P.P.	No Photo	XXA (Thorn)
2874371		
Mathewson, John		XXA (Thorn)
2058649		
Mathieson, George	No Photo	344 (Lamsdorf)
2879210		
Mathieson, J.H.	No Photo	XXA (Thorn)
3318776		
Matthewson, James	No Photo	344 (Lamsdorf)
3319008		
Maver, James		344 (Lamsdorf)
2876555		
McAllan, Norman		XXA (Thorn)
2881901		
McAllister, Hector	No Photo	344 (Lamsdorf)
2871360		
McAllister, Mungo	No Photo	344 (Lamsdorf)
2882986		
McAvoy, R.	No Photo	XXB (Marienburg)
3318826		
McBain, Alexander		IXC (Muhlhausen)
2879031		
McBain, Bertie	No Photo	XXB (Marienburg)
2878709		

Name / Army Number	Photo	PoW Camp
McBain, David / 2870474		XXA (Thorn)
McBean, J. / 2876871		XXA (Thorn)
McBeath, Robert / 2879211	No Photo	IXC (Muhlhausen)
McCabe, Peter / 2883133	No Photo	IXC (Muhlhausen)
McCallum, Ian / 2876585		XXB (Marienburg)
McCALLUM, WILLIAM / 2881197	No Photo	KIA
McCappin, Henry / 2882988	No Photo	344 (Lamsdorf)
McCarron, Philip / 2883301		Escaped
McCaskie, William / 2879480	No Photo	XXB (Marienburg)
McCleary, John / 2879523	No Photo	344 (Lamsdorf)
McCloskey, John / 2883254	No Photo	IXC (Muhlhausen)
McCLoy, Hugh / 2883924	No Photo	O.VIIB (Eischstätt)
McCormack, John / 2879227		Killed escaping

Name / Army Number	Photo	PoW Camp
McCowan, A.M. / 2816382	No Photo	XXA (Thorn)
McCRAW, LAWRENCE / 2876126	No Photo	KIA
McCulloch, J. / 3318824	No Photo	344 (Lamsdorf)
McCulloch, John / 2883285	No Photo	XXA (Thorn)
McDermott, George / 2874843	No Photo	XXID (Poznan)
McDermott, Peter / 2865960	No Photo	344 (Lamsdorf)
McDonald, David / 2881979		IXC (Muhlhausen)
McDonald, James / 2881371	No Photo	XXB (Marienburg)
McDonald, Matthew / 2883259	No Photo	Amputee; evacuated
McDonald, Percy / 2874995	No Photo	XXB (Marienburg)
McDonald, Robert / 2878962	No Photo	IXC (Muhlhausen)
McDONALD, ROBERT / 2883065	No Photo	KIA
McDonald, W. / 2830713	No Photo	344 (Lamsdorf)
McDonald, William / 2878097	No Photo	XXB (Marienburg)
McDonald, William / 2880155	No Photo	344 (Lamsdorf)

Name	Photo	PoW Camp
Army Number		
McDonald, Wilson	No Photo	IXC (Muhlhausen)
2880026		
McDougall, James	No Photo	XXA (Thorn)
2873853		
McDowall, Charles	No Photo	XXB (Marienburg)
2872464		
McEwan, T.	No Photo	XXA (Thorn)
3309454		
McFall, Harry		344 (Lamsdorf)
6075617		
McFarlane, John	No Photo	XXA (Thorn)
2883423		
McGarry, D.	No Photo	344 (Lamsdorf)
3247827		
McGarva, James	No Photo	344 (Lamsdorf)
866949		
McGeary, C.	No Photo	XXA (Thorn)
3319038		
McGhee, R.	No Photo	XXID (Poznan)
2191518		
McGillivray, James	No Photo	XXB (Marienburg)
2871836		
McGILLIVRAY, JOHN	No Photo	KIA
2883116		
McGregor, George	No Photo	XXB (Marienburg)
2879255		
McGregor, Isaac	No Photo	Evacuated wounded
2881329		
McGregor, James	No Photo	344 (Lamsdorf)
2879265		
McHardy, James	No Photo	XXA (Thorn)
2882995		

Name	Photo	PoW Camp
Army Number		
McHardy, William		383 (Hohenfels)
2873988		
McInnes, James	No Photo	XXB (Marienburg)
2871219		
McIntosh, Alexander		XXB (Marienburg)
2876912		
McINTOSH, ALEXANDER	No Photo	Died at XXB (Marienburg)
2882997		
McINTOSH, ANDREW	No Photo	KIA
2882848		
McIntosh, David		344 (Lamsdorf)
2872386		
McIntosh, Hector		IXC (Muhlhausen)
2871877		
McIntosh, James	No Photo	IXC (Muhlhausen)
2875905		
McIntosh, John	No Photo	344 (Lamsdorf)
2877101		
McIntosh, William	No Photo	344 (Lamsdorf)
2874620		
McIntyre, Robert	No Photo	XXB (Marienburg)
2882847		
McIvor, C.	No Photo	N/a – Escaped
2818602		
McKay, Albert	No Photo	344 (Lamsdorf)
2876413		

Name	Photo	PoW Camp
Army Number		
McKay, Daniel		344 (Lamsdorf)
2879467		
McKay, Edward		VIIIB (Teschen)
2876124		
McKAY, GEORGE	No Photo	shot escaping XXA (Thorn)
2871882		
McKay, G.H.	No Photo	IXC (Muhlhausen)
3319039		
McKay, John	No Photo	Repatriated 1943
2881503		
McKay, Maurice		XXB (Marienburg)
2875445		
McKay, Robert	No Photo	344 (Lamsdorf)
2883985		
McKee, Robert	No Photo	XXID (Poznan)
2883925		
McKENZIE KENNETH	No Photo	Died at XXIA (Schildberg)
2875808		
McKenzie, Alexander		XXID (Poznan)
2876008		
McKenzie, Alfred		BAB 20 (Hydebreck)
2881706		
McKenzie, Ian	No Photo	XXA (Thorn)
2879288		
McKibben, R.	No Photo	XXB (Marienburg)
3051455		
McKie, Frank	No Photo	XXB (Marienburg)
2879510		

Name	Photo	PoW Camp
Army Number		
McKie, W.	No Photo	XXB (Marienburg)
3319040		
McKinnon, John		IXC (Muhlhausen)
2876825		
McLaren, Frederick		VIIIC (Kunau Kz Sprottan)
2883842		
McLaren, Thomas	No Photo	XXB (Marienburg)
2883000		
Mclaughlan, C.	No Photo	344 (Lamsdorf)
3247904		
McLean, Alexander		344 (Lamsdorf)
2882998		
McLean, Charles	No Photo	344 (Lamsdorf)
2875693		
McLean, Donald	No Photo	XXID (Poznan)
2875261		
McLean, James	No Photo	N/a – Escaped
2879425		
McLean, William		IXC (Muhlhausen)
2875450		
McLennan, Donald	No Photo	XXB (Marienburg)
2881809		
McLennan, George		344 (Lamsdorf)
2875946		
McLENNAN, JOHN		KIA
2875150		

Name	Photo	PoW Camp	Name	Photo	PoW Camp
Army Number			Army Number		
McLeod, Alex		344 (Lamsdorf)	McPherson, James		VIIIA (Gorlitz)
2883100			2877792		
McLeod, Thomas	No Photo	XXB (Marienburg)	McPherson, J.S.	No Photo	O.VIIB (Eischstätt)
2875460			99714		
McMahon, Neil	No Photo	XXB (Marienburg)	McPherson, Peter	No Photo	XXB (Marienburg)
2873538			2867489		
McMaster, J.	No Photo	344 (Lamsdorf)	McPherson, William	No Photo	XXB (Marienburg)
310588			2883788		
McMillan, Farquhar	No Photo	344 (Lamsdorf)	McPhillips, Andrew	No Photo	Escaped
2882359			3318402		
McMILLAN, GEORGE	No Photo	KIA	McRae, Allan		XXA (Thorn)
2873515			2876733		
McNair, James	No Photo	XXB (Marienburg)	McRae, James	No Photo	XXA (Thorn)
2879478			2871182		
McNaught, J.	No Photo	XXB (Marienburg)	McRAE, JAMES DONNELLY		KIA
3318809			2876807		
McNee, William		XXA (Thorn)	McRae, William		344 (Lamsdorf)
2883002			2876054		
McNeil, James	No Photo	XXB (Marienburg)	McRobb, George		344 (Lamsdorf)
2883306			2871665		
McPartlin, Mark	No Photo	344 (Lamsdorf)	McRobbie, Andrew		IXC (Muhlhausen)
2883309			2882437		
McPhee, David		N/a – Evacuated	McWilliam, George	No Photo	Repatriated 1943
2876016			Unknown		
McPherson, Charles		XXID (Poznan)			
2867488					
McPherson, George	No Photo	IXC (Muhlhausen)			
2880514					

Name / Army Number	Photo	PoW Camp
McWilliam, John 2883821		XXB (Marienburg)
McWilliam, William 2876617		XXB (Marienburg)
Meek, S. 3318852	No Photo	XXB (Marienburg)
Meighan, Edward 2876811		XXB (Marienburg)
Meldrum, John 2879336	No Photo	344 (Lamsdorf)
Melville, A. 810600	No Photo	XXB (Marienburg)
Melville, John 2028923	No Photo	XXA (Thorn)
Melville, Robert 166641		XXB (Marienburg)
Mercer, Thomas 2879430	No Photo	XXID (Poznan)
Mess, Alexander 2882860	No Photo	XXA (Thorn)
Methven, Andrew 7344854	No Photo	N/a – Escaped
Michie, Alan 2874199	No Photo	XXB (Marienburg)
Michie, Harry 2882802	No Photo	XXA (Thorn)
Middleton, James 2874491		XXB (Marienburg)

Name / Army Number	Photo	PoW Camp
Middleton, William 2876064	No Photo	XXB (Marienburg)
Milburn, A.A. 4272866	No Photo	XXB (Marienburg)
Miles, J 3319009	No Photo	344 (Lamsdorf)
Millar, William 2876578		XXB (Marienburg)
MILLER, ANDREW 2883233	No Photo	KIA
Miller, Benjamin 2879260	No Photo	383 (Hohenfels)
Miller, David 2872003		IXC (Muhlhausen)
Miller, Thomas 2883151	No Photo	344 (Lamsdorf)
Miller, William 2876578	No Photo	XXB (Marienburg)
Milne, Albert 2882833	No Photo	IXC (Muhlhausen)
Milne, Alexander 2875037	No Photo	XXB (Marienburg)
Milne, Alexander 2873955	No Photo	344 (Lamsdorf)
Milne, Andrew 2882065	No Photo	XXB (Marienburg)
Milne, Archibald 2879044		344 (Lamsdorf)
Milne, Douglas 2883804	No Photo	344 (Lamsdorf)
Milne, Fergus 2882618	No Photo	344 (Lamsdorf)
Milne, Henry 2882814		XXB (Marienburg)

Name	Photo	PoW Camp
Army Number		
Milne, James 2879091		XXB (Marienburg)
Milne, John 2882805	No Photo	VIIIB (Teschen)
Milne, John Edward 2882979		XXA (Thorn)
Milne, John Penny 2880605	No Photo	XXB (Marienburg)
Milne, Lawrence 2881707	No Photo	IXC (Muhlhausen)
MILNE, NORMAN 2873909	No Photo	KIA
MILNE, ROBERT 2882908	No Photo	Died at XXB (Marienburg)
Milne, Robert D. 2882788	No Photo	XXB (Marienburg)
Milne, Robert P. 2000378		XXB (Marienburg)
Milne, Thomas 2871350	No Photo	XXB (Marienburg)
Milne, William 2867276		Unknown
Milne, William 2870706	No Photo	XXA (Thorn)
MILNE, WILLIAM 2871184	No Photo	KIA

Name	Photo	PoW Camp
Army Number		
Milne, William 2882810		XXB (Marienburg)
Milne, William 2884045	No Photo	17B (Gneizendorf)
Milne, William J. 2880536		XXB (Marienburg)
MILNER, JAMES 2875495		KIA
Milton, Bruce 2881874		IXC (Muhlhausen)
Milton, James 2881686	No Photo	344 (Lamsdorf)
Milton, W. 2820785	No Photo	344 (Lamsdorf)
Minty, John 875402	No Photo	XXID (Poznan)
Minty, Jack 2872766	No Photo	VIIA (Moosburg)
Mitchell, Alexander 2883782	No Photo	344 (Lamsdorf)
Mitchell, Charles 2883809		344 (Lamsdorf)
Mitchell, George 2876150		344 (Lamsdorf)
Mitchell, Herbert 2876966	No Photo	O.IXA (Spangenburg)

Name	Photo	PoW Camp
Mitchell, John 2882360	No Photo	XXA (Thorn)
Mitchellson, John 2869152	No Photo	383 (Hohenfels)
Moggach, James 2874506		Escaped
Moir, Alexander 2870129		Escaped
MOIR, GEORGE 2874561	No Photo	XXB (Marienburg)
Moir, James 2873432		IXC (Muhlhausen)
Moir, Leslie 2882791		IXC (Muhlhausen)
Moir, Walter 2883960	No Photo	XXB (Marienburg)
Moir, William 2880028	No Photo	XXA (Thorn)
Monaghan, Hugh 3318831	No Photo	Escaped
Moncur, Alaistair 2882885	No Photo	XXB (Marienburg)
Montague, Michael 2883949	No Photo	XXB (Marienburg)
Montgomery, James 2883047	No Photo	XXB (Marienburg)
Montrose, J. 2975287	No Photo	Evacuated wounded

Name	Photo	PoW Camp
Mooney, H. 3244908	No Photo	IXC (Muhlhausen)
MOREY, WILLIAM 2875482		KIA
Morgan, F.D. 71571		O.VIIB (Eischstätt)
Morgan, Harry 2879306	No Photo	XXB (Marienburg)
Morgan, W. 3708825	No Photo	Evacuated
Morran, W.D. 3319011	No Photo	XXA (Thorn)
Morren, David 68074		O.VIIB (Eischstätt)
Morrice, Arnold 2882760	No Photo	IXC (Muhlhausen)
Morrice, Gilbert 2882886	No Photo	344 (Lamsdorf)
Morrice, John 2879333		IXC (Muhlhausen)
Morrice, Thomas 2882368		344 (Lamsdorf)
Morrison, Charles 2881803		XXA (Thorn)
Morrison, Charles J. 2053380		XXB (Marienburg)

Name	Photo	PoW Camp
Army Number		
Morrison, James	No Photo	XXB (Marienburg)
861396		
MORRISON, JAMES	No Photo	KIA
2869038		
Morrison, James	No Photo	XXB (Marienburg)
2877303		
Morrison, John	No Photo	XXB (Marienburg)
2877334		
Morrison, John	No Photo	XXB (Marienburg)
2882982		
MORRISON, KENNETH		KIA
2879058		
Morrison, Marshall	No Photo	Repatriated 1943
Unknown		
Morrison, Robert D.	No Photo	344 (Lamsdorf)
2869878		
Morrison, W.A.	No Photo	O.VIIB (Eischstätt)
52686		
Morrison, William		344 (Lamsdorf)
2878420		
MORRISON, WILLIAM		KIA
2879046		
Morrison, W.S.	No Photo	344 (Lamsdorf)
2874464		
Morse, Sidney	No Photo	IXC (Muhlhausen)
2882983		
Mossom, J.	No Photo	IXC (Muhlhausen)
3319032		

Name	Photo	PoW Camp
Army Number		
Moultrie, George		383 (Hohenfels)
2868419		
Mountford, W.	No Photo	XXB (Marienburg)
4855931		
Mowat, Charles		XXB (Marienburg)
2584363		
MOWAT, GORDON	No Photo	KIA
2874701		
Mowberry, John	No Photo	XXB (Marienburg)
2879431		
MUIR, DAVID		KIA
2876697		
Muirhead, K.E.		O.VIIB (Eischstätt)
56782		
Mullan, J.	No Photo	3D (Berlin-Steglitz)
7010617		
Mullins, W.	No Photo	IXC (Muhlhausen)
3319034		
Mumme, Francis		Escaped
2876964		
Mundie, Alexander	No Photo	XXB (Marienburg)
2882509		
Munro, Lewis		XXB (Marienburg)
2874412		
Munro, William	No Photo	344 (Lamsdorf)
2881487		

Name / Army Number	Photo	PoW Camp
Murdoch, John / 2877135	No Photo	344 (Lamsdorf)
Murning, James / 2883283	No Photo	344 (Lamsdorf)
Murphy, Francis / 2882985	No Photo	344 (Lamsdorf)
Murphy, John / 2873901	No Photo	XXB (Marienburg)
Murphy, Maurice / 793525	No Photo	IXC (Muhlhausen)
Murphy, T. / 3319035	No Photo	IXC (Muhlhausen)
MURRAY, ALEXANDER / 2881507		Died XXA (Thorn)
MURRAY, GEORGE / 2877916		Died 344 (Lamsdorf)
Murray, J.R.D. / 102277	No Photo	O.VIIB (Eischstätt)
Murray, James / 2875532		XXB (Marienburg)
Murray, James / 2879233	No Photo	IXC (Muhlhausen)
Murray, James / 2884029	No Photo	344 (Lamsdorf)
Murray, John / 2880503	No Photo	344 (Lamsdorf)
Murray, Patrick / 2871789	No Photo	XXA (Thorn)
Murray, Thomas / 2876750		VIIIB (Lamsdorf)

Name / Army Number	Photo	PoW Camp
Murray, W. / 2214662	No Photo	XXB (Marienburg)
Murray, Walter / 2877214		XXB (Marienburg)
Mustard, Peter / 2877289	No Photo	XXB (Marienburg)
Mustarde, William / 2883282	No Photo	XXB (Marienburg)
Mutch, George / 2875302	No Photo	XXB (Marienburg)
Mutch, Harry / 2873241	No Photo	383 (Hohenfels)
Mutch, Peter / 2882066	No Photo	IXC (Muhlhausen)
Myles, David / 2879368	No Photo	344 (Lamsdorf)
NAISMITH, JOSEPH / 2883006	No Photo	KIA
Neill, Archie / 2883173	No Photo	Escaped
NEILSON, WILLIAM / 2872687		KIA
Nestor, Terence / 2186091	No Photo	XXB (Marienburg)
Nichol, Robert / 2883936	No Photo	IXC (Muhlhausen)
Nicholson, Joseph / 2876917		344 (Lamsdorf)

Name	Photo	PoW Camp
Army Number		
Nicol, Frank		IXC (Muhlhausen)
919912		
Nicol, J.	No Photo	XXB (Marienburg)
405344		
Nicol, James		XXB (Marienburg)
2880206		
Nicoll, James Ogg		XXA (Thorn)
2882151		
Nish, John	No Photo	344 (Lamsdorf)
2872482		
Noble Charles		XXB (Marienburg)
2882300		
Noble, A.	No Photo	XXID (Poznan)
2865728		
Noble, Alexander	No Photo	XXA (Thorn)
2882846		
Noble, John	No Photo	XXID (Poznan)
2871851		
Noble, Peter	No Photo	344 (Lamsdorf)
2880453		
Noble, Robert		344 (Lamsdorf)
2878888		
Noble, William		383 (Hohenfels)
2879022		
Normington, John	No Photo	IXC (Muhlhausen)
2879314		

Name	Photo	PoW Camp
Army Number		
Norrie, Andrew		344 (Lamsdorf)
2879171		
Norrie, James	No Photo	IXC (Muhlhausen)
2874469		
Norrie, Richard	No Photo	IXC (Muhlhausen)
2882435		
Ogden, J.H.	No Photo	XXB (Marienburg)
6205296		
Ogen, Thomas		Evacuated wounded
2879301		
Ogg, John	No Photo	XXB (Marienburg)
2878376		
Ogg, William	No Photo	357 (Kopernikus)
2872781		
Ogilvie, John	No Photo	344 (Lamsdorf)
2877246		
Ogilvie, John	No Photo	344 (Lamsdorf)
2880616		
Ogilvie, Raonuill		O.VIIB (Eischstätt)
95655		
Ogston, Charles	No Photo	XXA (Thorn)
2875925		
Ogston, J. Ernest	No Photo	XXB (Marienburg)
2882774		
O'Hara, (Alias Keith), Robert		XXB (Marienburg)
2879059		
Omara, James	No Photo	XXA (Thorn)
2883188		

Name	Photo	PoW Camp
Army Number		
O'Neill, Alexander		344 (Lamsdorf)
2876470		
O'Raw, William	No Photo	XXB (Marienburg)
2884056		
Ord, Andrew R.	No Photo	344 (Lamsdorf)
2872600		
Ord, John	No Photo	XXB (Marienburg)
2869492		
Ormiston, William	No Photo	XXB (Marienburg)
2883247		
O'Shae, Vernon		344 (Lamsdorf)
2877000		
Paget, A.	No Photo	383 (Hohenfels)
5567248		
Park, Alexander		344 (Lamsdorf)
2877038		
Park, James	No Photo	344 (Lamsdorf)
2880402		
Park, Robert		XXA (Thorn)
2876947		
Park, William		344 (Lamsdorf)
2876948		
Parley, Andrew		XXB (Marienburg)
2880696		
Paterson, Albert	No Photo	France - Hospital
2879212		
Paterson, Andrew	No Photo	344 (Lamsdorf)
2870483		

Name	Photo	PoW Camp
Army Number		
Paterson, George		IXC (Muhlhausen)
2880027		
Paterson, Harold	No Photo	XXB (Marienburg)
2877871		
Paterson, H.	No Photo	XXID (Poznan)
3318830		
Paterson, Robert A.	No Photo	344 (Lamsdorf)
2875030		
Paterson, Robert S.	No Photo	IXC (Muhlhausen)
2882510		
Paton, Alexander		XXIA (Schildberg)
2881878		
Patterson, Forbes	No Photo	XXB (Marienburg)
2871685		
Patterson, S.W.	No Photo	344 (Lamsdorf)
3318862		
Patterson, Walter	No Photo	XXA (Thorn)
2878776		
Paulin, Andrew	No Photo	XXID (Poznan)
2874952		
Peel, David	No Photo	IXC (Muhlhausen)
2883207		
Pegler, Donald		BAB 20 (Hydebreck)
2875254		
PEGLER, GEORGE	No Photo	KIA
2875255		
PERCIVAL, ALBERT	No Photo	Died of wounds
2873510		
Petrie, Andrew	No Photo	IXC (Muhlhausen)
2877786		

Name / Army Number	Photo	PoW Camp
Petrie, Herbert / 2877777		XXB (Marienburg)
Philip, Charles / 2874950	No Photo	XXA (Thorn)
Philip, James / 2883835		344 (Lamsdorf)
Philips, Hubert S. / 2878966		XXB (Marienburg)
Philips, Walter / 2880285	No Photo	N/a – Escaped
Phillips, James / 2874331	No Photo	344 (Lamsdorf)
Pirie, Charles / 1663214		VIIIA
Pirie, James S. / 2882854		344 (Lamsdorf)
Pirie, William / 2881539	No Photo	XXB (Marienburg)
Pirie, James / 2869629	No Photo	IXC (Muhlhausen)
Pittendreigh, James / 2878101	No Photo	XXID (Poznan)
Porter, Bruce / 2876715		XXB (Marienburg)

Name / Army Number	Photo	PoW Camp
Porter, George / 2883299	No Photo	XXB (Marienburg)
Porter, William / 2883153		XXB (Marienburg)
Pow, Andrew / 2883214	No Photo	Escaped
Prest, Albert / 2874419		IXC (Muhlhausen)
Price, Iain / 113550	No Photo	O.IVC (Colditz)
Pyper, J. / 3318856	No Photo	XXID (Poznan)
Rabone, John / 2876804		XXID (Poznan)
Rae, Angus / 2883128	No Photo	XXB (Marienburg)
Rae, Frank / 2879298	No Photo	XXB (Marienburg)
Rae, Neil / 2875385	No Photo	N/a – Escaped
Rae, S.D. / 88383		O.VIIB (Eischstätt)
RAEBURN, ALEXANDER / 97432		KIA
Raeburn, Frank / 2876996		XXB (Marienburg)

Name	Photo	PoW Camp
Army Number		
Raeburn, George		O.VIIB (Eischstätt)
88490		
Raines, George		IXC (Muhlhausen)
2879024		
Rainnie, Jack		Evacuated
2878834		
Raitt, Walter		383 (Hohenfels)
2878636		
Ralston, Henry	No Photo	XXA (Thorn)
2883305		
Ralston, William		344 (Lamsdorf)
2876970		
Ramage, Robert		XXB (Marienburg)
2876789		
Ramsay, Alex.	No Photo	IXC (Muhlhausen)
2883175		
Ramsay, Donald	No Photo	XXB (Marienburg)
2882903		
Ramsay, James		XXB (Marienburg)
2883063		
Ramsay, W.	No Photo	XXB (Marienburg)
2879433		

Name	Photo	PoW Camp
Army Number		
Rankin, Robert	No Photo	IXC (Muhlhausen)
2882326		
Rattray, Charles		IXC (Muhlhausen)
2872007		
Rattray, George	No Photo	IXC (Muhlhausen)
2882900		
Rattray, William	No Photo	XXB (Marienburg)
2884027		
Reaper, William		BAB 20 (Hydebreck)
2883961		
Reid, Albert	No Photo	344 (Lamsdorf)
2882877		
REID, ALEXANDER	No Photo	KIA
2875552		
Reid, Alexander		IXC (Muhlhausen)
2883069		
REID, ALEXANDER BURR		KIA
2883972		
Reid, Andrew	No Photo	344 (Lamsdorf)
2874180		
Reid, Angus		XXB (Marienburg)
2876836		
REID, DUNCAN		KIA
2875642		
Reid, Frederick	No Photo	XXB (Marienburg)
2869498		

Name	Photo	PoW Camp
Army Number		
Reid, George	No Photo	XXB (Marienburg)
2881422		
Reid, George	No Photo	344 (Lamsdorf)
2884043		
Reid, George G.		XXB (Marienburg)
2874067		
Reid, Gilbert	No Photo	XXA (Thorn)
2883964		
Reid, Gordon	No Photo	344 (Lamsdorf)
2880224		
Reid, Gordon	No Photo	XXB (Marienburg)
2882817		
Reid, Gordon S.		XXB (Marienburg)
2880758		
Reid, James Masson	No Photo	IXC (Muhlhausen)
2881540		
Reid, James Murray	No Photo	344 (Lamsdorf)
2883280		
REID, JOHN	No Photo	KIA
2881328		
Reid, Joseph	No Photo	XXB (Marienburg)
2873433		
Reid, Wallace		XXB (Marienburg)
2876708		
Reith, William	No Photo	VIIIB (Lamsdorf)
2882839		
Rennie, George		XXA (Thorn)
2873958		

Name	Photo	PoW Camp
Army Number		
RENNIE, GEORGE A.		KIA
2878470		
Rettie, Wilson	No Photo	344 (Lamsdorf)
2872721		
REYNOLDS, JAMES	No Photo	KIA
2883958		
Rhodes, John		0.9A/Z (Rotenburg Fulda)
95527		
Rhynd, J.	No Photo	XXB (Marienburg)
763748		
Rhynd, Robert	No Photo	344 (Lamsdorf)
2881199		
Riach, Fred		XXB (Marienburg)
2883845		
Rice, Joseph		XXA (Thorn)
2883136		
RICE, WILLIAM	No Photo	KIA
2883318		
Riddell, John	No Photo	XXA (Thorn)
2879479		
Riddell, William	No Photo	XXID (Poznan)
2880011		
Riley, Charles Summers		XXA (Thorn)
2882866		
Riley, Thomas	No Photo	344 (Lamsdorf)
2874489		

Name / Army Number	Photo	PoW Camp
Ritchie, A.D. / 93989		O.VIIB (Eischstätt)
Ritchie, Alexander / 2878887	No Photo	344 (Lamsdorf)
Ritchie, Andrew / 2879503	No Photo	XXA (Thorn)
Ritchie, Andrew G. / 2883796		VIIA (Moosburg)
Ritchie, George / 2879222	No Photo	XXA (Thorn)
RITCHIE, JOHN / 2878626		KIA
Ritchie, John / 2879400	No Photo	XXA (Thorn)
Ritchie, William / 2874634	No Photo	344 (Lamsdorf)
Roan, Patrick / 2883182	No Photo	XXB (Marienburg)
Robb, George / 2873210	No Photo	IXC (Muhlhausen)
Robb, James / 2870705		344 (Lamsdorf)
ROBBIE, DAVID / 2877117		KIA

Name / Army Number	Photo	PoW Camp
Robertson, Albert (Spud) / 2875213		344 (Lamsdorf)
Robertson, Alexander / 2877200	No Photo	XXB (Marienburg)
Robertson, Allan / 2882019	No Photo	IXC (Muhlhausen)
Robertson, Charles / Unknown	No Photo	Repatriated 1943
Robertson, Douglas / 2879095		IXC (Muhlhausen)
Robertson, Frank / 2881200	No Photo	IXC (Muhlhausen)
Robertson, George / 2868023	No Photo	XXB (Marienburg)
Robertson, Henry / 2883813	No Photo	XXA (Thorn)
Robertson, J. / 3318350	No Photo	344 (Lamsdorf)
Robertson, James / 2883827	No Photo	IXC (Muhlhausen)
Robertson, James A. / 2882832	No Photo	344 (Lamsdorf)
Robertson, James Gilchrist / 917921	No Photo	XXA (Thorn)
Robertson, James G. / 2883015	No Photo	344 (Lamsdorf)
Robertson, James P. / 2880070	No Photo	XXA (Thorn)

Name	Photo	PoW Camp
Army Number		
Robertson, John	No Photo	XXID (Poznan)
2876718		
Robertson, Morris Samuel		XXA (Thorn)
2215196		
Robertson, Robert	No Photo	XXB (Marienburg)
2883054		
Robertson, William	No Photo	XXB (Marienburg)
2884013		
Robertson, William McD.	No Photo	344 (Lamsdorf)
2882764		
ROBINSON, GEORGE	No Photo	KIA
3319045		
Robson, George	No Photo	344 (Lamsdorf)
2874025		
Robson, William	No Photo	XXB (Marienburg)
2881708		
Rodgers, Andrew	No Photo	XXA (Thorn)
2879492		
ROGER, ROBERT	No Photo	KIA
2878835		
Rorrison, Edward		344 (Lamsdorf)
3186018		
Rose, Hugh	No Photo	XXID (Poznan)
2884046		
Rose, J.	No Photo	XXID (Poznan)
2822236		
Ross, Alexander	No Photo	XXB (Marienburg)
2881902		
Ross, Charles		VIIIB (Teschen)
2877611		

Name	Photo	PoW Camp
Army Number		
Ross, Charles	No Photo	XXB (Marienburg)
2881327		
Ross, David	No Photo	IXC (Muhlhausen)
2883313		
Ross, Henry	No Photo	IXC (Muhlhausen)
2881523		
ROSS, JAMES	No Photo	KIA
2876574		
Ross, John	No Photo	XXA (Thorn)
2879499		
Ross, Joseph	No Photo	N/a – Escaped
3318412		
Ross, Nelson	No Photo	XXB (Marienburg)
2872471		
Rothney, William		XXB (Marienburg)
2878315		
Rough, John	No Photo	344 (Lamsdorf)
2871880		
Russell, William	No Photo	XXA (Thorn)
2882899		
Ryan, J.	No Photo	XXB (Marienburg)
3049777		
Sangster, Leonard		IXC (Muhlhausen)
2876283		
Sangster, William		XXB (Marienburg)
2881333		
Savage, T.	No Photo	344 (Lamsdorf)
4855570		
SCORGIE, ALBERT	No Photo	KIA
2873925		

Name	Photo	PoW Camp
Army Number		
Scott, Alexander	No Photo	383 (Hohenfels)
2873930		
Scott, Edward	No Photo	XXB (Marienburg)
2873438		
Scott, John	No Photo	XXB (Marienburg)
2883018		
Scott, Norman	No Photo	IXC (Muhlhausen)
2882315		
Scott, Peter	No Photo	344 (Lamsdorf)
2878633		
Scott, Wilfred	No Photo	344 (Lamsdorf)
2880663		
Scott, William		344 (Lamsdorf)
2879088		
Scully, James	No Photo	IXC (Muhlhausen)
2883934		
Selbie, Robert		VIIIB (Teschen)
2878695		
Semple, Andrew	No Photo	344 (Lamsdorf)
2883926		
Shand, Harry	No Photo	O.VIIB (Eischstätt)
99735		
Shand, Len	No Photo	XXB (Marienburg)
2881719		
Shand, Robert		IXC (Muhlhausen)
2881980		
Shand, Ronald		Evacuated
2881630		

Name	Photo	PoW Camp
Army Number		
Shand, William		344 (Lamsdorf)
2873998		
Shand, William J.	No Photo	XXB (Marienburg)
2877735		
Shankley, J.		O.VIIB (Eischstätt)
76239		
Shanks, Francis	No Photo	IXC (Muhlhausen)
2883780		
Shaw, Charles	No Photo	Killed escaping
2874858		
Shaw, James Kerr	No Photo	344 (Lamsdorf)
2883019		
Shaw, Morrison		Mixed Medical Board Repatriation
2876553		
Shearer, Kenneth		IXC (Muhlhausen)
2876633		
Shearer, Robert		Escaped
807218		
Shearer, Victor		344 (Lamsdorf)
2882857		
Shearer, William	No Photo	XXB (Marienburg)
787964		
Sheed, Alexander	No Photo	344 (Lamsdorf)
2874513		

Name / Army Number	Photo	PoW Camp
SHEPHERD, GEORGE / 4267594		Died XXB (Marienburg)
Shepherd, James / 2871272	No Photo	XXB (Marienburg)
SHEPHERD, WILLIAM / 2927120	No Photo	KIA
Sheppard, James / 2873422	No Photo	XXB (Marienburg)
SHERRIFFS, HENRY / 2873477	No Photo	KIA
Sheves, Don / 2882056		IXC (Muhlhausen)
Shewan, George / 2883802	No Photo	XXB (Marienburg)
Shiach, James / 2882489	No Photo	XXB (Marienburg)
Shirran, Alexander / 2873648		3D (Berlin-Steglitz)
Shore, David / 2875301		383 (Hohenfels)
Silver, James / 2877186		XXB (Marienburg)
Silver, John / 2878411		XXB (Marienburg)

Name / Army Number	Photo	PoW Camp
Sim, Alexander / 2882855	No Photo	IXC (Muhlhausen)
Sim, John / 2883847		XXA (Thorn)
SIMPSON, ALEXANDER / 2881755	No Photo	KIA
Simpson, Charles / 2869382	No Photo	XXID (Poznan)
Simpson, Ezekiel / 2191573	No Photo	344 (Lamsdorf)
Simpson, George / 2876855		XXID (Poznan)
Simpson, Harold / 2879581	No Photo	383 (Hohenfels)
Simpson, Henry / 2883846		344 (Lamsdorf)
Simpson, James / 2879076		344 (Lamsdorf)
Simpson, James / 2879117		XXB (Marienburg)
Simpson, James / 2876117	No Photo	XXB (Marienburg)
Simpson, James D.G. / 2872010	No Photo	XXB (Marienburg)

Name	Photo	PoW Camp
Army Number		
SIMPSON, JOHN		KIA
2873697		
Simpson, Joseph	No Photo	XXA (Thorn)
2882797		
Simpson, Robert	No Photo	XXA (Thorn)
836211		
Simpson, Ronald		XXB (Marienburg)
2876721		
Simpson, Roy	No Photo	XXB (Marienburg)
2883829		
Simpson, Wilfred		344 (Lamsdorf)
2878882		
Simpson, William	No Photo	XXB (Marienburg)
2873714		
Simpson, William	No Photo	344 (Lamsdorf)
2881439		
SINCLAIR, GEORGE		Died of wounds
2876913		
Sinclair, James		O.IXA/H (Spangenburg)
45141		
Sinclair, William	No Photo	344 (Lamsdorf)
2884038		
Singer, Alexander	No Photo	IXC (Muhlhausen)
2883806		
Singer, John		XXB (Marienburg)
2883779		

Name	Photo	PoW Camp
Army Number		
Sivewright, Alex	No Photo	344 (Lamsdorf)
846964		
Sivewright, George	No Photo	344 (Lamsdorf)
2692373		
Skene, Alexander	No Photo	XXID (Poznan)
2879311		
Skilling, John	No Photo	XXB (Marienburg)
2883302		
Skinner, Joseph		XXID (Poznan)
2867945		
Skinner, William		383 (Hohenfels)
2874138		
Skinner, Walter		IXC (Muhlhausen)
2881709		
Slater, David	No Photo	XXA (Thorn)
2881981		
Slessor, Alexander		XXB (Marienburg)
2077853		
Sloan, J.T.	No Photo	344 (Lamsdorf)
3188286		
Small, James	No Photo	IXC (Muhlhausen)
2874243		
Smart, Alexander		344 (Lamsdorf)
2881423		
Smart, Duncan	No Photo	IXC (Muhlhausen)
2882403		

Name	Photo	PoW Camp
Army Number		
Smart, Robert		IXC (Muhlhausen)
2881424		
Smith, Alexander	No Photo	XXB (Marienburg)
2873972		
Smith, Anderson		XXA (Thorn)
2873850		
Smith, Arthur		XXID (Poznan)
2876315		
Smith, Charles	No Photo	344 (Lamsdorf)
2879028		
Smith, E.	No Photo	VIIIB (Teschen)
4272825		
Smith, Ernest	No Photo	XXB (Marienburg)
2881733		
Smith, F.G.V.	No Photo	383 (Hohenfels)
4973967		
Smith, Frank	No Photo	357 (Kopernikus)
811914		
Smith, George		XXA (Thorn)
2876944		
Smith, George M.	No Photo	383 (Hohenfels)
2873441		
Smith, Henry	No Photo	344 (Lamsdorf)
2879310		
Smith, Herbert	No Photo	IXC (Muhlhausen)
2883024		
Smith, J.	No Photo	XXA (Thorn)
2982635		

Name	Photo	PoW Camp
Army Number		
Smith, James	No Photo	IXC (Muhlhausen)
2881710		
Smith, James	No Photo	IXC (Muhlhausen)
2879369		
Smith, James	No Photo	Untermassfeld
2882348		
Smith, James C.		XXID (Poznan)
2879176		
Smith, John	No Photo	344 (Lamsdorf)
2882434		
Smith, John L.	No Photo	344 (Lamsdorf)
2882535		
Smith, John W.	No Photo	IXC (Muhlhausen)
2880537		
Smith, John W.J.	No Photo	XXA (Thorn)
2881658		
SMITH, KEITH		KIA
2869825		
Smith, Norman	No Photo	344 (Lamsdorf)
2877353		
Smith, Robert		XXID (Poznan)
2873056		
Smith, Robert	No Photo	XXA (Thorn)
2873839		
Smith, Robert F.	No Photo	344 (Lamsdorf)
2883317		
Smith, Robert J.	No Photo	344 (Lamsdorf)
2881331		

Name / Army Number	Photo	PoW Camp
Smith, Thomas / 2873063	No Photo	XXB (Marienburg)
Smith, Thomas / 2875488	No Photo	344 (Lamsdorf)
Smith, W.C. / 28773117	No Photo	XXB (Marienburg)
Smith, William / 2883117	No Photo	IXC (Muhlhausen)
Smith, William C. / 2871387	No Photo	XXA (Thorn)
Smollett, James / 2875228	No Photo	XXID (Poznan)
Snape, C / 6538279	No Photo	XXA (Thorn)
Sneddon, James / 2873565	No Photo	344 (Lamsdorf)
Sneddon, James / 2883930	No Photo	IXC (Muhlhausen)
Sneddon, Thomas / 2883180	No Photo	IXC (Muhlhausen)
Somerville, John / 2883955	No Photo	344 (Lamsdorf)
SPENCE, GERALD / 117820	No Photo	Died of wounds
SPENCE, JOHN / 2882248		KIA
SPENDLOVE, ROY / 2575766	No Photo	KIA
SPINK, DAVID / 2881442		KIA
Sproule, William / 2879507	No Photo	344 (Lamsdorf)

Name / Army Number	Photo	PoW Camp
Stables, Norman / 2880448		IXC (Muhlhausen)
Stables, William / 2877665	No Photo	357 (Kopernikus)
Stansfield, J.deB. / 36880	No Photo	O.VIIB (Eischstätt)
Starrs, James / 2883951	No Photo	XXA (Thorn)
Steel, Allan / 2877872		XXA (Thorn)
Steel, Francis / 2873626		N/a
Steel, William / 2874225		344 (Lamsdorf)
Stephen, Andrew / 2869875	No Photo	344 (Lamsdorf)
Stephen, Arthur / 2880759	No Photo	XXB (Marienburg)
Stephen, Charles / 2869935	No Photo	KIA
Stephen, George / 2882852	No Photo	XXA (Thorn)
STEPHEN, GEORGE MAIR / 859072	No Photo	KIA
Stephen, William / 2881514	No Photo	344 (Lamsdorf)
Stephen, William / 2882319	No Photo	XXID (Poznan)
Stevenson, George / 2880754	No Photo	XXA (Thorn)

Name	Photo	PoW Camp
STEVENSON, JAMES	No Photo	KIA
2883029		
Stewart, Alexander		IXC (Muhlhausen)
2881366		
Stewart, David	No Photo	XXA (Thorn)
2881490		
Stewart, George	No Photo	XXID (Poznan)
881491		
Stewart, James	No Photo	XXID (Poznan)
2873216		
Stewart, James	No Photo	IXC (Muhlhausen)
2882433		
Stewart, John	No Photo	XXID (Poznan)
2879459		
Stewart, John	No Photo	344 (Lamsdorf)
2880525		
Stewart, John G.		IXC (Muhlhausen)
2881982		
STEWART, PATRICK (Peter)		KIA
2866870		
Stewart, Robert		XXB (Marienburg)
2883105		
Stewart, William		IXC (Muhlhausen)
2882442		
Stewart, William F.		344 (Lamsdorf)
2883064		

Name	Photo	PoW Camp
Stirton, John	No Photo	XXID (Poznan)
2883819		
STODDART, THOMAS		KIA
2873284		
Storrie, Alexander		VIIIC (Kunau Kz Sprottau / Sagan)
2883120		
STRACHAN, GEORGE	No Photo	Killed VIIIB (Teschen)
2879199		
Strachan, Wilfred		XXID (Poznan)
2876979		
Strachan, William	No Photo	IXC (Muhlhausen)
2881016		
Strachan, William	No Photo	XXB (Marienburg)
2881757		
Strathdee, Stewart	No Photo	344 (Lamsdorf)
2875973		
Straughan, Malcolm		Escaped
2876101		
Stuart, Charles		344 (Lamsdorf)
2881864		
STUART, JAMES	No Photo	KIA
2872692		
STUART, JAMES	No Photo	KIA
2878825		
Stuart, James	No Photo	XXID (Poznan)
2879429		

Name / Army Number	Photo	PoW Camp
Stuart, William G. / 2882884	No Photo	VIIIB (Teschen)
Summers, John / 2878669		383 (Hohenfels)
SUTHERLAND, DUNCAN / 2878884	No Photo	KIA
SUTHERLAND, GEORGE / 2881711		Accidental drowning
Sutherland, Robert / 2874306		IXC (Muhlhausen)
Sutherland, W. / 2881759		344 (Lamsdorf)
Swanson, James / 2883028	No Photo	Wollstein
Sword (Dennistoun Sword), John Colin / 66373	No Photo	O.VIIB (Eischstätt)
Symon, C. / 74226		O.VIIB (Eischstätt)
Symonds, J.B. / 5824456	No Photo	XXB (Marienburg)
Tait, T.D. / 4270782	No Photo	XXB (Marienburg)
Tapley, H.C. / 6090667	No Photo	XXB (Marienburg)

Name / Army Number	Photo	PoW Camp
Taylor, Alexander / 2874461	No Photo	344 (Lamsdorf)
Taylor, Charles / 2877674	No Photo	344 (Lamsdorf)
Taylor, David / 2881413	No Photo	IXC (Muhlhausen)
Taylor, Frank / 2873790	No Photo	XXID (Poznan)
Taylor, George / 2878206	No Photo	383 (Hohenfels)
Taylor, George G. / 2884007		XXB (Marienburg)
Taylor, George W. / 2876513		383 (Hohenfels)
Taylor, James / 2875490	No Photo	XXA (Thorn)
Taylor, James / 2875523		VIIIA (Gorlitz)
Taylor, James / 2879085		357 (Kopernikus)
Taylor, James / 2979131		XXB (Marienburg)
Taylor, James / 2883953	No Photo	XXB (Marienburg)
Taylor, John / 2191422		XXA (Thorn)

Name	Photo	PoW Camp
Army Number		
Taylor, John 2883060	No Photo	344 (Lamsdorf)
Taylor, John A. 2871361	No Photo	383 (Hohenfels)
Taylor, John G. 2879312	No Photo	IXC (Muhlhausen)
Taylor, John Philip Pagan 67198		O.VIIB (Eischstätt)
Taylor, John W. 2879343	No Photo	IXC (Muhlhausen)
Taylor, Robert A. 2875502		XXB (Marienburg)
Taylor, Robert L. 2879472	No Photo	344 (Lamsdorf)
Thom, David 2881444		XXB (Marienburg)
Thom, Henry 2874112	No Photo	XXB (Marienburg)
Thom, R.C. 117305	No Photo	O.VIIB (Eischstätt)
Thompson, Hector 2878967		344 (Lamsdorf)
Thomson, Andrew 2880101	No Photo	344 (Lamsdorf)
Thomson, D.A. 2881721	No Photo	344 (Lamsdorf)
Thomson, Francis 2884040	No Photo	344 (Lamsdorf)

Name	Photo	PoW Camp
Army Number		
Thomson, George 2878777		XXA (Thorn)
Thomson, Gordon 2876640		XXB (Marienburg)
Thomson, James 2882825	No Photo	344 (Lamsdorf)
Thomson, John 2877323	No Photo	XXB (Marienburg)
Thomson, Thomas 2871744	No Photo	383 (Hohenfels)
Thomson, William 2879063		XXB (Marienburg)
THOW, ALEXANDER 2885276	No Photo	IXC (Muhlhausen)
Thow, Dugald 2873889		XXB (Marienburg)
Tilney, Thomas 2881085	No Photo	Repatriated 1943
Titley, George 2866742		344 (Lamsdorf)
Tobin, H. 2868637		Unknown

Name / Army Number	Photo	PoW Camp
Tobin, Henry (Harry) Joseph / 2878125		IXC (Muhlhausen)
Tobin, Henry Joseph / 2878965	No Photo	357 (Kopernikus)
Tocher, Harry / 844525	No Photo	344 (Lamsdorf)
Tocher, William / 2880404		344 (Lamsdorf)
Todd, (Alias Wood) William / 2876821		344 (Lamsdorf)
Todd, George / 2873136	No Photo	383 (Hohenfels)
Todd, George S. / 2879252	No Photo	344 (Lamsdorf)
Todd, Robert / 2883933	No Photo	XXB (Marienburg)
Torry, Fred / 2876788		XXA (Thorn)
Turner, George / 2879083		XXA (Thorn)
Turner, W. / 3049913	No Photo	XXB (Marienburg)
Ure, Richard / 2883147	No Photo	XXID (Poznan)
Usher, Charles / Unknown		Evacuated

Name / Army Number	Photo	PoW Camp
Usher, H.M. / 47767		O.VIIB (Eischstätt)
Waddell, J. / 6205225	No Photo	XXA (Thorn)
Waddell, W.C. / 2889221	No Photo	XXB (Marienburg)
Wadsworth, Hubert / 2878422		XXA (Thorn)
Walker, A.E. / 4856691	No Photo	344 (Lamsdorf)
Walker, Allan / 2869658		IXC (Muhlhausen)
Walker, Charles / 2881524		XXB (Marienburg)
Walker, D. / 7582713	No Photo	XXB (Marienburg)
Walker, Evan J. / 2874981		344 (Lamsdorf)
Walker, James / 2881515		IXC (Muhlhausen)
Walker, J.D. / 3318248	No Photo	XXB (Marienburg)
Walker, John W. / 2883169	No Photo	IXC (Muhlhausen)

Name	Photo	PoW Camp
Army Number		
Walker, Peter	No Photo	344 (Lamsdorf)
2879324		
Warkup, C.	No Photo	XXB (Marienburg)
4272117		
Warner, William	No Photo	XXB (Marienburg)
2876460		
Warrell, R.J.	No Photo	XXB (Marienburg)
4386344		
Warren, James	No Photo	344 (Lamsdorf)
2872995		
Waterman, Charles		344 (Lamsdorf)
2873181		
Waterhouse, J.	No Photo	IXC (Muhlhausen)
4343658		
Watson, Alexander		344 (Lamsdorf)
2879080		
Watson, Archibald	No Photo	XXA (Thorn)
2883237		
Watson, George		344 (Lamsdorf)
2881205		
Watson, James	No Photo	344 (Lamsdorf)
2874387		
Watson, John	No Photo	XXIB (Schubin)
2879387		
Watson, Walker	No Photo	XXB (Marienburg)
2875347		
Watson, Walter	No Photo	344 (Lamsdorf)
2879490		

Name	Photo	PoW Camp
Army Number		
Watson, William	No Photo	344 (Lamsdorf)
2882799		
Watt, Alexander	No Photo	344 (Lamsdorf)
2871083		
Watt, Alexander M.		XXA (Thorn)
2875918		
Watt, Atholl		XXB (Marienburg)
2882843		
Watt, Charles	No Photo	344 (Lamsdorf)
2873883		
Watt, Charles A.L.		O.VIIB (Eischstätt)
74696		
Watt, Douglas	No Photo	383 (Hohenfels)
2875553		
Watt, G	No Photo	383 (Hohenfels)
3186009		
Watt, James		XXB (Marienburg)
2881470		
Watt, William	No Photo	XXB (Marienburg)
2873195		
Webster, Irwin		N/a
2867178		
Webster, Ralph	No Photo	344 (Lamsdorf)
2883035		
Wedderburn, Fred		344 (Lamsdorf)
2879178		

Name / Army Number	Photo	PoW Camp
WEDDERBURN, PETER / 811676		Died of wounds
Weir, Joseph / 2879319	No Photo	XXA (Thorn)
WELLS, DONALD / 2873899	No Photo	KIA
Welsh, Edward P. / 2883219	No Photo	XXA (Thorn)
Welsh, Edward J. / 2883037	No Photo	XXB (Marienburg)
WELSH, FREDERICK / 2881779	No Photo	KIA
West, James / 2881679		344 (Lamsdorf)
Westland, Stanley / 2879102		N/a – Escaped
WEYERS, GERT / 2879191	No Photo	KIA
Wheildon, Norman / 2883036	No Photo	344 (Lamsdorf)
Whitelaw, Walter / 2883159	No Photo	XXID (Poznan)
Whiteman, C.J. / 5615199	No Photo	344 (Lamsdorf)
Whyte, Andrew / 2878837		BAB21 (Blechammer)

Name / Army Number	Photo	PoW Camp
Whyte, Donald / 2883123	No Photo	344 (Lamsdorf)
Whyte, Gilbert / 2883039	No Photo	IXC (Muhlhausen)
Whyte, Irvine / 2877241	No Photo	IXC (Muhlhausen)
Whyte, Robert / 2872478	No Photo	383 (Hohenfels)
Wight, James / 2875849	No Photo	IXC (Muhlhausen)
Wilkinson, James / 2879315	No Photo	344 (Lamsdorf)
Will, Fergus / 2881714	No Photo	IXC (Muhlhausen)
WILL, NEIL / 2879275		KIA
Will, Robert / 2882311	No Photo	344 (Lamsdorf)
Will, William J. / 2876344	No Photo	VIIIC (Kunau Kz Sprottau/Sagan)
Williams, James / 2876866		XXB (Marienburg)
Williams, John / 2875977	No Photo	XXB (Marienburg)
Willis, Thomas / 2883195	No Photo	XXB (Marienburg)
Willox, William / 2879125		IXC (Muhlhausen)

Name / Army Number	Photo	PoW Camp
Wilson, Albert / 2880698		XXB (Marienburg)
Wilson, Alexander / 2871863	No Photo	344 (Lamsdorf)
Wilson, Alexander / 2877426	No Photo	XXB (Marienburg)
Wilson, Alfred G. / 2875210	No Photo	344 (Lamsdorf)
Wilson, Duncan / 2882357	No Photo	XXA (Thorn)
Wilson, Edgar / 2883315	No Photo	344 (Lamsdorf)
Wilson, Eric / 2866266		Medical Repatriation
Wilson, Frank / 2883076		344 (Lamsdorf)
Wilson, Gavin / 2883946	No Photo	XXA (Thorn)
Wilson, George / 2873830	No Photo	344 (Lamsdorf)
Wilson, George William / 2881903		IXC (Muhlhausen)
WILSON, HARRY / 2879304		KIA

Name / Army Number	Photo	PoW Camp
Wilson, James / 2879153		344 (Lamsdorf)
Wilson, James B. / 2879511	No Photo	344 (Lamsdorf)
WILSON, JAMES H. / 2876830		KIA
Wilson, John / 2880738	No Photo	XXB (Marienburg)
Wilson, John F. / 2882891	No Photo	XXB (Marienburg)
Wilson, John T. / 2883999	No Photo	XXB (Marienburg)
Wilson, John / 2878331	No Photo	XXA (Thorn)
Wilson, Leslie / 2879366	No Photo	Escaped
Wilson, N. / 2815490	No Photo	383 (Hohenfels)
Wilson, Robert / 2872180	No Photo	383 (Hohenfels)
Wilson, Stephen / 2880798		IXC (Muhlhausen)
WILSON, THOMAS / 3709260	No Photo	KIA
Wilson, William / 2880032	No Photo	XXB (Marienburg)
Wilson, William / 2881888		383 (Hohenfels)

Name / Army Number	Photo	PoW Camp
Wink, George / 2883837	No Photo	XXID (Poznan)
Winton (De Winton), Peter / 105341	No Photo	O.IVC (Colditz)
Wood, A.M. / 3127279	No Photo	IXC (Muhlhausen)
Wood, James / 2874031	No Photo	344 (Lamsdorf)
Wood, James / 2877290	No Photo	XXA (Thorn)
Wood, William G. / 2882801	No Photo	383 (Hohenfels)
Wood, William S. / 2882909	No Photo	XXA (Thorn)
WOODLEY, WILLIAM / 2611924	No Photo	KIA
Wright, Charles / 2883072		VIIIC (Kunau Kz Sprottau / Sagan)
Wright, Gordon / 2875253		XXA (Thorn)
Wright, Harry / 9289		O.IXA/H (Spangenburg)
WRIGHT, JAMES / 2880066		KIA

Name / Army Number	Photo	PoW Camp
Wright, Luke / 2883140	No Photo	XXB (Marienburg)
Wrigley, A. / 4686045	No Photo	344 (Lamsdorf)
Wyllie, Alexander / 2883042	No Photo	344 (Lamsdorf)
Yeates, Joseph / 2883042		XXB (Marienburg)
Young, Arthur / 2880180	No Photo	344 (Lamsdorf)
Young, David / 2873659	No Photo	XXB (Marienburg)
Young, G. / 3130002	No Photo	IXC (Muhlhausen)
Young, George / 2880555	No Photo	XXB (Marienburg)
Young, Henry / 401619	No Photo	344 (Lamsdorf)
Young, John / 2883181	No Photo	XXB (Marienburg)
Young, John A. / 2883131	No Photo	XXIA (Schildberg)
YOUNG, PETER / 2876087	No Photo	KIA
Young, R. / 2879223	No Photo	344 (Lamsdorf)
Young, Walter / 2873535	No Photo	N/a – Escaped
Yule, Robert / 2881326	No Photo	XXB (Marienburg)

Four battalions of Gordon Highlanders (1st; 4th; 5th and 6th) served in France in 1940 and the table above lists all the men known to have been killed or captured that year. Unfortunately, there is no definitive list of those captured in 1940 and so the table was compiled from a number of sources. This involved using archive material from the Gordon Highlanders' Museum, contemporary newspaper reports, the records of the Commonwealth War Graves Commission, family records and information from the National Archives. The majority of the men listed served with the 1st and 5th Battalions and were captured at St Valéry-en-Caux whereas the bulk of the 4th and 6th Battalions were evacuated through Dunkirk. Every effort has been made to make this list as accurate as possible but it is not exhaustive. If any error or discrepancy has occurred, I apologize in advance. (The names of the men who were killed in action, died of wounds or died for any reason while they were PoWs are written in upper case.)

Index